Politikwissenschaft

Problems of Democratic Transitions in Multi-Ethnic States

Comparison Between the Former Yugoslavia and Present Days Myanmar

Inaugural-Dissertation

Zur Erlangung des Doktorgrades

der

Philosophischen Fakultät

der

Westfälischen Wilhelms-Universität

zu

Münster (Westf.)

vorgelegt von

Saw Myat Sandy

aus Yangon

34 Jahre

Tag der mündlichen Prüfung: 25. April 2007

Hauptfach: Politikwissenschaft

Prüferin: Prof. Dr. Susanne Feske

Nebenfach: Englische Philologie

Prüfer: Prof. Dr. Bernfried Nugel

Saw Myat Sandy

PROBLEMS OF DEMOCRATIC TRANSITIONS
IN MULTI-ETHNIC STATES

Comparison Between the Former Yugoslavia
and Present Days Myanmar

ibidem-Verlag
Stuttgart

Bibliografische Information der Deutschen Nationalbibliothek
Die Deutsche Nationalbibliothek verzeichnet diese Publikation in der
Deutschen Nationalbibliografie; detaillierte bibliografische Daten sind im
Internet über http://dnb.d-nb.de abrufbar.

Bibliographic information published by the Deutsche Nationalbibliothek
Die Deutsche Nationalbibliothek lists this publication in the Deutsche Nationalbibliografie;
detailed bibliographic data are available in the Internet at http://dnb.d-nb.de.

∞

Gedruckt auf alterungsbeständigem, säurefreien Papier
Printed on acid-free paper

ISBN-10: 3-8382-0014-4

ISBN-13: 978-3-8382-0014-9

© *ibidem*-Verlag
Stuttgart 2009

Lebenslauf

Persönliche Angaben:

Name: Saw Myat
Vorname: Sandy
Geburtsdatum: 17.08.72
Geburtsort: Yangon
Familienstand: Verheiratet
Staatsangehörigkeit: Deutsch
Sprachen: Burmesisch, Deutsch, Englisch, Französisch, Thailändisch

Schulischer Werdegang:

1976 – 1986   Staat Hochschule Nr. (2) Sanchaung, Yangon, Myanmar.
                     Abiturzeugnis

Hochschulausbildung:

1986 – 1991   Universität Yangon, Yangon, Myanmar.
                     Bachelor of Art (Anglistik)

04/2000 – 03/2003   Westfälische Wilhelms Universität Münster, Münster.
                     Magister (Politik Wissenschaft u. Anglistik)

Zusätzliche Kurse:

10/1998 – 03/2000   Sprachzentrum, Lehrgebiet Deutsch als Fremdsprache,
                     Westfälische Wilhelms Universität Münster, Münster.
                     Zertifikat – DSH (Zertifikate für die Deutsche
                     Sprachprüfung für den Hochschulzugang ausländischer
                     Studienbewerber)

01/1998 – 07/1998   Bildungsinstitut Münster e. V., Münster, Deutschland.
                     Zertifikat für Deutsch für Aussiedler, Asylberechtigte und
                     Kontingentflüchtlinge

09/1990 – 08/1993   Alliance Française de Yangon, Yangon, Myanmar.
                     Zertifikat – C. E. F. P. (Certificat Elémentaire de Français
                     Pratique)

Veröffentlichungen:

2001   "Sexuality and Burmese Culture." *Scholar Forum* Nr.4 –
                     Winter 2001 (The Journal of the Open Society Institute)

Abstract

This dissertation deals with theoretical and empirical analysis of the political transitions in former Yugoslavia and Burma, the present day Myanmar. It covers the transition period of both states from the late 1980s until present. The study examines the democratic transition in both states, wherein the process has been either unsuccessfully accomplished, after a very promising beginning, sooner or later undermined by formidable challenges which threatened the reversal of democratic gains. In this dissertation, it is argued that the democratic transition in both states became an 'extended process of transition' because of its multi-ethnic societies. The democratisation in former Yugoslavia led to disintegration and in Myanmar it is proving to be an intractable one and has become almost un-resolvable to anyone's satisfaction. Myanmar today suffers from on-going political instabilities that cause political and social fragmentations, but do not demonstrate that it will fall into conventional Balkan scenarios.

This dissertation analyses, if Myanmar political transition will follow the former Yugoslavian fate, by using the transition theoretical frame-work and highlighting the empirical facts on the problems of ethnicity and other political factors that relate to these democratisation processes. The theoretical approaches are based on the 'democratic transition and consolidation theories' argued by Juan J. Linz, Alfred Stepan and Samuel Huntington. As opposed to many quantitative studies, relevant dimensions will gradually appear in this qualitative case study. The theoretical perspectives, which apply are equally significant and supplement each other and relate to its national experience. However, this study aspires to contribute to the conventional theoretical debate and aims to offer the understanding for the need to expand the link between ethnicity and political transitions in transition theories that is lacking, wherein it will be evidenced in analysing the case of former Yugoslavia and Myanmar. It will propose a heuristic method to integrate the dynamic of ethnicity in political transitions theories.

CONTENTS

Acknowledgement

My study on democratic transitions in multi-ethnic states, which is in comparison between former Yugoslavia and Present Day Myanmar has in many ways been a challenge. One motivating force behind this study is my long-held desire to understand why the democratic transition fails in multi-ethnic countries. During my years of research, I have been fortunate to have met a number of people who have contributed and supported me on this doctoral thesis. First of all, I would like to thank Prof. Dr. Susanne Feske, my supervisor, who has over the entire period supported my research endeavours. I also want to express my sincere appreciation to Prof. Dr. Volker Grabowsky, who has not only contributed comments on various drafts but also provided constant encouragement and support during the 'ups and down' of my work as a doctoral student. I appreciate the efforts of all those who, despite their hectic schedules, took the time to read and edit the preliminary manuscript. My thanks go to John Quigley of the European Institute for Asian Studies, Brussels for several detailed helpful comments and suggestions for improvement and clarifications. I extend my gratitude to the many insightful comments from my husband Arthur Minsat, who imparted a theoretical perspective to my work. All in all, I am grateful to the Friedrich-Ebert-Foundation (FES) for granting me the whole doctoral study.

Glossary

Bama/ Bamar/ Myanma	is an adjective, such as Burmese
Bogyoke	General
Chetniks	(Serbian: четници or *četnici*) were members of a Serbian nationalist and royalist guerrilla organization named after a 19th century Serbian movement opposing Ottoman rule.
Daw	for aunts, or older women
Dinar	Currency of Macedonia and Serbia
Dobama Asi-Ayone	We the Burmans Association that formed to fight for independence from Britain
Hsaya San	Hsaya San rebellion is the most significant anti-colonial peasant movement in Burma in 1930
Jr.	Junior
Kuna	Croatian Currency
Kyat	Currency of Myanmar
Maung	for younger brothers, boys
Naing-ngang	Nation
Otpor	(Cyrillic: *ОТПОР*, in English: *Resistance*) was a pro-democracy youth movement in Serbia which has been widely credited for leading the eventually successful struggle to overthrow Slobodan Milošević in 2000.
Pyidaung-zu	Union
Reforma-pactada ruptura-pactada	a reform-willing government and moderate opposition forces made a possible transition
Sangha	the Buddhist Monkshood
Saophas or Sawbwa	Shan Kings or Prince
Tatmadaw	the Myanmar armed forces
Thakin	a prefix that means 'Master', proclaiming they were the true masters of their own land.

Theravāda	(Pāli: *theravāda*; Sanskrit: *sthaviravāda*; literally, "the Way of the Elders") is the oldest surviving Buddhist school.
Thirty Comrades (Yèbaw thoun gyeik)	constituted the embryo of the modern Burmese army called the Burma Independence Army (BIA) which was formed to fight for independence from Britain.
Tolar	Slovenian Currency
U	for uncles, or older men
Ustaše	(singular Ustaša or Ustasha) was a Croatian organization put in charge of the Independent State of Croatia by the Axis Powers in 1941, in which they pursued Nazi policies.

List of Abbreviations

Brig.	Brigadier
cf.	compare
Dr	Doctor
e.g.	for example
et al.	and others
etc.	and so forth, and so on
i.e.	that is
ibid	Latin-Abbreviations (When referring to the same work as in the citation immediately preceding, use the abbreviation "Ibid." for the second reference. This is acceptable even if several pages of text separate the first and second references. The abbreviation "Ibid." is followed by a page number if the page from which the second reference is taken is different from the first. If the pages are the same, no number is necessary.
Lieut.	Lieutenant
n. d.	no date of publication given
n. p.	no place of publication given
n. p.	no publisher given
n. pag.	No pagination given
N.B.	note well
P.S.	postscript
Ret.	Retired
Sr.	Senior

List of Acronyms

ABMU	All Burma Muslim Union
ABSDF	All Burma Students Democratic Front
ABFSU	All Burma Federation of Students Unions
AFPFL	Anti-Fascist People's Freedom League (Burma)
AM	Alliance for Macedonia
APWB	Autonomous Province of Western Bosnia
ASEAN	Association of South-East Asian Nations
ASEM	Asia-Europe Meeting, The
BCP	Burma Communist Party
BH	Bosnia
BJP	Bharatiya Janata Party (India)
BSPP	Burma Socialist Programme Party
CD	Christian Democrats (in Slovenia)
CDU	Croatian Democratic Union
CMEA	Council for Mutual Economic Assistance, The
CNF	Chin National Front
CPB	Communist Party of Burma
CPP	Croatian People's Party
CRPP	Committee Representing of People Parliament
CSCE	Conference on Security and Cooperation in Europe
CSLP	Croatian Social Party
DAB	Democratic Alliance of Burma
DDSI	Directorate of the Defence Services Intelligence (Myanmar)
DEMOS	Democratic Alliance of Slovenia
DEPOS	Democratic Movement (*pokret*) of Serbia
DKBA	Democratic Karen Buddhist Army
DP	Democratic Party (in Serbia)

DPM	Democratic Party of Macedonia
DPMNE	Democratic Movement for Macedonian National Unity
DPNS	Democratic Party for a New Society
DPS	Democratic Party of Serbia
DPS MN	Democratic Party of Socialists of Montenegro
DPVM	Democratic Party of Hungarians in Vojvodina
EC	European Community
EU	European Union
FAO	Food and Agriculture Organisation
FES	Friedrich Ebert Foundation
FRJ	Federal Republic of Yugoslavia
FYRM	Former Yugoslav Republic of Macedonia
GSC	General Strike Committee, 1988, Burma
HB	Herzeg Bosnia
HBS	Heinrich Böll Foundation
IDP	Internally Displaced People
IGO	International Governmental Organisation
ILO	International Labour Organisation
JNA	Yugoslav Peoples Army
KIO	Kachin Independence Organisation (armed wing: Kachin Independence Army)
KNDO	Karen National Defence Organisation
KNU	Karen National Union (armed wing: Karen National Liberation Army)
LCY	League of Communists of Yugoslavia
LDC	Least Developed Countries
LDP	Liberal Democratic Party (in Slovenia)
LP	Liberal Party (in Macedonia)
LP MN	Liberal Party (in Montenegro)
MI	Military Intelligence
MLO	Muslim Liberation Organisation (Burma)
MNDO	Mon National Defence Organisation

MY	Movement for Yugoslavia
NATO	North Atlantic Treaty Organisation
NCGUB	National Coalition Government of the Union of Burma
NCUB	National Coalition of the Union of Burma
NDF	National Democratic Front (Burma)
NGO	Non-Governmental Organisation
NIC	Newly Industrialising Countries
NLD	National League for Democracy, The
NMSP	New Mon State Party (armed wing: Mon National Liberation Army)
NP MN	Narodna (People's) Party of Montenegro
NUFA	National United Front of Arakan
NUP	National Unity Party (Burma)
OBLF	Overseas Burmese Liberation Front
OKO	Overseas Karen Organisation
OSCE	Organisation for Security and Cooperation in Europe
PDA	(Muslim) Party of Democratic Action (in BH)
PDC	Party of Democratic Change (in Croatia)
PLA	Palaung Liberation Army
PLF	People's Liberation Front (Burma)
PVO	People Volunteer Organisation (Burma)
RBH	Republic of Bosnia
RC	Republic of Croatia
RIT	Rangoon Institute of Technology
RM	Republic of Macedonia
RMN	Republic of Montenegro
RS	Republic of Serbia
RSK	Republic of Srpska Krajina
RSl	Republic of Slovenia
RSr	Republika Srpska (in BH)
SC	(UN) Security Council
SDP	Serbian Democratic Party (in BH)

SDP MN	Social Democratic Party of Montenegro
SDPM	Social Democratic Party of Macedonia
SFR	Socialist Federal Republic
SFRY	Socialist Federal Republic of Yugoslavia
SLORC	State Law and Order Restoration Council
SNP	Slovenian National Party
SP	Socialist Party (in Slovenia)
SPDC	State Peace and Development Council
SPS	Socialist Party of Serbia
SRP	Serbian Radical Party
SSA	Shan State Army
UMNO	United Malays National Organisation
UN	United Nations, The
UNAIDS	Joint United Nations Programme on HIV/AIDS
UNDC	United Nations Development Corporation
UNESCO	United Nations Educational, Scientific and Cultural Organisation
UNHCR	United Nations High Commissioner for Refugees
UNICEF	United Nations Children's Fund, The
UNODC	United Nations Office on Drugs and Crime
UNPA	United Nations Protected Areas
UNPF	United Nations Protection Force
UWSA	United Wa State Solidarity Army, The
UYM	Union of Young Monks, The
VMRO	Macedonian Revolutionary Organisation (Inner)
YPA	Yugoslav People's Army

List of Figures

List of Tables

Introduction

We must try to find out what it is that causes
our cities to be so badly governed and
what prevents them from being governed well?
(Socrates in Book V, Plato: The Republic.)[1]

Since the Third Wave of Democratisation, many studies have been conducted about the particular transition processes.[2] Decisive for the selection of the case studies became the defunct character of their democratisation process. In both former Yugoslavia and present day Myanmar, the democratic transition process was unsuccessfully accomplished, after a very promising beginning, sooner or later undermined by formidable challenges which threatened the reversal of democratic gains. To some degree these democratisation processes can even be labelled an 'extended process of transition.' Both states, which consist of multi-ethnicities, have problems in settling a peaceful and meaningful transition to democracy. The democratisation in former Yugoslavia led to disintegration and in Myanmar it is proving to be an intractable one and has become almost un-resolvable to anyone satisfaction. Myanmar today suffers from on-going political instabilities that cause fragmentations, but do not demonstrate in conventional Balkan scenarios. Hence, this comparative study aims to answer the question, if Myanmar political transition will follow the former Yugoslavian fate, by using the transition theoretical frame-work and highlighting the empirical facts on the problems of ethnicity, involvement of the international community and other political factors that relate to the democratisation process.

---

[1] Plato (c.427 – c.347 BC) was an immensely influential ancient Greek philosopher, a student of Socrates, writer of philosophical dialogues, and founder of the Academy in Athens where Aristotle studied. *The Republic* was written by Plato in 360 B.C.E.

[2] Huntington argues that three waves of democratisation have occurred in the modern world. The dates of these waves of regime changes are as mentioned: First, long wave of democratisation between 1828 – 1926, first reverse wave between 1922 – 42; Second, short wave of democratisation between 1943 – 62, second reverse wave between 1958 – 75; and Third wave of democratisation between 1974 – 1990s (see Huntington 1999).

Figure 1-1. Map of the Union of Serbia and Montenegro

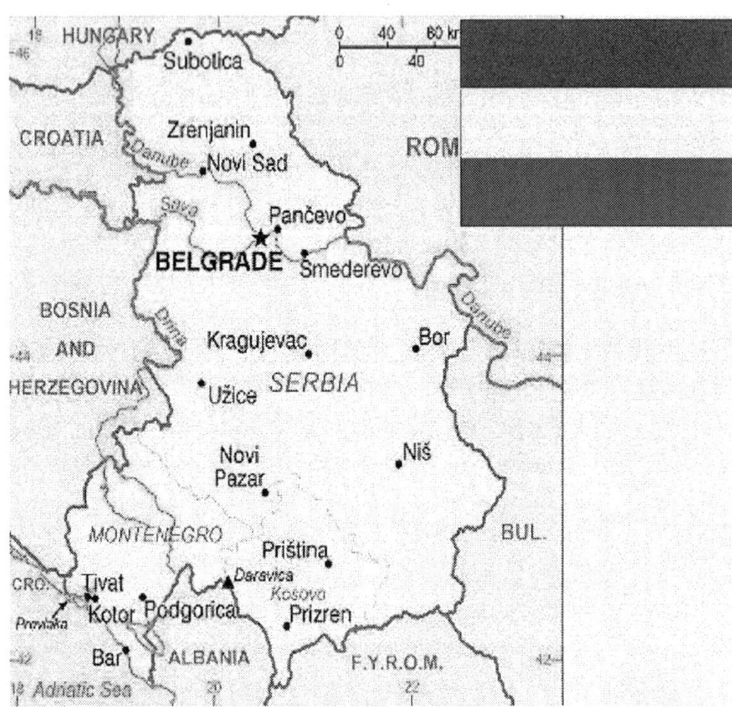

Source: (see *The World Fact Book*)

Figure 1-2. Map of the Union of Myanmar

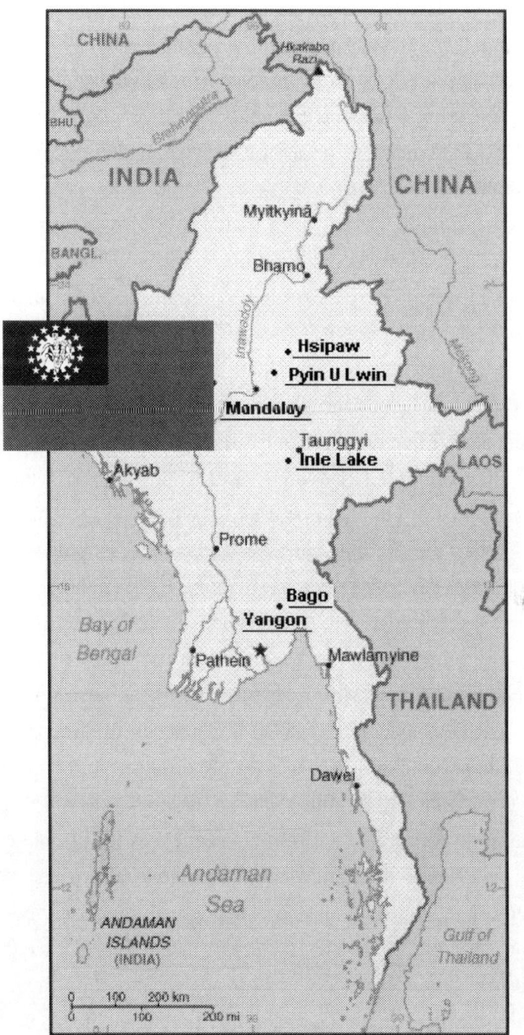

Source: (see Ibid)

1.1. Why Should Myanmar be compared to the Former Yugoslavia?

The recurring ethnic conflicts in the Balkans constitute a significant element of the term, 'balkanisation.' The Balkans became a symbol of something that is torn into pieces and that has lost any connection to a unifying whole. When any dramatic disintegration was to be vividly characterised, the term 'balkanisation' was used (see Pantev, May 2001). The term was specially applied to reflect conflicts and wars with an ethnic basis, which is claimed to be a case in Myanmar, both from the ruling SPDC and the democratic opposition.

Nevertheless, re-emerging after the Cold war, and following Edward Said's denotation of a post-colonialist organised system of knowledge, 'Orientalism,' the terms 'Balkanism' or 'Balkanisation' have been coined around a 'sense of binaries, rational and irrational, centre and periphery, and civilisation and barbarism, arranged hierarchically so that the first, the Europe which is always primary and definitional of the second is the Balkans' (see Dusan *et al.* 2002: 3). The Balkanism and Balkanisation, have become fragmentation, ethno-egoism and ethno-primitivism, a synonym of endless divisions and demarcations (see Mircev, 2003), which similar to the Orientalism has become discourse to be used in other contexts when analysing a political transition in other multi-ethnic countries and becomes a policy prescription.

This comparative case study between two countries is important due to the knowledge base that is required for making responsible decisions in the fields of foreign policy, security, and international relations in the post-Cold War era. The lack of a modern regional economy, infrastructure and the existence of political, social, and cultural disparities have created either a distorted or an incomplete picture of the Balkan situation, and this has been negatively reflected in the general knowledge of the subject (see Pantev, May 2001). The endurance of the old foreign-policy stereotype of 'balkanisation' has had harmful consequences for all interested actors in the local, bottom-up drive to modernisation and progress also in the other part of the world. This stereotype overlooks the new and prevailing social, political, economic, cultural, and strategic tendencies that more accurately depict the region's profile. This is why the knowledge of the historical origins and present realistic threats of the ethnic conflicts in the Balkans are fundamental for understanding whether 'Balkanisation' takes place elsewhere.

The 'Balkanism' and 'Balkanisation' are the discourses which connect to the basic of this case study,[3] which finds its roots in former Yugoslavia wars. The term Balkanisation begun to be used in other contexts, describing a disintegration process. However, these are new fields of discourses as well as a new definition of Western scholarship, in which 'Balkan' is paired in opposition to 'West' and 'Europe.' Thus, Balkan scenarios became a concept to imply to the problems of other multi-ethnic states. Consequently, media, observers, transition specialists and Myanmar scholars are making assumptions on if or not - the possible balkanisation exits in Myanmar, since it is put together in the same category of being multi-ethnic countries with former Yugoslavia. Hence I shall analyse in this study that if there is a great danger of Myanmar breaking up like former Yugoslavia, facing inter-ethnic strife, and after all - if the balkanisation scenario exists in Myanmar.

In terms of geography, Burma and Yugoslavia are far apart. In terms, however, of the common sufferings they have gone through in the past and the common ideals and goals towards which they strive for in the future, there are few nations so close to each other as these two nations (see Tito 1995: 76). Their nationalist struggle against foreign invaders and for national liberation, under the heroic leadership of Tito in Yugoslavia,[4] and Aung San in Burma,[5] is a well known historical fact.

---

[3] 'Balkanism' is a definition which means the rediscovery of the East and Orientalism as independent semantic values and means to divide it a country, territory into small, quarrelsome, ineffectual states. The Balkans is left in Europe's thrall; anti-civilisation, alter ego, and the dark side within (see Stein 1966: 113). Balkanisation has emerged in response to small-scale independence movements and the increasing trend of mini-nationalisms (or micro-nationalisms), as they occur along ethnic, cultural and religious fault lines (see "Balkanisation").

[4] Josip Broz Tito (1892 - 1980) was born near Zagreb. In 1920, he became a member of the Yugoslavian Communist Party. In 1934, he was a member of the Political Bureau of the Central Committee of the YCP (where he used nickname 'Tito'). During the Nazi occupation of Yugoslavia, resistance leader Marshal Tito proclaimed a provisional democratic Yugoslav government in exile. He was Secretary-General (and later President) of the Communist Party of Yugoslavia (1939–80), Supreme Commander of the Yugoslav Partisans National Liberation Army (1941–45) and the Yugoslav People's Army (1945–80), Marshal (1943–80), Prime Minister and Minister of Foreign Affairs of Yugoslavia (1945–53), and President (1953–80) of Yugoslavia. In 1961, Tito co-founded Non-Aligned Movement with Gamal Abdel Nasser of Egypt and Jawaharlal Nehru of India. On 7 April 1963, he was named 'President for Life.' He died on 4 May 1980, in Ljubljana [now in Slovenia] (see "Josip Broz Tito").

[5] Aung San (13 February 1915 – 19 July 1947) was a revolutionist, nationalist, general, and politician who led a nationalist movement to build Burma as an independent nation. The national hero was assassinated during an Executive Council meeting on 19 July 1947, together with six other Councillors before Burma's independence which was agreed upon in 1947 was gained on 4 January 1948 (see Win 1997).

Moreover, the political history has proven that when the ethnic identities are focused at the centre of one nation State, it can either lead to the outbreak of civil wars and disintegration of the states like in former Yugoslavia, or can end up in a dead-lock of transition by regime experimenting with political-institutional openings designed to stabilise military-technocratic authority and focusing on the steady major crackdown on the democratic opposition like in Myanmar. The SPDC in Myanmar, provides all the ammunition they need to justify their grip on power, claiming that they prevent the country at risk of following 'former Yugoslavia's fate,' as there is a great danger of fragmentation of former Yugoslavia alike, or facing inter-ethnic strife and blood-shed as in Bosnia.[6] The State Peace and Development Council (SPDC) states that:

> 'the *Tatmadaw*[7] while safeguarding the nation from dangers for over 50 years is also sacrificing much life, blood and sweat in serving in the forefront to ensure non-disintegration of the Union and strengthening of national solidarity.'[8]

According to former schools of thought in the academic literature regarding democracy and ethnic relations, democracy leads to more ethnic conflicts. The scholars suggests that it is especially difficult to sustain a democracy in a society where 'political parties, interest groups, media of communication, schools and voluntary associations,' are divided along 'religious, ideological, linguistic, regional, cultural, racial, or ethnic' lines (see Wachman 1994: 31). Former theories suggest that the more democratic the regime is, the more conflicts it will experience, because the pluralism of a political system provides an opportunity for all kinds of political activities in a deeply divided multi-ethnic society, and political leaders can use ethnicity to attain their benefits as in former Yugoslavia. The democratisation produces a political enigma in the country, the guarantee of universal democratic rights becomes distorted, and country population groups may rally behind ethnic or religious banners. Conversely, if ethnic or religious groupings are given genuine political expression and territorial identity within a democratic federal system, this may simply lead to calls at a future time for secession of that ethnically-defined region. As a result, establishing democracy in a multi-ethnic State quite often breeds more conflicts than peace. The democratisation permitted the release of old conflicts after the end of the

---

[6] The Government of Croatia reported that the country had suffered 13,583 deaths and nearly 40,000 injured in the 'homeland war' of 1991-5, and neighbouring Bosnia-Herzegovina experienced perhaps 200,000 deaths in the same period (see Smith, Anthony D. 1995: vii).

[7] *Tatmadaw* means the Burmese government's armed forces.

[8] Conclusion of '*Union Spirit*' (see www.myanmar.com).

Cold War in former socialist countries. Thus, the former theories conclude that the strongly centralised regimes are better suited to keeping multi-ethnic States together.

The opposition leader Aung San Suu Kyi belabours her point that, in order to build up a peaceful nation, there is a need for trust among the different groups.[9] There has to be openness and room to discuss. She further argues that former Yugoslavia is a very good example of a country where there was not sufficient dialogue to resolve the problems. Her argument aligns with later schools of thought regarding democracy and ethnic relations:- the establishment of democracy ought to reduce conflict between ethnic groups; the problems shall be solved at the negotiation table through dialogue.[10]

Democratisation has been described as a complex, open-ended, dynamic process leading from a democratic transition marked by uncertainty over the 'rules-of-the-game,' to relatively stable, consolidated political systems (see G. Schmitz *et al.* 1992: xii), and democracy alone will not be sufficient to prevent from 'balkanisation' because the aspiration for ethnic equality and rights and for a genuinely federal union must be secured. They have been an integral and fundamental part of political

---

[9] Aung San Suu Kyi, since 1988, one of the world's most renowned pro-democracy activist, born on 19 June 1945, to General Aung San, the architect of Burma's independence, who was assassinated in 1947. Aung San Suu Kyi was educated in Burma, India (when she accompanied her Ambassador mother) and the UK. She married a British scholar Dr Michael Airs and has two sons, Alexander and Kim. After living in Oxford for many years, she returned to Burma in April 1988 to nurse her ailing mother. When the nationwide movement started, she was asked to take a leading role in the movement by the student leaders. She co-founded the NLD - a political party that won a landslide victory in the general election 1990. Aung San Suu Kyi has been held under of house-arrest many time ever since. She was held from 1989-1995, from 2000-2002, and from 2003 to present. She has won numerous international awards, including the Nobel Peace Prize, the Sakharov Prize from the European Parliament, the United States Presidential Medal of Freedom, and the Jawaharlal Nehru Award from India.

[10] The verity of ethnicity: the former Yugoslavia consists of Serbs, Croats, Muslim, Slavs, Slovenes, Macedonians, Montenegrins and other ethnic groups (7.7% Albanians and 1.9% Hungarians); Burma consists of 68% Burman, 9% Shan, 7% Karen, 4% Rakhine, 3% Chinese, 2% Mon, and other 5%. As the Burman group forms the largest ethnic group, thus the name of the country is derived; and the ideological factors such as 'the non-alignment' block and 'putting together Federalism.' The religious factors; in Yugoslavia, the religious factor is heterogeneous: in 1990 – there were 30% Roman Catholic, 50% Serbian and Macedonian Orthodox, 9% Muslim, 1% Protestant and 10% others. Burma is homogenous with 89% Buddhist, 4% Christian (3% Baptist and 1% Roman Catholic), 4% Muslim, 1% animist beliefs, and 2% others. As far as historical legacies; language factors are concerned, Yugoslavia is homogeneous: predominantly Serbo-Croatian. In Burma, it is heterogeneous - although Burmese is official state language, major ethnic language groups such as Shan, Karen, Chin, Mon and Kachin are widely spoken. Geographical location leads to major differences in their transition phase; interests of neighbouring countries and Great Power; and the role of international involvements and inventions.

discourse in Myanmar since 1948 (see Yawnghwe, Chao-Tzang, 2003). On the one hand, the proponents of ethnic reconciliation argue that ethnic conflict in Myanmar is unlike the situation that existed in Rwanda or Somalia or Yugoslavia (see Aung Naing Oo, 2002), and on the other hand, some ethnic groups demand for future self-determined States and some for the secession of their States (recent developments regarding some Shans' demands) by taking the former Yugoslavia's example.

Others argue that neither democracies nor autocracies are very likely to lead to conflicts, because democracies open many ways for solving conflicts without resorting to violence, while autocracies repress any possibility of mobilising for violent conflict. Thus transitional period is more likely to experience civil war than either democracies or autocracies, and institutionally consistent democracies and stark autocracies are equally unlikely to experience war (see Hegre *et al.* 2001). It is also possible that violent ethnic conflicts disappear at higher levels of democratisation and are replaced by institutionalised ethnic conflicts. Ethnicity has become the most important force of the 1990s, although the phenomenon is not a new one. Ethnic conflicts based on nationalism did erupt in the era of bipolarity for example in Myanmar, Burundi and Kashmir before the 1990s. Burma, during the late 1950s, already faced what would become known as the 'balkanisation' scenario.

The process, which led the former Yugoslavia to disintegrate, began by the ethno-nationalistic overestimation of the Serbs accompanied by a concomitant demonisation of the Albanians of Kosovo, the Croats and the Serbs-Muslims. The changes to the borders in the Balkans reawakened old hatred and ethnic hostilities causing unprecedented human suffering, which was quelled only by the intervention of the international community and finally led to the emergence of new States from Tito's Yugoslavia. The expectation that a liberal democracy would soon replace former totalitarian regimes in that region has only partly been realised. Ethnic-nationalism is considered to be the central object of former Yugoslavia's disintegrations.[11] As for former Yugoslavia, the claim of historical ethnic animosities are ways of dismissing from consideration what collapsed and why. The former Yugoslavia was unique, and no lessons can be learned from its tragedy (see Woodward 1995: 13-21).[12]

---

[11] It is often forgotten that ethnic community has a long history and that nationalism, as an ideology and a movement, has been a powerful force in world politics since the French and American Revolutions.

[12] Most of these conflicts are neither ethnic nor religious, though they are presented and perceived as such, in most cases the underlying causes are political or economic (see Ivanov 1996: 12).

Democratic transition in Myanmar continued to be at an impasse, even though the 'challenge of democracy' became an unavoidable reality in Southeast Asia with the global wave of democratisation in the 1990s. On account of its civil wars and ethnic conflict over 50 years, Myanmar lacks the fertile soil for the development of a sustainable democracy (see Taylor *et al.* January 2005: 3). Myanmar's military apparatus is devoid of all legitimacy, rather depending on power through its monopoly of the means of violence and legitimacy largely resides in the repressed opposition. In short, this comparative study will provide a current empirical illustration of the challenges such as historical legacies, states borders and multi-ethnicities (which vary in religion) involving in democratic transitions in multi-ethnic States. It aims at generating an improved theoretical understanding of it. Hence, it will deal with the problem of both countries' political transitions based on their basic similarities and their differences.

1.2. The Elaboration of Terms

I wish to explain the usages of certain terms in my work as follows before I start with other aspects of this work: -

1) Yugoslavia (Serbian: *Jugoslavija*) is used for three separate periods but successive political entities that existed during most of the 20th century on the Balkan Peninsula in Europe. In this work, the *first Yugoslavia* indicates the Kingdom which was formed in 1 December, 1918 as the Kingdom of Serbs, Croats and Slovenes, and which was re-named the *'Kingdom of Yugoslavia'* on 6 January, 1929 and existed under that name until it was invaded on 6 April, 1941 by the Axis powers. Capitulating only eleven days later, it ceased to exist 17 April, 1941; The second Yugoslavia signifies a Socialist state established immediately after World War II on 29 November, 1945 as Democratic Federation of Yugoslavia (DFY), which in 1946 became the Federal People's Republic of Yugoslavia (FPRY) and in 7 April, 1963 the Socialist Federal Republic of Yugoslavia (SFRY). This remained in place until 15 January, 1992, at which time four of its six constituent republics - Slovenia, Croatia, Macedonia and Bosnia and Herzegovina - had seceded. The second Yugoslavia and the third Yugoslavia – the Union of Serbia and Montenegro will be implied as 'former Yugoslavia' in this study: and third Yugoslavia was called Federal Republic of Yugoslavia (FRY), was formed in 1992 on the territory of the remaining republics of Serbia (including the autonomous provinces of Vojvodina and of Kosovo, officially known as Kosovo and Metohija) and Montenegro. In 2001, the name Yugoslavia was to be officially abolished when the state would transform into a loose commonwealth called Serbia and Montenegro which finally happened on 4 February, 2003. On May 21, 2006, Montenegro held a referendum to seek full autonomy and with the final official results of the votes, formally declared independence on June 3, 2006. The separation of Kosovo from Serbia seems on the way. However, the researches for this dissertation have started in early 2003 and ended at the decease of Milošević at March 2006, and for reasons of practical constraints, further factors later than that date have not been taken into account.

2) The SPDC of what is now officially known as *Myanmar Naingngan* (the State of Myanmar) abandoned the older and more familiar name of the country, Burma (or the Union of Burma) in 1989. For the reason that lies in the nature of the mili-

tary regime, the United States and EU have refused to recognise the change in nomenclature, as have some of the regime's political opponents; in particular Aung San Suu Kyi and her party the National League for Democracy (NLD).[13] In this work, generally 'Burma' is used to describe the period before 1988 and 'Myanmar' for the period of the SLORC/SPDC period. No political connotations are implied by this, and none should be inferred.

3) I wish to make a clear distinction between the words 'Burmese' and 'Burman.' Among scholars - there is an understanding that 'Burmese' refers to all ethnic groups, a term denoting the citizens or people of Burma. The term 'Burman' refers to the Burmese speaking ethnic group, comprising the majority (around 40 – 60 percent) of the population. Therein lies a problem because 'Burmese' is the language of the Burman, and used to signify things of Burman essence, like Burmese dance, food, etc. Although 'Burmese' is considered to be more inclusive, ethnically neutral like 'British,' it is actually not (see Yawnghwe, Chao-Tzang, September 2002). 'Myanmar' is to refer to all the citizens of Burma/ Myanmar and 'Burmans' for the country's majority ethnic group. During the colonial period (1824–1948), the term 'Myanmar,' previously used for the territory under the kings of the central Irrawaddy valley, and the term, 'Burma' became the common name that was derived from the idea of the territory of the Burmans (Bama). By the late colonial period the term 'Myanmar' had largely fallen from common usage. Instead, 'Burman/ Burmese' (Bama) became most frequently used. The 1948 Constitution further complicated the terms 'Myanmar' that have become the collective name for all the ethnic groups and territories.[14] The term 'Myanmar' is back in the controversial period of military government in 1989. Belonging to the Burman ethnic group, I feel obliged to make these elaborations as there is an inseparable link between politics and scholarship.[15]

---

[13] The NLD has been Myanmar's leading opposition party since 1988 and won a landslide victory in the May 1990 elections. The party was founded on 24 September 1988 by retired Brigadier-General Aung Gyi (Chair), retired General Tin Oo (Vice Chair), and Aung San Suu Kyi (General Secretary).

[14] The United Kingdom of Great Britain and Northern Ireland is a sovereign state occupying much of the British Isles. It is often shortened to 'United Kingdom,' 'UK' or 'Britain.'

[15] One has never devised a method for detaching the scholar from the circumstances of life, from the fact of his/ her involvement (conscious or unconscious) with a class, a set of beliefs, a social position, or from the mere activity of being a member of a society (see Said 1995: 10).

1.3. From Epistemological Queries to Methodological Strategies

This comparative study will deal with transition theories, which relate to national experience. The theoretical approaches are the 'democratic transition and consolidation theories' argued by Juan J. Linz, Alfred Stepan and Samuel Huntington. However, this study will aspire to contribute to the conventional theoretical debate, and aim to offer the understanding for the need to expand the link between ethnicity and political transitions in transition theories that is lacking, which will be evidenced in analysing the case of former Yugoslavia and present day Myanmar.

The theoretical perspectives applied in this study will be equally significant and supplement each other. Applying these dimensions to this comparative study, a descriptive analysis is made to investigate how the regime type prior to the elite system could effect both nations' democratic transition and how the pro-democratic forces and the authoritarian regimes interacted in the political process of liberalisation.

An analytical framework, which highlights an agent-structure approach and situated actors, may thus contribute to an enhanced understanding of the interactions between intention, motivation, restraints and possibilities of the winners and losers in such transitions of multi-ethnic societies. Hence, with this analytical framework, we are able to improve knowledge of the intricate and dynamic processes of transitions and contribute to the advancement of the theories of democratic transitions. As such, it is not the theories that lead the practices but *vice-versa*. The theoretical model and empirical analysis will complement each other in this work. The qualitative analysis also attempts to provide an academic foundation for the development of adequate policies in support of democracy.

The testing of the hypotheses pre-supposes the availability of data on democratisation as well as data on the degree of ethnic heterogeneity and on the degree of ethnic conflict and its two aspects: institutionalised ethnic conflict and violent ethnic conflict. All data are measured at the interval level. It will frame out of stereo-type of ethnic researches on Burma. This case-study may provide empirical insights that are of interest not only to scholars but also to practitioners. It may also, for instance, be seen as an attempt to 'bridge the gap' between theory and practice in that it involves an analysis of current events, including Myanmar's unfinished struggle for democracy and the former Yugoslavia's 'imagined democracy.' One has to recognise that analysis of a current event has limitations regarding archival material, obstacles that are not encountered in studying a historical case. Nonetheless, the ambition of this dissertation is to provide improved knowledge and understanding of contemporary problems of transition through a political scientific analysis.

A Note on Interviews

A series of interviews have been carried out for this study, especially necessary as the Myanmar part is still a more recent event. This is also the reason why I have given priorities to interviews mainly with activists, rebels, journalists, politicians, Myanmar scholars and international political actors who are involved in the case of Myanmar. The interviews may be described as open discussions. The interview can be conceived of as a face-to-face 'conversation with a purpose' (see Gubrium *et al.* 2002). In this study, there are different types of interviews including qualitative interviewing, in-depth interviewing, life story interviewing and elite interviewing. Qualitative and in-depth interviewing in this work is more exploratory, theory driven, and collaborative. The aim of 'qualitative interviewing' is to ascertain those qualities and their social organisation. 'In-depth interviewing' commonly elicits highly personal information about specific individuals who are involved in political arena. My own approach to life story, which is based on a naturalistic, person-centered view, has evolved from an interdisciplinary context. The life story interview is inherently interdisciplinary and a highly contextualised, highly personalised approach to the gathering of qualitative information about the human experience featured in this case-study. I have conducted life story interviewing because it can help the teller, the listener, the reader and the scholar to understand a broad range of psychological, sociological, political, mystical-religious and cosmological-philosophical issues. Upon formally requesting an interview, I realised that persistence and patience were required virtues when I attempted to arrange 'elite interviews.' The term 'elite' is closely linked with the operation of power and privilege. Any analysis of elites also depends on broader interpretations of hegemony and society, and on an understanding of the intersection of respective environments. The elite interviewing in this study is linked with theoretical understanding of power, status and society. It is important to present an unbiased study and therefore I pursue both the privileged and the activists.

1.4. Outline of the Dissertation

This dissertation is based on theoretical and empirical analysis, which covers the transition period (from the late 1980s until present). This thesis consists of ten chapters that are divided into four parts: 1. Introduction, 2. Theoretical Analysis, 3. Empirical Factors, and 4. Conclusion. Although the third part is explicitly mentioned as Empirical Factors, some chapters are combined and demonstrated with the theory.

Chapter II of the second part which follows the introduction is the *Theoretical Part* that describes how an innovative framework for the analysis of transition phase is constructed. Chapter II entitled 'Theorising Transition: Transition Theories and their Implications in Democratic Transitions' highlights how the political theories are implicated into political practices. Chapter II is divided into three sub-chapters, which demonstrate the highlighted empirical factors with theoretical considerations.

The third part, the *Empirical Factors*, consists of five chapters. It traces the evolution of the State's approach to the issue in post-transitional Yugoslavia and Myanmar at its *status quo*. The basic factual material of the monograph, past political history and its legacies are provided in Chapter III. In that Chapter, Marshall Tito and General Ne Win are compared,[16] as well as their legacies and how did they rule their respective. The current governments and its nature are explained in Chapter IV. The democratic opposition of both countries is comparatively analysed in Chapter V.

The Chapter VI highlights some insights into the manifestation of the politics of ethnicity and its role in political transitions in multi-ethnic countries, and the possi-

---

[16] General Ne Win (a) Shu Maung (24 May 1911 - 5 December 2002) was the leader of Burma from 1962 to 1988. He was born in Paungdale. He began to involve in the Burmese independence movement during the mid-1930s. He was one of Aung Sans 'Thirty Comrades' who joined the Burma Independent Army (BIA). After Burma's independence in 1948, he became Home and Defence Minister. In 1950, under Ne Win's command, the army was able to contain both the Karen revolt and the insurgency by the Chinese-backed Burmese Communist Party (BCP). In 1958, as the Prime Minister U Nu asked General Ne Win to form a temporary military government; he ruled the country in caretaker mode for 18 months. U Nu returned to power between 1960-62, and General Ne Win returned to power in a bloodless coup in 1962. By 1971, he had transformed Burma into a one-party policy State led by the Burma Socialist Programme Party (BSPP). He was a President of Burma from 1974-81 under a Constitution adopted in 1974 and the country was renamed the Socialist Republic of the Union of Burma. Burma became isolated and impoverished under General Ne Win. Admitting economic mismanagement and as a response to the country-wide protests in 1988, he resigned. General Ne Win remained out of government in relative seclusion near Rangoon. In March 2001 he was placed under house arrest following the arrest of some number of his family members. His three grandsons were sentenced to death for treason on 26 September. The former dictator died on 5 December 2002 (see Maung 1969; see "Former Burma Dictator Ne Win dies").

bilities to overcome it. There is also an analysis of the long-term origins and complexities involved in the making of ethnicity, nationalism and national identity in the same Chapter. Both are presented empirically but also imply different theories of ethnicity, nationalism and federalism. They examine the implications of the resurgence of ethnicity and nationalism for the democratic transition from the erstwhile dictatorship structure of power to Western-style liberal capitalist democracies. It depicts the challenges that the countries are facing in their transition and tries to answer the question whether federalism is an answer to their problems.

The overall international interests in both countries are thoroughly explained in Chapter VII. The Chapter VII discusses the interests of the international society in both crises. The international society has widely misunderstood ethnic dimension of transition. The analysis of outbreaks of civil wars is centered on the implications of the ethnic *Intifada*[17] in both countries for the level of agent and structure, which are 'state-to-be' against society.

In this study, the view of the very different dimensions – historical, political, and sociological - of the minorities issue in both countries, the proportion of data and theory varies from Chapter to Chapter, until it reaches its conclusion. The final and concluding part, Chapter VIII 'The Conclusion,' will highlight the adaptive interplay between the theoretical concepts and the empirical analysis throughout this study to understand how a multi-ethnic state has undergone the transition phase and considers whether Balkan scenario exists in Myanmar.

---

[17] *Intifada* (also Intefadah or Intifadah) is an Arabic term for 'uprising.'

Theorising Transitions: Transition Theories and their Implications in Democratic Transitions

"Die Theorie bleibt in letzter Instanz ihr Hüter
. . . . die Praxis folgt der Wahrheit, nicht umgekehrt."[18]
(Rudi Dutschke 1965)[19]

The overall objective of this chapter is to present key theoretical arguments for how democratic transition can be analysed and interpreted, and also to combine known empirical facts of former Yugoslavia and present day Myanmar. The theories are always applicable, although a variety of analytical approaches in transition theory may be discerned, such as structural, strategic, process, behavioural, and integrative. It is also a difficult task if one is to achieve the theoretical level, that is, to find general tendencies of development by comparing processes, which are different in time and space. Although not all transitions achieve democracy, by tracing the efforts both of successful and unsuccessful transitions, one can gain a wide base for comparison, typology and models of transition. One consequence of this is the problem of distinguishing between the scholar's perspective of transition, and the practitioners' frames of transition. The objective of this part of the thesis is to present a theoretical overview which relates to both cases. In the first section, an overview of transition research will be presented, with a particular emphasis on how transitions are defined and understood. The second and third sections will compare how various approaches theorise and the dynamics of transition. On the basis of a critical approach to the study of democratic transition, a meta-theoretical model is outlined at the end of this chapter.

---

[18] English Translation: at last instance, theory remains in its authority, but practise follows the truth, not vice-versa.

[19] Rudi Dutschke (7 March, 1940 in Schönefeld, Germany – 24 December, 1979, Århus, Denmark) was the most prominent spokesperson of the German students' movement in 1960s. Dutschke died in 1979 from an epileptic seizure as a consequence of the brain damage that he had from the assassination attempts. The public assessment of Dutschke's political activities had undergone several changes in 1960s to a broad recognition that the movement for which he was a leading spokesperson who played an essential role in the democratisation in the post-World War II period.

2.1. Theoretical Considerations

This section aims to present an overview of transition research in order to discuss how various perspectives theorise about political actors, structures, change and continuity of the world-politics. This section will also explain why the democratic transitions are irrelevant to many cases. Approaches to democratic transition and consolidation argued by Juan J. Linz, Alfred Stephan and Samuel Huntington explain the dynamics of the political process in both countries which actually brings out its circumstances.

Transition does not necessarily mean transitions from the non-democratic regimes toward a democratic one. It could actually be the contrary. Even if it is not the contrary case, there is no guarantee or inevitability about democratisation succeeding as if by some process of unstoppable evolution. Transitions can also develop into widespread, violent confrontations, eventually giving way to revolutionary regimes, which promote changes going far beyond the political realm. The term "democratic transition", does not mean "democracy". It conveys an *ongoing process*, which begins with the transformation of a one-party regime, the military regime and/ or the apartheid regime leading to a new order based upon the "will of the people". The process of transition from non-democratic to democratic regimes, and especially to the political dynamics of the consolidation of post-authoritarian democracies is being theorised. The starting point of theorising transition was the Eastern and Central European cases.[20] Theorising transition tries to answer this important question through a variety of studies of the complex transformations occurring in the world that moved away from strong State-direction of their societies.

Transition is not a one-way process of change from one hegemonic system to an-

---

[20] In last thirty years, transition could be observed in three Southern European countries namely Spain, Portugal, and Greece. In South America, Brazil, Argentina, Chile, and Uruguay – all had democratic breakdown in the 1960s and 1970s. These regimes demobilised popular organisations, repressed civil societies, were (unlike the countries in Southern Europe) led by hierarchical military regimes, and were "presidential" instead of "parliamentary" in their institutional and cultural legacies. As late as 1987, the outcome in of these four countries was highly uncertain, so we had the chance to observe directly possible transitions and possible failures. In post-Communist Europe, there are former USSR, Poland, Hungary, Czechoslovakia, Romania, and Bulgaria to be looked at it. In Southeast Asia and East Asia it has been observed that development causes democratisation. Post-war Latin American politics and interwar European history provide suitable lessons about how countries may embark on and make it through democratic transition but then fail the tests of democratic consolidation. Thereafter, one may speak of a growing probability that new democracies will become consolidated (see Pridham 2000).

other. Rather, transition constitutes a complex reworking of old social relations in light of processes distinct to one of the boldest projects in contemporary history – the attempt to construct a form of capitalism on and with the ruins of the communist system. Mainstream transition theory has, then, largely been written in terms of the discourses and practices of liberalisation. Early attempts by anti-Stalinist socialists and social democrats within the democracy movements of Eastern and Central Europe are to frame a transition 'with a human face' failed in the euphoria of 1989.

The geopolitical consequences of the end of a 'two-world' order and the consolidation of what George Bush called 'the New World Order' have become clear in recent years. Super-power singularity supervises the emergence of regional power blocs and, once again, narrows the option open to individual state planners in all countries. From the boycott of Cuba, the blockading of Iraq, to the 'openness' towards Vietnam and China, a variety of strategies are being deployed to sustain transitions with the goal of building post-communist, open markets and stable relations for the flow of goods and capital.

There is diversity and complexity in transition. The process of transition varies from one setting to another depending on the nature of regimes. There are various attitudes to transition, and different interpretations of it. To elucidate how transitions are situated in time and place, I will discuss outlooks of democratic transition and facilitating and restraining structural features circumventing democratic transitions, which are often neglected in the predominantly actor-oriented transition theories. For example, the politics of ethnicity and the different dimensions of transformation of the former Yugoslavia may have retarded the democratic consolidation of present day "the Union of Serbia and Montenegro", and the democratic transition in "the Union of Myanmar."

However, there is something very convincing about regarding the 1990s as the decade of transition. The global waves of democratisations that started in the 1990s not only stimulated the theory of transition to explain the changes. They also produced much broader pessimism about the applicability of democracy in developing countries and they contributed to concern about the viability and workability of democracy among the developed countries where it has existed for years. Obviously, the events of the collapse of the Soviet Union, Yugoslavia's ethnic wars, the disintegration of the eastern block in Europe, and the situation in Southeast Asia in the decades of rapid transitions resisted the expectations of theory. This left the West with the opportunity and challenge of confronting head-on the issue of the maintenance of stability and democratic institutions, and also giving the new-input to the transition studies of political science.

The theoretical arguments of the democratic transition which are used in this study are mainly based on the transition theories of Samuel P. Huntington, Juan J. Linz and Alfred Stepan, though Huntington expresses that, inevitably, no theory can explain fully a single event or group of events (see Huntington 1991: xiii). Transition theory is relevant to only a few cases, because the causes of the democratic transition differ from one case to another and from one time to another. Thus we may discern the following:

1. No single factor is sufficient to explain the development of democracy in all countries or in a single country.
2. No single factor is essential to the development of democracy in all countries.
3. Democratisation in each country is the result of a combination of causes.
4. The combination of causes producing democracy varies from country to country.
5. The combination of causes generally responsible for one wave of democratisation differs from that responsible for other waves.
6. The causes responsible for the initial regime changes in a democratisation wave are likely to differ from those responsible for later regime changes in that wave. (see Ibid 37-38).

Transition, transformation, and democratisation theories have emerged from vital Western interests.[21] Based on those theories, analyses were made upon the transitions. Immediately following the changes, social scientists shifted gears and began to produce substantial literature on the preconditions for democratisation, the process by which it occurs and, in due course, the democratic consolidation problems of new democratic regimes (see Ibid 16-17). Therefore, it is not always feasible to apply the theories to the situation of developing countries. These difficulties are outlined in both the Yugoslavian and Burmese cases.

---

[21] All the political theories diverged from Western perspectives, monopole of the imperial powers (until World War II was in the hands of English and French, and to the present is in the hands of the Americans) (see McCargo *et al.* 1996: 210-5).

2.2. Stage of the Transition Process in both Cases

In this section, in order to specify the focus of this study, a broad definition of a transition will be made, before going through the deep analysis of the stages of the transition process in both cases. Democratic transition is not a one-day switch from a non-democratic to a democratic order. Huntington also underlines: "the critical point in the process of democratisation is the replacement of a government that was not chosen [...] by one that is selected in a free, open, and fair election" (see Ibid 139). It is a broad threshold that commences with the empowerment of individual citizens, groups that eventually leads to the installation of the winner of an election and his survival in the office of who rules. Theoretical categorisation is made in order to discuss the present state of transition research in this work. Three broad approaches are identified in the study of transition for both cases, including: (1) Liberalisation, (2) Democratic Transition, and (3) Democratic Consolidation. The process of transition is frequently divided into the following three phases:

- 'pre-transition,' is a phase in which the outgoing regime disintegrates and the course is set for eventual regime change,
- 'democratic transition' is a phase of regime change, a process commencing at the point where the previous authoritarian regime begins to be dismantled,
- and, 'democratic consolidation' is often a lengthier stage but also one with wider/ deeper effects. It involves the full institutionalisation of the new system, the internalisation of its rules and procedures and dissemination of democratic values (see Pridham *et al.* 1994: 2).[22]

In order to explain the stages of the transition process in both cases of my work, I

---

[22] Consolidated democracy normally means a country has regular, fair elections, contests by voting for leaders and citizen participation and influence on government. Firstly, three conditions must happen before there can be any possibility of democratic consolidation: (a) a State has to exist, (b) Democratic transition has to be brought to completion (free and contested elections), and (c) Rulers must govern democratically; Secondly, consolidated democracy is a political regime where democracy, a complex system of institutions, and its rules become the only political process in a country such as: (a) *Behaviourally:* Democratic regime has no threats from other actors wanting a non-democratic regime, (b) *Attitudinally:* Public opinion, even during times of economic hardship and political turmoil, holds belief that democratic procedures are the best method of governance, and (c) *Constitutionally:* Conflict resolution performed through specific laws, procedures and institutions sanctioned by the new democratic processes; Thirdly, five inter-connected conditions are necessary for consolidation of democracy: (a) conditions must exist for development of free and lively society, (b) autonomous political society, (c) all political actors must be subject to rule of law and elections, (d) existing State bureaucracy for new democratic government to use, and (e) institutionalised economic society (see Linz and Stepan 1996: 5).

shall apply to the stages below:

Figure 2-1. The Politics of Liberalisation

Phase 1	*Phase 2*	*Phase 3*	
Decline of Fear	Struggle over Rules of the Game	Decisions to extend the Liberalisation Process	
Decline of a sense of anti-populist or counter-revolutionary fear	Governmental experiments with political-institutional openings designed to stabilise military-technocratic authority	Repression/ toleration calculus of military and capitalist elites	
	Development of a liberalising opposition, led or supported by middle-sector groups	Where cost of repression exceed cost of toleration	further lib-eralisation
		cost of toleration exceeds cost of repression	crackdown

Source: (see Huntington 1991: 40-45).

Theoretically, there are four ideal alternatives of the future development at the initiation of liberalisation process: -

Table 2-1. The Process of Liberalisation

Ideal-alternatives	Circumstances	Result
1st case	Reformers maintain weak position; are challenged by strong opposition; popular mobilisation threatens the elites; involved the security apparatus.	An internal coup occurs and power passes to the hardliners. The attempt to liberalise the society is aborted and the repressive actions are renewed.
2nd case	The possibility for the regime to accept reform, which doesn't change the structure of the authoritarian system, but enables to renew its legitimacy.	The regime with its liberalised appearance can function in the long-term perspective without the phase of democratisation.
3rd case	Political elites of non-democratic regime understand that they are not able to challenge the activity of the opposition and surrender power.	The phase of liberalisation is very short and elections are quickly announced. The old elites don't gain any guarantees for the future.
4th case	Most popular among scholars because of its results related to the criteria of democracy.	Often it is called transition by pact, transition through transaction or negotiated transition.

Source: (see Dvorakova 1994).

An effective definition of a transition is needed in order to specify the focus of this study. O'Donnell and Schmitter define transition rather broadly as "the interval between one regime and another." Transitions are delimited, on the one hand, by the launching of the processes of dissolution of an authoritarian regime and, on the other, by the installation of some form of democracy, the return to some form of authoritarian rule, or the emergence of a revolutionary alternative (see O'Donnell *et al.* 1986). The analysis must distinguish between a successful and an unsuccessful transition, if this definition is to be adopted. Transitions can start with the aim of establishing a well-functioning democracy. The consolidation phase shows if it is successful or not. The stabilisation and maturation of an already existing democratic system takes place here. These two stages must be differentiated. In 1998, Altermark provided a broad definition of a transition:

> A transition is initiated when signs of liberalisation and relaxation start emerging in the authoritarian or totalitarian regime and is accomplished when a democratic system has been established (in the case of success) or when there is an authoritarian backlash and the start of a new authoritarian regime (in the case of failure) (see Altermark 1998: 11).

Altermark's broad definition does not describe political and judicial bodies and their characteristics after a transition. These must be specified for an understanding of the requirements. Linz and Stepan define a transition phase in the following way:

> A democratic transition is complete when "sufficient agreement has been reached about political procedures to produce an elected government, when a government comes to power that is the direct result of a free and popular vote, when this government *de facto* has the authority to generate new policies and when the executive, legislative, and judicial power generated by the new democracy does not have to share power with other bodies *de jure*" (see Linz *et al.* 1996: 3).

The behavioural elements in Linz's theory are excluded, where are requirements for democratic consolidation. The integrative perspective records the actors' goals through their behaviour during this process. Consolidation is often defined as the period, which begins after free elections are held and new constitutional arrangements have been put in place (see Linz 1990: 157). During consolidation, the institutional arrangements installed in the transition phase take a definitive shape and actors become habituated to the new rules of the game. It must be stressed, however, that transition phases do not necessarily follow each other, and that not all regimes in transition end up as consolidated democracies. Moreover, the transition does not necessarily is a democratic transition. In fact, most scholars studying the transition believe that not all transitions will be successful and that some countries may revert to authoritarian or totalitarian regimes or end up in a grey zone between democracy and some form of dictatorship or oligarchy (see Dimitrova 1996).

Former Yugoslavia "the Union of Serbia and Montenegro": Referring the second table, the third case of the process of liberalisation could apply to development of the liberalisation process in "the Union of Serbia and Montenegro", if one would look only at the changes that occurred in 2000, after 24 September. The decade-long experience of "transition" in the former Yugoslavia demonstrates that the varied paths of individual countries differ significantly and that transition within a particular country occurs through processes with multiple meanings and with multiple directions. There is increasing agreement among scholars that "transition" is in fact a generic name for numerous different patterns of change with highly individual dynamics and consequences (see Heinrich 1999). Transition in the former Yugoslavia followed the stages of transition phases step by step and its transitions turned out to be most difficult and unpredictable one in Eastern Europe. It started with Tito's death. In the absence of the sole holder of the nation, difficulties arose for the leaders who were left to deal with his political legacy and the declining economy. The 1974 Constitution was amended and with the multi-party elections in the 1990s, the democratisation of the former Yugoslavia commenced. Conversely, it was overshadowed by instability and ethnic conflicts, because of the absence of a necessary condition for the formation of democracy. The nationalist programmes were implemented during the 1990 election and willingness to achieve consensus of different ethnic groups led toward the tragedy of civil wars. Through to the end of the 1980s, Yugoslavia remained a one-party State. As the 1990s began, the political culture of Yugoslavia was in an unprecedented state of flux. To reach his goal of separating his government completely from Communist domination, Prime Minister Markovic[23] pushed new laws that would allow national, multi-party elections in 1990. The death of Tito deprived the party of its only unifying element and, after 1980, the League of Communists of Yugoslavia (LCY) suffered from the same fragmentation and diffusion of power as the government institutions. His proposals met with substantial opposition in the Federal Assembly and the Presidency, especially because at the time of the proposed changes only Slovenia and Croatia had already committed themselves to a multi-party system at the Republic level. The first phase of liberalisation took place with the beginning of implementing democracy by holding elections in

---

[23] Ante Markovic was the Prime Minister of the SFR Yugoslavia (SFRY) between 1989 and 1991.

1990s, but it led to the out-break of ethnic civil wars and resulted in a failed democratic transition of the former Yugoslavia as a whole, but different democratic transition processes in the newly emerged countries – Bosnia and Herzegovina, Croatia, Macedonia, Slovenia, Serbia and Montenegro.

Table 2-2. Outline of Successor Countries of the Former Yugoslavia

	Area (km^2)	Population (mil.)	Currency
Bosnia and Herzegovina	51,129	3.2	Convertible Mark
Croatia	56,538	4.54	Kuna
Macedonia	25,713	2.03	Denar
Montenegro	13,812	0.56	DEM (EURO)
Serbia	88,361	8.98	Serbian Diner
Slovenia	20,251	2.0	Tolar

Serbian transition is an extreme and exceptional case. It is an exception because it used to be part of the former Yugoslavia, a country that had historically been a special case, in many ways. In Serbia, "transition" is specifically linked to the wars in which the regime played a decisive role and subsequently it became the target for NATO intervention. Serbia is also extreme because of the level of destruction of institutions, the creation of an institutional blockade, the sacrifice of its own and other countries' population and the extraordinary price, which its citizens have had to pay which, in total, combine to characterise the Serbian situation as one of "perverted transition". Ever since 1989-90, non-regime alternative opposition and regime-alternative co-existed in parallel with Milošević's authoritarian rule, which plays a role in the former Yugoslavia's transition. Transition impacts ethnic minorities to a greater extent, thus ethnic groups have been forced to draw on the cultural resources of their communities.

In September 2000, Slobodan Milošević called elections, because the country was crippled after NATO's bombing which arose out of his standoff with the West over Kosovo, where he abolished the autonomy of Kosovo and sponsored "ethnic cleansing" in 1998. The different opposition groups in Yugoslavia can be presented as set out in the table below.

Table 2-3. Groups in Opposition to Milošević's Regime since 1990[24]

	Regime alternative	*Non-regime alternative*
Non-violent struggle	Traditional opposition[25]	Business elite
Violent Struggle		Muslim Secessionists,[26] Different Ethnic Rebellions Groups

The fall of Milošević was argued that, it is not achieved by Western sanctions or NATO bombing but, rather, that it was a people's revolution that brought him down.[27]

---

[24] The Democratic Opposition of Serbia was formed as an alliance of political parties against the ruling Socialist Party of Serbia and its leader, Slobodan Milošević: the Democratic Party of Serbia (DSS) led by Vojislav Koštunica, was to form a part of the Democratic Opposition of Serbia, but split from the group in 2001 into the Democratic Party and the G17 Plus group (see "Democratic Opposition of Serbia.").

[25] Democratic Opposition of Serbia or DOS (a coalition of many small parties including DSS) [leader N/A]: Alliance of Vojvodina Hungarians or SVM [Jozsef, Kasza], Democratic League of Kosovo or LDK [Dr Ibrahim Rugova, President], Democratic List for European Montenegro or DLECG [Milo Djukanovia and Ranko Krivokapic], Democratic Party or DS [collective interim leadership led by Cedomir Jovanovic], Democratic Party of Serbia or DSS [Vojislav Koštunica], Democratic Party of Socialists of Montenegro or DPS [Milo Djukanovic], Party of Serb Unity or SSJ [Borislav Pelevic], Serbian Radical Party or SRS [Tomislav Nikolic], and Social Democratic Party or SDP [Rasim Ljajic] (see "Serbia and Montenegro.").

[26] Former Yugoslavia was confronted by active secessionists: Croats and Muslims bent on going their own ways and the rebellion of the Kosovo Albanian separatists against Serbs. The general view of the wars of 1991 to 1995 is turned on its head; and the press becomes a malevolent force mysteriously engaged in 'demonisation' of the Serbs.

[27] Slobodan Milošević ruled former Yugoslavia (1989-2000). He was born in 1941 in Pozarevac, Serbia, and graduated as a lawyer from the University of Belgrade in 1964. He started his career as economic adviser to the Mayor of Belgrade. He became the head of the local Communist Party in 1987, and then emerged as the leading force in Serbian politics. By 1988, he replaced the party leaders in Kosovo and Vojvodina. Milošević was first elected President of Serbia in 1989. He was re-elected as President in the direct elections of 1990 and 1992. His opposition to confederation led to Croatian and Slovenian declarations of independence in 1991. Milošević backed Serbian rebels throughout three years of civil war. He signed a peace agreement only in 1995 to end the civil war in Bosnia. He became President of the new Yugoslavia Republic in 1997. Ethnic violence and unrest continued in Kosovo. He agreed to withdraw from Kosovo after NATO's bombing in 1999. Milošević's rejection of claims of a first-round opposition victory in new elections for the Federal Presidency in September 2000 led to mass demonstrations in Belgrade in October which led to the collapse of the regime's authority. Opposition leader Vojislav Koštunica took office as a President in October. Milošević was arrested in 2001 and handed over by the Serbian government to the United Nations International Criminal Tribunal. The trial began at The Hague in 2002 with Milošević defending himself though refusing to recognise the court's jurisdiction. He died in March 2006 in prison.

On 24 September 2000, he was defeated overwhelmingly at the polls by opposition candidate Vojislav Koštunica,[28] the regime "alternative traditional" opposition of Serbia since the death of Tito, then the transition took place in present day "the Union of Serbia and Montenegro."

The battle against Milošević had at least temporarily united the nineteen political parties that supported the opposition's candidate, Vojislav Koštunica (see Kramer, October 2000). Yet, the problems facing the opposition in Yugoslavia were tremendous. The democratic consolidation seemed to be at *status-quo* because it was reconstructing the very basis of its statehood, the most basic level of its political systems that defined national identity and State identity. A multi-level framework tends to fill out the picture of the former Yugoslavia as having passed through transition and being recognisably on the road towards democratic consolidation, and it powerfully influences the chances for these then fragile new democracies to consolidate themselves. Hence its transition turned out to be more of a difficult phase rather than a semi-permanent structural condition inhibiting consolidation. This follows the pattern of the majority of post-Communist States in the Balkans, which have simultaneously carried the burden of State- and nation-building. This is hardly surprising given the enormous difficulties of the new democratic system in the former Yugoslavia, with multiple transformations imposed on routine government overload; but some improvement is probably necessary eventually for securing democratic consolidation.

Burma – "The Union of Myanmar": Referring to Table 2, the first case of the process of liberalisation can generally be applied to the development of Myanmar

---

[28] Vojislav Koštunica was the Prime Minister of Serbia. He studied law at the University of Belgrade. He lost his job in 1974 after criticising Tito's government. In 1989, he became one of the founders of the Democratic Party. Later, he became the leader of the new Democratic Party of Serbia. Koštunica was a populist politician with no connection to the old Communist Party. He was supported both by the democratic and nationalistic voters, so the Democratic Opposition of Serbia backed him in the presidential election of September 2000. After the turbulent events in 2000, Koštunica was finally declared the winner of the election and remained President of the Federal Republic of Yugoslavia until 2003, when the State was replaced by Serbia and Montenegro and the position he held was abolished. Koštunica opposed the extradition of Slobodan Milošević and has stated his opposition to the Hague Tribunal several times. He also refused to remove Milošević's former police chief Rade Markovic from office. Following the parliamentary elections in December 2003, in which the DSS emerged as the largest of the democratic parties, Koštunica became Prime Minister in March 2004 at the head of the new minority government of Serbia with the support of the Socialist Party of Serbia (see "Vojislav Koštunica.").

which is - contrary to Serbia case where the whole democratic transition process regressed to its beginning – the liberalisation phase. Liberalisation precedes democratisation. It starts when at least some of the elites in power are aware of the impossibility of maintaining their position in the long run, without changing. During periods of liberalisation, regimes make certain concessions to the opposition and offer limited amounts of liberty; there is a decline in repression and sometimes the hardliners can be alternated with the reformers. The system itself is not changed and it maintains most of its authoritarian features. If there are elections during this period, they occur only in situations in which the elites can secure continuation of their control of the country's political life after the vote. Hence, elections in this phase do not permit a true shift of power. This leads Linz and Stepan to regard a transition as completed after the first elections if these are regarded as free and fair. This is just a narrow definition of a transition and it orients transition study. It excludes the consolidation phase. The main actors regard winning free elections as the only means to achieve power in a consolidated democracy: "To put it simply, democracy must be seen as the only game in town" (see Linz 1990: 38). However, it is not the case of Myanmar's democratic transition. Myanmar's impetus for liberalisation can be elaborated in three points as follows:

1. "loss of legitimacy" theories of regime transformation must make two good claims: 1) that legitimacy is irreducible to anything else, whatever it might be (self-interest and fear being the prime candidates), and (2) the legitimacy is a necessary condition of stable domination. If legitimacy is reducible, then it cannot be the source of the dynamic of regime transformation;

2. one obstacle to understanding the processes of liberalisation and democratisation is the difficulty of identifying on *a priori* grounds the actors relevant to these processes;

3. and, the other approach is to focus on the strategic postures directly and to distinguish the hard-liners and the soft-liners within the ruling bloc, and the moderates and maximalists (and perhaps the principalists or moralists) among the opposition.

According to the three points, Myanmar's liberalisation is analysed as followed:

Legitimacy question: In 1990, the regime held elections for a multi-party parliament in which the NLD, led by Aung San Suu Kyi who was then under house arrest, won a majority of the seats. However, the junta ignored the result of the election and the elected parliamentary representatives never took office. The regime imprisoned hundreds of pro-democracy supporters, including elected members of parliament. Thousands more fled the country. Since the military claims that it is a legitimate coercive force, society cannot prevent itself from a military takeover and, at the same time, foster and sustain a military strong enough to protect society from threats to its integrity (see Schiff 1995: 11). Several years ago, Timothy Garton Ash, the noted student of Eastern European social movements and a friend of the late Michael Aris,[29] made an observation that "the Lady", has all the legitimacy, but the generals have all the guns. He argues that, the NLD and its most avid supporters are not only equally emphatic in saying 'no' to this claim, they go a step further and proceeding from the so-called hostage theory, assert that progress under an authoritarian rule is a sheer impossibility. Their policy of boycott and isolation is based on this understanding. The SPDC regards this as defamatory to their intentions, to the positive steps they are taking and also as obstructionism with the aim of sabotaging the process towards peace and development (see Ash, May 2000). Unlike in Serbia, neither the non-violent struggle nor the violent struggle co-exists as a regime alternative in Myanmar. Myanmar's on-going violent struggle consisting of different armed groups (ethnic and non-ethnic) for the past five decades could not be considered as a regime alternative movement because of these groups' weak conditions and their inability to challenge the ruling junta. For example, the exile Government, the National Coalition Government of the Union of Burma (NCGUB) led by Dr Sein Win,[30] is not in a position to become an alternative regime.

Myanmar seems to have reached an impasse between two forces with two quite different natures; one that is strong in terms of power but lacks legitimation and the

---

[29] Michael Aris was the late husband of Aung San Suu Kyi.

[30] Dr Sein Win is the Prime Minister of the NCGUB and the former leader of the Party for National Democracy PND). In late 1990, he went to the Thai-Burma border and set up the NCGUB. Dr Sein Win is the son of U Ba Win, the elder brother of General Aung San, who were assassinated together. In 1965, Dr Sein Win graduated from Rangoon University in Mathematics, later went to Hamburg University and obtained a Master of Science in 1974 and a Doctorate in Mathematics in 1979. After the 1988 uprisings, he was the Treasurer of the Information Department of the NLD and in PND. The PND was then banned in December 1990 and he was charged with breaking the Political Parties Registration Act. The Election Commission subsequently dismissed him as an MP. Dr Sein Win left Burma and co-founded the NCGUB on the Thai-Myanmar border in December 1990 and MPU in 1995. He was elected Prime Minister of the NCGUB receiving 17,511 valid votes or 50% of ballots cast in the 1990 elections, at Paukkhaung, Pegu Division. He currently lives in the US (see "Brief Biographies of Exiled Members of Parliament of Burma").

other which has the legitimation of the voters but is weak. The heart of the Burmese problem is that Aung San Suu Kyi has all the legitimacy and the SPDC has all the power. If the NLD had a little element of real power, and the SPDC had a little more legitimacy, a negotiated transition would be easier to imagine (see Ibid). Opposition groups in Myanmar can be categorised as set out in the table below:

Table 2-4. Groups in Opposition to Myanmar Ruling Regime from 1947 until Present

	Regime alternative	*Non-regime alternative*
Non-violent struggle	The National League for Democracy (NLD) since November 1988	Exile Government: The National Coalition Government of the Union of Burma (NCGUB), since 1990
Violent Struggle		- Different Ethnic Minorities Rebellion Groups,[31] and Communists Military Rebels,[32] since after independence - All Burma Students Democratic Front (ABSDF),[33] since 1988

Difficulty of identifying on a priori grounds the actors relevant to transition processes: Ash argues that the analysis of Myanmar's problem is only half-right, because it is a strategic blunder to reduce a country's or a people's liberation movement to a single icon, however great an asset the icon may be to the movement as a whole in

---

[31] Myanmar has experienced a long history of migration and conflict among various ethnic groups along fluid frontiers. Under British control, diverse peoples were brought under at least nominal central administration. Yet many areas remained effectively self-ruled, with only a thin veneer of imperial oversight. During World War II, while many Burman joined Japanese forces to fight against the British and many minority ethnic groups remained loyal to Britain. This reflected a genuine desire for independence on the part of both groups. Burma became independent in 1948 only after extensive negotiations led by General Aung San. The Panglong Agreement of 1947 outlined minority rights and specifically gave the Shan and Karenni peoples the option to secede from the Union a decade after independence. After Aung San's death, almost immediately upon independence, Burma was thrown into a series of brutal ethnic wars that have continued with varying intensity to this day (see http://www.burmaproject.org).

[32] Thakin Soe, Thakin Aung San, Thakin Ba Hein, Bo Latyar and Ko Ba Tin originally founded the CPB in the 1930s. Thakin Soe and Thakin Than Htun were the intellectuals who sided Aung San until the early 1940s. When ideological differences drew them apart, the CPB chose the armed struggle after the independence in 1948, despite all Aung San's efforts for the negotiations.

[33] After the "8.8.88." movement, most of the students left their homes and went to the border areas where they hoped to obtain military training to fight against the army to give up its political power. In November 1988, they founded the world's first student-army named the "All Burma Students Democratic Front (ABSDF)" on the Burma-Thai border. The KNU was the first ethnic organisation to welcome and accommodate the students.

terms both of public relations values and internal political significance. The first thing that needs to be done if we are to correct this serious mistake is to recognise that there is both Aung San Suu Kyi *and* the movement, and that they co-exist in a dialectical relationship. The movement has enabled Aung San Suu Kyi, one of the two surviving children of the architect of Burma's independence, to become an important political leader in her own right. Equally, she has rejuvenated activists' hope and strengthened their resolve to stay committed to the movement (see Zarni, September 2003). The military government appears unwilling to compromise with its weaker rival, but election-legitimised opponent, the NLD. Encouraged by its supporters in Washington, London and Brussels, the NLD, for its part, refused to accommodate the SPDC as it reiterates their democratic principles, but took an unrealistic stand against the military junta. The extreme imbalance of power between the military leaders and the civilian democratic forces is a major impediment towards possible change. This is the barrier toward the country's progress. A deeply felt sense of siege mentality inflicts all sides, creating a highly polarised situation.

Hard-liners and soft-liners: One of the most common paths away from a non-democratic to a democratic regime is via a "pacted transition." Linz and Stepan explains that in a "pacted transition" there are four players composed of hard-liners and soft-liners in the regime, and moderates and radicals in the opposition. Theoretically and politically, there are two structural preconditions of such a pacted transition to democracy: 1) the existence of an organised, nationally known and non-violent democratic force in civil and political society; and 2) the existence of soft-liners in the regime who have the desire and autonomy to negotiate a "pacted reform" (see Linz *et al.* 1996: 356). However, the democratic opposition groups in Myanmar, the non-violent struggle led by Aung San Suu Kyi and the NLD, the armed struggle of different ethnic groups since 1950s and the former ABSDF, do not fit into conventional "hard-liners versus soft-liners" theories. As far as the military regime of Myanmar is concerned, "hard-liners versus soft-liners" and "hard-liners versus moderates" analyses were based on the assumption of the former power struggle between military intelligence and the battalion forces. Such conclusions were reached after power struggle between SPDC's Vice-Chairman General Maung

Aye,[34] the hard-liner, and a former Prime Minister, General Khin Nyunt, former Chief of the National Intelligence Bureau (NIB), a moderate politician.[35] Myanmar specialists, international observers, mediators and different groups in opposition regard the former Prime Minster as a "soft-liner" or a "moderate-man", although he did not fulfil any criteria to be one. The former Prime Minster was definitely a pragmatic man according to any definition, who tried to protect his territories by any means, as a Military Intelligence official. The empirical facts demonstrate that in the major theories of democratic transition, a conclusion can be drawn that Myanmar's "regime change" processes are unlikely to take place via a "pacted transition". Power without legitimacy unhinged illegitimate regimes elsewhere and it will continue to elude the Burmese political scene, where legitimacy largely resides in the repressed opposition. Hence, there also left a narrow marginal chance for Myanmar's liberalisation to continue from where it ended.[36]

---

[34] General Maung Aye is the Vice-Chairman of the SPDC who graduated from the Defence Services Academy (1st Batch) in Maymyo. He joined the military in 1959 and, from 1975, served as a Lieut. Colonel in the Infantry Battalion No. 68. He was promoted to Colonel in 1979 and became the Commander of the North-East Region in 1986. In 1988, he became the Commander of the Eastern Region with the rank of Brigadier General. He was promoted to Major General in 1990 and Lieut. General in 1993, when he was summoned to Yangon to become Deputy Commander-in-Chief. He became the Vice-Chairman of the SLORC in 1994 and later of the SPDC.

[35] Lieut. General Khin Nyunt was appointed Prime Minister in 2003 and the Head of the MI. He graduated from the Officer's Training School (25th Batch) in 1960 and holds a BA. He became Commander of Infantry Battalion No. 20 in 1960, and served as a Staff Officer at the Defence Ministry's Bureau of Special Operations in the 1970s. In 1982, he was a Tactical Operations Commander of the 44th Light Infantry Division. He was called to Rangoon to take over as Head of the Directorate of Defence Services Intelligence (DDSI) after North Korean terrorist attack in 1984. He was close to General Ne Win and was instrumental in suppressing the 1988 uprising. He announced a 'roadmap' for democracy after his appointment as Prime Minister. He is placed under house arrest since 19 October 2004.

[36] The result of the free and fair elections of 1990, organised and later ignored by the SLORC, the whole democratic transition process went back to the beginning of its liberalisation phase. The last flame of Myanmar's liberalisation phase occurred in 1996 and was far from a precursor to revolution, for which the only claim to fame was that there was once a riot in Rangoon. Myanmar's junta announced it was changing the old name of the "State Law and Order Restoration Council (SLORC)" and adopting the new name of the "State Peace and Development Council (SPDC)", in November 1997, in order show that there was a change.

2.3. Theory and Practice

This section offers selected structural and actor-orientated approaches to transition theory and theoretical implication to both cases. A transition could be understood as an interval between the first opening of an established non-democratic regime and the introduction of a new stable regime, which is not necessarily democratic. Linz and Stepan's typology of non-democratic regimes, the transition and consolidation tasks associated with them are presented. The problems that Eastern Europe and especially the former Yugoslavia and Myanmar have confronted, have been considerably greater than the political problems of any of the South American or even Central European cases (see Ibid 1996), as both former Yugoslavia and Myanmar are multi-ethnic States. They do not relate to Huntington' influential formulation, which says "democratisation occurs most frequently and also most easily in countries that have reached the upper-middle income levels of economic development" (see Huntington 1993). Linz and Stepan argue that there is a model for the implications of prior non-democratic regime types for paths to democratic transition, because the arena of characteristics and its leader has an exclusive position in the sultanistic regimes,[37] as differentiated from authoritarian and totalitarian versions as demonstrated as below.

Table 2-5. The Prior Non-democratic Regime Type for Democratic Consolidation

Arena Characteristics	*Authoritarian*	*Totalitarian*
Civil society autonomy	medium to high	low
Political society autonomy	low to medium	low
Constitutionalism and the rule of law	low to high	low
Professional norms and autonomy of State bureaucracy	low to high	low
Economic society with a degree of market autonomy and plurality of ownership forms	medium to high	low (Communist) or medium (Fascist)

Source: (see Linz *et al.* 1996)

---

[37] The term originated from Ottoman Empire. The ruler may or may not be present in economic or social life. It was originally coined by Max Weber to describe "an extreme form of patrimonialism" involving "an administration and a military force which are purely personal instruments of the master" (see Weber 1978).

As the object of the research of the transitions is more narrowly specified by the presence of the desirable goal and value – democracy - the trend toward democracy is one of the criteria from the beginning of the transition process. Democracy is characterised by the presence not of subjects but of citizens, so a democratic transition often puts the polis/ demos questions at the centre of politics. From all that has been said so far, following assertions can be made:

1. The more the population of the territory of the State is composed of pluri- national, lingual, religious or cultural societies, the more difficult agreement on the fundamentals of a democracy becomes.

2. Even though this does not mean that democracy can not be consolidated in multi-national States, it means that considerable political crafting of democratic norms, practices and institutions must take place (see Ibid).

The character of the arenas in the prior non-democratic regime in the period relatively close to the start of the transition is of the greatest importance for the tasks democratic leaders will face. The less developed the arena, the greater the tasks democratic leaders will have to accomplish before the new regime can become a consolidated democracy. Even though "dictatorship" is the common usage for non-democratic and non-traditional legitimate governments, main non-democratic regime types are proposed as authoritarianism, totalitarianism, post-totalitarianism and sultanism (see Ibid 44-56). In this regards, the former Yugoslavia can be differentiated as an authoritarian regime and Myanmar as totalitarian one, though it is not easy to categorise different ruling systems according to the types of regimes. For example, in "totalitarian regimes" in the past, the pseudo-fascism of Balkan, Eastern European and Baltic States had not corresponded to the German or even the Italian model. Many of the differences between systems or within the same system over time are to be understood in terms of the relationship of people in those positions to the ideology (see Linz 2000: 53-77). *Totalitarianism* is defined as: -

> 1) a totalist ideology; 2) a single party committed to this ideology and usually led by one man, the dictator; 3) a fully developed secret police and three kinds of monopoly or more precisely monopolistic control; namely, that of (a) mass communications; (b) operational weapons; and (c) all organisations including economic ones, thus involving a centrally planned economy (see Friedrich 1969: 126).

Totalitarianism is any political system, that of an extreme form of dictatorship, in which a citizen is totally subject to a governing authority in all aspects of day-to-day life. It goes well beyond dictatorship or typical police-State measures and even beyond those measures required to sustain total war between States. It involves constant indoctrination achieved by propaganda to erase any potential for dissent, by anyone, including most especially the agents of government. Totalitarian regimes can break down under following circumstances:

1) After the death of regime's charismatic leader, totalitarian regimes begin to change (e.g., Stalin in USSR) or break down (e.g., Tito in former Yugoslavia)

2) The regime is defeated in a war which results in the collapse of existing political system (e.g., Nazi Germany, Fascist Japan, Saddam's Iraq or Afghanistan).

3) The regime falls as a result of internal upheaval perhaps either a "revolution" or a *"coup d'état"* (e.g., France in 1940) (see Friedrich 1954; Linz 1964).[38]

Myanmar is experiencing a very unstable system, in contrast to stable totalitarian systems where pre-existing business, religious organisations and even the role of the army is at a secondary level. The subordination of military authority is one of the distinctive characteristics of totalitarian systems in contrast to other non-democratic systems. Until now no totalitarian system has been overthrown or changed fundamentally by the intervention of armed forces, even when in crisis moments, one or another faction might have reinforced its power through the support of the military (mostly in terms of hierarchical military). Conversely, many "authoritarian regimes" are founded by military coups and headed by military men. A category of military authoritarian regimes includes too many and quite different regimes. Military men can carry out a deep cultural revolution like Mao Zedong in China or bring about important social and ideological changes like Tito in Yugoslavia, can displace traditional regimes and realise a social revolution after a break within tradition with counter-revolutionary intent, like Franco in Spain. Authoritarianism is defined as: -

> Political system with limited, not responsible, political pluralism, without elaborate and guiding ideology but with distinctive mentalities, without extensive not intensive political mobilisation, except at some points in their development, and in which a leader or occasionally a small group exercises power within formally ill-defined limits but actually quite predictable ones (see Linz 1964: 255).

---

[38] All classic concomitants of "revolution" were absent at the end of the Second World War, unless we count the Czech *"coup d'état"* as an example (see Kecskemeti 1954: 345-360).

Tito's Yugoslavia was defined more as totalitarian regime, whereas the former Yugoslavia under Milošević as an authoritarian regime because Milošević was a civilian leader. Regardless of the office he occupied, civil-military relations in former Yugoslavia have been heavily dominated not by an institution but by one person – by Milošević (see Vankovska 2000). It seems that a typology distinguishing military and non-military authoritarian is not an easy task.[39] The political nature and the purpose of the military intervention in assuming power is different from case to case. Authoritarian regimes can break down under following circumstances:

1) The authoritarian regime has met the functional needs that led to its establishment. It is, therefore, no longer necessary and it collapses.

2) The regime has, for one reason or another, lost its "legitimacy" and disintegrates sometimes due to (1).

3) Conflicts within the ruling bloc, deriving often from (2), particularly within the military cannot be reconciled and some ruling faction decides to appeal to outside groups for support. Thus, the ruling bloc disintegrates *qua* bloc.

4) Foreign pressures to "put on a democratic face" lead to compromises, perhaps through the mechanism of (3).

Nonetheless, Huntington argues that "regime change" does not depend on the nature of regime:

> Why did some thirty countries with authoritarian regimes but not some one hundred others shift to a democratic political system? And why did regime changes in these countries occur in the 1970s and 1980s and not some other time? It does seem unlikely that these transitions within a decade and half could be purely coincidental (see Huntington, 1991: 40-45).

The regimes that moved toward democracy in the third, included one-party systems, military regimes, personal dictatorship and the racial oligarchy in South Africa. These regimes can be characterised as below.

---

[39] The most bizarre situation arises from the collision that still exists between the Serbian and Federal Constitution in regard to the respective President's competencies in the defence sphere. According to the Constitution, the Republic of Serbia is still a State within (a federal) State, having kept the position of Supreme Commander of the (non-existing) armed forces, who is also authorised to declare a state of war or of emergency, to declare mobilisation *et cetera*. The President of the Republic does not have any great authority, but he is the Commander-in-Chief of the armed forces and Chair of the Supreme Defence Council. Prior to Milošević, two men - Dobrica Cosic and Zoran Lilic, held this office. Their 'success' in the position was determined by their loyalty to the President of Serbia (see Vankovska 2000).

Table 2-6. Transformation in Different Waves

Functions	Total	Partial
Instrumental	Totalitarian	Tutelary
	Stalinist Russia, Maoist China, Nazi Germany, "Stalinist" East Europe	Tunisia, Tanzania, Tito's Yugo-slavia, Ataturk's Turkey,
Expressive	Chiliastic	Administrative
	Fascist Italy, Nkrumah's Ghana, Mali, Guinea, Cuba, Ben Bella's Algeria	Mexico

Source: (see Linz 2000: 172).

Milošević's regime was pressured by foreign countries (both the US and the EU) with both diplomatic and military means (NATO intervention in 1999 for the Kosovo crisis) to give up power and, in that way, his regime came to an end. The facts which concern the SPDC in Myanmar the most are: 1) US-led military attacks on grounds of a nuclear threat, which is an unlikely scenario; and 2) an internal coup which encourages a mass uprising. Short of the emergence of any of these, the SPDC feels confident and is determined to pursue its own agenda.

Some people also dub all fascist and communist regimes as *totalitarian* even though some fascist regimes, such as Franco's Spain, and Mussolini's Italy before World War II, and some communist regimes, such as Yugoslavia under Tito, the People's Republic of China under Deng Xiaoping and Cuba under Fidel Castro, have authoritarian rather than totalitarian characteristics. Within each category of regime type, some countries did not democratise during the fifteen years after 1974: China as a one-party system; Myanmar as a military regimes; Cuba as a personal dictatorship. Therefore, Huntington comes to the conclusion that the nature of the regimes, consequently, can not explain why some regimes transited to democracy and others did not (see Huntington 1991: 41). In the Asia-Pacific, Malaysia and Myanmar are frequently mentioned as authoritarian States and North Korea as a totalitarian State. However, Myanmar is sometimes mentioned as a totalitarian and sometime as an authoritarian State, because it shares characteristics from both definitions. Myanmar is characterised as authoritarian because it favours absolute obedience to authority, as against individual freedom, and relates to or expects unquestioning obedience. It is today considered as a totalitarian regime, which is relating to, being, or imposing a form of government in which the political authority exercises absolute and centralised control over all aspects of life, the individual is subordinated to the State, and opposing political and cultural expressions are suppressed. Theoretically, there is another explanation regarding transition. Other than the regime type, there are four different types of State elites: 1) a hierarchical military, 2) a non-hierarchical military, 3) a civilian elite, and 4) the distinctive category of sultanistic elites. The institutional characteristics of the State elites are elaborated in the table below.

Table 2-7. The Institutional Characters of the State Elite

State Elite	How favourable affect democratic transition?
Hierarchical Military	Shares characteristic that is potentially favourable to democratic transition: a) the hierarchical leaders of the military-as-institution come to the decision that the costs of direct involvement in non-democratic rule are greater than the costs of extrication, and b) it is likely to acquiesce that their reserve domains of power be eliminated.
Non-hierarchical Military	Have some characteristics that make it less of a potential obstacle to democratic transition: a) the incentive for the military-as-institution to re-establish hierarchy military, and b) likewise, the colonels have established para-state intelligence operations that are perceived as threats even to the military.
Civilian Leadership	Will characteristically have greater institutional, symbolic and absorptive capacities than either military or sultanistic leaders to initiate, direct and manage a democratic transition.
Sultanic Regime	Presents an opportunity for democratic transition because, should the ruler (his or her family) be overthrown or assassinated, the sultanistic regime collapses, otherwise, there is very little place for a democratic transition.

Source: (see Linz *et al.* 1996: 66-83).

Both Milošević's and the SPDC regimes were backed by a hierarchical military, but democratic transition took place in the former Yugoslavia and not in Myanmar. If the path of democratic transition type has to depend totally on the State elites of prior non-democratic regime types, it is hard to speculate in the Myanmar case, since the latest power struggle in Myanmar resulted in the removal of former Prime Minister, General Khin Nyunt, together with more drastic action of dissolving the National Intelligence Bureau where the former Prime Minister was the head of the institution.

Theories that explain democratisation include: a high overall level of economic wealth; relatively equal distribution of income; a market economy; economic development and social modernisation; a feudal aristocracy at some point in the history of society; the absence of feudalism in the society; 'a strong bourgeoisie' ("no bourgeois, no democracy," in Barrington Moore's succinct formulation); a strong middle class; high levels of literacy and education; an instrumental rather than consummatory culture; Protestantism; social pluralism and strong intermediate groups; the development of political contests before the expansion of political participation; democratic authority structures within social groups, particularly those closely connected to politics; low levels of civil violence; low levels of political polarisation and extremism; political leaders committed to democracy; experience as a British colony; traditions of toleration and compromise; occupation by a pro-democratic foreign power; influence by a pro-democratic foreign power; elite desire to emulate democratic nations; traditions of respect for law and individual rights; communal (ethnic, racial, religious) homogeneity and/ or heterogeneity; consensus on political and social values; and absence of consensus on political and social values. With regard to democratic transition, one always argues along these lines below. Different types of paths to democratic transition are mentioned as follows:

1.   *Reforma-pactada, ruptura-pactada* (for example Spain).
2.   Defeat in war and externally monitored installation (for example Germany, Italy and Japan).
3.   Interim government after regime termination not initiated by regime (coup by non-hierarchical military, armed insurgents, or mass uprising and regime collapse, for example Portugal).
4.   Extrication from rule by hierarchically led military (crisis of a non-hierarchical military, for example Greece).
5.   Internal restoration after external re-conquest (for example the Netherlands and Norway, Denmark and Belgium).
6.   Internal reformulation (for example France).
7.   Re-democratisation initiated from within the authoritarian regime.
8.   Re-democratisation initiated by the Civilian Political Leadership (for example Spain).
9.   Re-democratisation initiated by "Military-as-Government" (for example Brazil).
10.   Re-democratisation led by "Military-as-Institution" (for example Pakistan).
11.   Society-led regime termination (for example the Philippines).

12. Party Pact with or without consociational elements (for example Indonesia, Nigeria).

13. Organised violent revolt coordinated by democratic reformist parties (for example Costa Rica).

14. Marxist-led revolutionary war (for example China, Yugoslavia, the Soviet Union, Vietnam and Cuba).

15. Or other regime-specific paths (a risk-prone consolidated democracy, for example Uruguay; a crises of efficiency, legitimacy, and democratic state, for example Brazil; from an impossible to a possible democratic game, for example Argentina; incomplete transition/ near consolidation?, for example Chile).

The transition studies also have tended to neglect the structural context in which human agency takes place. The focus on political regimes has made these studies too State and elite centred. The analysis of the State has also been rather narrowly focused on the main political institutions on a national level. Building a democratic State requires institutional change (the form of the State), and representative change (which has influence over policies) as well as functional transformation (what the State does) (see Grugel 2002: 69-70). "Transitologists" focuses on institutional and representational change, but have not paid sufficient attention to the functional aspects (see Ibid 66), which are different from its geographical, historical and cultural background. For example, the relative de-decolonisation of post-totalitarian regimes in Eastern Europe, South America and the Asia-Pacific have not been the same.

The different characteristics of the Western and the major non-Western States are also reasons for the different impacts of transition. Of all the transitions which took place in Southern Europe, Spain, Portugal and Greece, none of them had a sultanistic,[40] a totalitarian or post-totalitarian origin, nor had they been governed by an authoritarian regime led by the hierarchical military. They also did not come from a basis of a strong single authoritarian party (see Linz *et al.* 1996: 139). In contrast to Europe, no Latin American country carried out an unconstrained constituent assem-

---

[40] Sultan originally is an Arabic abstract noun meaning "strength", "authority", or "rulership". Later, it came to be used as the title of certain Muslim rulers who claimed full sovereignty in practical terms. The dynasty and lands ruled by the Sultan is called Sultanate. But the ideal type of a contemporary sultanistic regime is based on personal rulership, loyalty to the ruler is motivated not by his embodying or articulating an ideology, nor by a unique personal mission, or any charismatic qualities, but by a mixture of fear and rewards to his collaborators (see Chelabi *et al.* 1998).

bly. Brazil tried and was constrained both by the military and the President. Democratic politicians in Chile are still slowly attempting to unshackle themselves from an authoritarian Constitution. Uruguay and Argentina opted for restoration formulas. In short, four South American cases are yet to be fully consolidated according to the Linz theory, which is in contrast to three Southern European cases, all of which are already consolidated (see Ibid 220-221). Even though the case of post-Communist Europe is complex, still the case of the former Yugoslavia can be well explained theoretically, when compared to Myanmar.

Nonetheless, in view of the lack of objective yardsticks about "free, open and fair" elections, singling out electoral politics as the crucial element of the democratisation process is apparently problematic. Moreover, questions of economic development and social justice in addition to political liberalisation seem to be increasingly attached to the process of democratisation in the Asian context. Until now, the literature on democratisation in Southeast Asia focused on the effect of rapid economic growth on the performance legitimacy of the regimes, the size and attitude of the middle class and the prospects for civil society (see Huntington 1993). The situation in Southeast Asia in the decades of rapid economic growth resisted the expectations of Huntington theory. Based on Karl Marx's industrial theories, some analysis classified the countries in the Asia-Pacific into three groups: Group I (Thailand, Taiwan and South Korea) - the case suggests that rapid development leads to democratic transition, Group II (Malaysia, Singapore and Indonesia) its development does not lead to democratic breakthrough or further democratisation, and strangely the democratic Philippines and authoritarian Myanmar are grouped as Group III only because of their similar poverty status (see Laothamatas 1997: 17). This grouping confirms that it is hard to theorise the transitions in Southeast Asia.

Transitions initiated by an uprising of civil society, by the sudden collapse of the non-democratic regime, by an armed revolution or by a non-hierarchically led military coup all tend toward situations in which the instruments of rule will be assumed by an interim or provisional government. Transitions are initiated by hierarchical State-led or regime-led forces (see Linz *et al.* 1996: 71). Myanmar was a country ruled by a dictator and, from 1988 to the present with non-hierarchical military structure. Some regime-specific possible transition paths and likely outcomes such as the collapse of non-democratic authoritarian regimes which were led by non-hierarchical military forces or a split in the leadership as in typical totalitarian regimes do not seem to be a forthcoming event. Myanmar's historical and most popular uprising '8.8.88' has initiated the transition period, which remains to be accomplished today. There is a definition of a modern democracy which says that it could be conceived of as being composed of five major inter-related arenas: civil society which has access to freedom of association and communication, political society, rule of law according to the Constitution of the country, State apparatus which is legitimate and economic society with institutionalised market (see Ibid 15). When one discusses 'civil society', during transitions from military dictatorships to democracy in Latin America from the 1980s onwards, the concept of 'civil society' re-emerged in the left-of-centre political discourse. By the late 1980s, the concept was adopted in Central America and referred to popular organisations linked to revolutionary opposition movements. The civil society that died under the BSPP era in Myanmar also had no chance to reappear under the continuous repression of the SPDC. The other facts such as access to freedom of association and communication, political society, rule of law, state apparatus, which is legitimate and economic society with institutionalised market, do not exist within the current set-up of the SPDC. The existing translation theories obviously fit well into the case of the former Yugoslavia rather than into Myanmar.

Connecting the Political Dimensions after the Second World War

The objective of the chapter is to present an overview of various understandings attached to the origin and past history of both the former Yugoslavia and present day Myanmar. However, the analysis of this study is confined to a comparative one, which connects the case not only with their present but also with their past that includes both similarities and differences.[42] There is a political and historical past that has to be compared. Without investigating the era of Marshall Tito in the former Yugoslavia and General Ne Win in Burma,[43] this study can not be a complete one, as it is one of the similarities of both countries. These men's legacies from the past have influenced both transition cases strongly, even though they are different. It is important to study the impacts of the legacies of one-man rule from the past in both cases. Thus, the aim of this chapter is to investigate the one-man-rule, of both countries under Marshall Josip Broz Tito and General Ne Win, their legacies and how they kept their countries together. They will be portrayed in this chapter thoroughly in addressing the time and changes, describing the differences and similarities, their role in the political history, how they managed to rule the country and how their legacies had influenced.

---

[41] Voltaire was a French author, humanist, rationalist, and satirist (1694 - 1778).

[42] The two countries have maintained a good relationship ever since the time of Marshall Tito and U Nu under the Non-Alignment Movement.

[43] The name "Burma" will be used in this chapter, as the timeline and analyses of the chapter reflects the time when the country was under General Ne Win and was named "The Socialist Republic of the Union of Burma."

3.1. Josip Broz Tito and Ne Win

The past of both Marshall Tito and General Ne Win can be compared, as they shared some similar past due to the period of time when they ruled their countries. Marshall Tito is still the subject of nostalgia among the people of the former Yugoslavia, as the father of the former Yugoslavia, when in the mind of many Burmese people until now, General Ne Win only remains as a negative figure, who had driven their country from prosperity to poverty. Many citizens of the former Yugoslavia regard Tito as a symbol of more peaceful and relatively prosperous times, when the former Yugoslavia enjoyed considerable prestige in both the East and the West.[44] For some, Marshall Tito remains a tyrant whose failure to begin democratisation in 1960s ultimately led to the rise of Serbian strongman Milošević and the tragedies of the 1990s (see Peranic, January 2004). Actually, it would have been more appropriate to compare Marshall Tito with late General Aung San of Burma, who was the living symbol of the army and a national hero of Burma, whose integrity was unimpeachable and patriotism was absolute, which was totally selfless. People of Burma love their '*Bogyoke*'. Even until today, they still talk stories about the austere *Bogyoke*, the dedicated leader, who became a legend (see Maung 1969: 132).[45]

However, while Tito's legacies might be dismantled with the disintegration of the former Yugoslavia yet, one does not deny the fact that Tito was the greatest politician in the former Yugoslavia history and also globally. As for General Ne Win, as his biographer claims, he was not a non-person. Historical turns and circumstances in post-independent Burma made General Ne Win a leader. He was a patriot who has served his country to the very best of his ability (see Ibid) and the current ruling generation of Myanmar is left with his legacies. They both launched one-man ruled in their countries, and changed the Constitutions of their countries in 1974, although in different ways, means and intentions.

---

[44] In the small northern Croatian village where Tito was born, people still mark the anniversary of his death. Every year, exact time of his death, the mourners honour the late leader with flowers and old partisan songs (see Peranic, Jan 2004).

[45] Unfortunately, before the Aung San era was to begin, he was assassinated. General Ne Win was absolutely loyal to Bo Aung San who was a younger man, and junior in many ways and his loyalty was not mere propriety in military behaviour towards an officer of higher rank. It was subordination of self not just to a man but to a mission (see Maung Maung 1969: 133). In 1955, he received the Yugoslav Banner (First Class) from Yugoslavian President Marshal Tito (see Aung Zaw, March-April 2001).

They came to the political stage along with the resistance movements against foreign rulers during World War II and their multi-ethnic countries together for decades, though in different ways. Josip Broz Tito, who was known as Marshall Tito, was already a medallist solider during World War I. In 1920, he became a member of Communist Party of the former Yugoslavia and started to use the party name "Tito". He remained involve in the Yugoslavian politics until he died in 1980. Tito's Yugoslavia was very famous for its social, political, and legislative experiments. General Ne Win became part of the anti-British nationalist group *Dobama Asi-Ayone* in the 1930s. In 1941 he was one of the *'Thirty Comrades'* led by Aung San, who were trained by the Japanese forces to command the Burmese Independent Army (BIA). When the BIA was formed, he changed his name from Shu Maung to Ne Win (Brilliant as the Sun or Sun of Glory). By 1943 he was the head of the BIA.

Tito called for the armed resistance against the former Yugoslavia when it was invaded by the Axis forces[46] in April 1941, and in the meantime he became the Chief Commander of the Yugoslav National Liberation Army (*Narodnooslobod-ilačka vojska/ armija-* NLA).[47] However, Japanese occupation during World War II was initially supported by the Burmese nationalists, including Aung San, who was made Minister of War, and Ne Win, who was given the rank of General and in 1943, became Chief-of-Staff of the pro-Japanese Burmese National Army (BMA). In March, with the defeat of the Japanese imminent, Aung San formed the Anti-Fascist People's Freedom League (AFPFL) and switched the BMA's allegiance to the Allies. British authority over Burma was restored in August, though the push by the nationalists for independence continued. General Ne Win had taken command of the 4th Burmese Rifles.

With the fall of several trustworthy leaders after Aung San's assassination and due to U Nu's AFPFL government weak managements, minority groups were disoriented and distrust from minorities leaders came to the surface. Following inde-

---

[46] Major Axis Powers: Germany under Chancellor Adolf Hitler, Italy under Primer Minister Benito Mussolini and Japan under Prime Minister Hideki Tojo and Emperor Hirohito.

[47] In 1941, the Germans declared war on Yugoslavia and occupied Belgrade and most of Serbia. The Croats had declared themselves an independent nation and established a fascist State of Croatia (*Nezavisna Država Hrvatska*– NDH) that sided with the Axis powers. The former nation of Yugoslavia was divided into three factions: the *Četniks,* believers in the monarchy and headed by the royalist government leader, *Draža Mihailović,* the Partisans, a resistance movement, headed by Josip Broz Tito; and the *Ustaša,* a fascist movement of mostly Croats, who subscribed to Nazi philosophy and collaborated with the Germans (see Jacobson n d)

pendence on 4 January, 1948, civil war broke out throughout the country.[48] In early 1949, General Ne Win was appointed as Chief-of-Chief in the fragmented army. In 1958, due to a conflict between leaders of AFPFL and U Nu's government failure to gain peaceful conditions throughout the country, General Ne Win was tasked by U Nu to raise 52 militia units to defend cities and towns and to relieve the army in fighting the rebels, and to rally the army and fight to hold the Union together.[49] At that time, the government was named by the media as Yangon or the 7th Mile Government, because the Karen insurgents swept down towards Yangon from Toungoo. The Battle at Insein was a vital test for General Ne Win. With their backs to the wall, General Ne Win's army broke the backbone of the insurrection and sent them to the hills and jungle areas.[50] General Ne Win was declared an interim Prime Minister and the army remained in power as a Caretaker Government from September 1958 to March 1960. General Ne Win's interim government was faced with several problems involving questions of political and national unity which were carried over from the preceding administration (see Silverstein 1960: 523). A meeting, called by U Nu in March 1962 for all minority leaders, to find a solution through frank discussions, by General Ne Win *coup d'etat* by stating that:

---

[48] The Burma Communist Party (BCP) went underground on 28 March 1948; other insurgents came into being all across Burma, and Karen uprising started in 1949.

[49] At that time General Ne Win was not interested in politics. He was considered a political lightweight. It was only after an indirect coup in 1958 initiated by his subordinates, Brig. General Tin Pe and Maung Maung and the 1960 elections which humiliated him, made him to become more engaged in military affairs and in turning the army into his political base (see Yawnghwe, Chao-Tzang 2002: 17).

[50] Lucian Pye writes that thus, neither U Nu nor Ne Win were able to project themselves as charismatic unifiers of Burma. Instead, the basic features of Burmese political culture generated divisions within the elite, which made effective public policies impossible (see Pye 1985: 106). U Nu was a founding leader of the nationalist 'Thakin Movement'. The British imprisoned him for belonging to "Dohbama Asi-Ayone". In 1942, he was released when Burma was invaded with the help of Japanese. The Japanese sponsored puppet government and installed Dr. Ba Maw as Foreign Minister. Being disillusioned with the Japanese, he co-founded Aung San's AFPFL, which advocated Burmese independence from both Japanese and British occupation during the 1940s. When the war ended, he was elected Vice-President of the AFPFL. He then served as the first Prime Minister of Burma between 1948 and 1956, again from 1957 to 1958, and finally between 1960 and 1962. U Nu dealt with opposition from various ethnic groups and communist factions. In 1958 he asked General Ne Win to take over but returned to power two years later and was overthrown by General Ne Win in 1962. Then Nu was put under house arrest. Several years later he was released and left Burma go into exile. He lived in India and Thailand. He later returned to Burma. In 1989 he was convicted for attempting to set up a rival government and was sentenced to house arrest. He was released in 1992 and passed away in 1995 (see Butwell 1969).

> The Revolutionary Council (RC) of the Union of Burma, having rescued the
> Union, not a moment too soon, from utter disintegration, now strives to recon-
> struct the social and economic life of all citizens the *Burmese Road to Socialism*
> (see *Constitution of the Burma Socialist Programme Party*).

Other than some students protests, his military coup was generally accepted by
the Burmese people because the *Tatmadaw* commanded by General Ne Win, which
was born under General Aung San's nationalist forces, was not only the sole de-
fender of Burma's beleaguered national unity but was also as the country's most
important administrative and political force (see Seekin 2000: 29). President Mahn
Win Maung, Prime Minster U Nu and their cabinet, and leaders of the different ethnic groups were arrested. The Constitution of 1947 and the Parliament were dissolved. General Ne Win declared that a *Revolutionary Council* of 17 senior military
officers under his leadership would govern.[51] With its declared socialist goals, the
RC reiterated its policy of freedom of religious faith and conscience (see Maung
Maung 1969: ix). Ever since, General Ne Win ruled Burma, from 1962 until 1988,
effectively.[52]

Tito implemented "Titoism" in the former Yugoslavia precisely and General Ne
Win launched the "Burmese Way to Socialism." "Titoism" was a new ideology, discourse and theory at that time comparable to Marxism, Stalinism and Capitalism[53]
but the "Burmese Way to Socialism" which General Ne Win instituted was a spe-
cialised form of totalitarianism involving elements of extreme nationalism, Marxism
and local religions. In 1974, both men made changes in their countries' Constitu-

---

[51] The RC was founded with the mission to replace the pluralism of U Nu era with orderly progress toward the creation of a socialist State. The BSPP closely followed the Leninist model of a
revolutionary party with a hierarchical structure and operated according to 'centralism'. The ideology of the RC was tepid and unimaginative; the intellectuals had no role in its formulation.

[52] The rule of General Ne Win can be divided into two institutionally well-marked periods: the
Revolutionary Council (RC) period 1962-1974, when the Chairman of the RC ruled by decrees;
and the Socialist Republic (SR) period since 1974 when Burma was given socialist Constitution
(see Gyi 1983: 191).

[53] "Titoism" is a term for nationalistic policies and practices based on the principles that in each
country the means of attaining ultimate communist goals must be dictated by national conditions
rather than by a pattern set. "Titoism" emphasises workers' self-management, non-alignment and
the decentralisation of political power. Tito himself had clearly and openly explained the place
which Titoism occupies in the overall strategy of imperialism in undermining the socialist countries from within. At that time, he declared that the Yugoslav model of socialism was valid not
only for Yugoslavia, but also for other socialist countries, which ought to follow and apply it. In
fact, Titoism became the inspirer of revisionist elements in the former Socialist countries.

tions. General Ne Win made the BSPP the single party of the country and changed the name of the country to the "Socialist Republic of the Union of Burma." The 1974 Constitution was framed to place the ruling authority of the country in the hands of the BSPP (see Son, June 2003).[54] The Yugoslav Constitution was revised in 1974 including reforms which gave more autonomy to the Serbian provinces Kosovo-Metohija and Vojvodina, and recognised the Bosnian Muslims as one of Yugoslavia's nations.[55] Tito, who was named 'President for Life' of the Republic in the 1974 Constitution, led the collective Presidency but, after his death, the position of President of the collective Presidency would rotate.

Tito and General Ne Win's greatest strength was suppressing nationalist insurrections and maintaining unity throughout the country. This ability of Tito was put to the test several times during his reign, notably during the Croatian Spring[56] when the government had to suppress both public demonstrations and dissenting opinions within the Communist Party, despite his own ethnic origin as a Croat. For national unity, Tito mostly used mutual guilt to draw a line under the history of ethnonational conflicts because while the Croats were haunted by the *Ustaše a* ghost, the Serbs were haunted by the spectre of the accusation of Great Serbian Hegemonism."[57] General Ne Win's "national unity" policy over the country was also known as "Burmanisation." Despite his family's Chinese immigrant background, hard rules

---

[54] General Ne Win founded BSPP in July 1962. He became a military dictator, and the Chairman of the BSPP as well as the President of Burma. In the 1970s, he was referred to elliptically as 'the President', 'the Chairman' or 'the Old Man.' Even when he was no longer Head of State but people would still drop their voice to talk about 'Number One'. He was addicted to spells, numerology and magical word plays, and was a keen gambler. He had shown obsessive an interest in Burma's past and Burma's culture. The authoritarian control of the military had obvious echoes of the totalitarian rule to the Burmese kings (see Silverstein 1960: 100).

[55] The Constitution 1946 gave wide autonomy to the six newly created Republics (Serbia, Croatia, Slovenia, Montenegro, Bosnia and Herzegovina and Macedonia) but power remained in the hands of Tito and the Communist Party.

[56] The Croatian Spring (*Hrvatsko proljeće*) was a political movement in the 1970s that called for rights for Croatia and its pride. It was set in motion when a group of influential Croatian poets and linguists published a *Declaration on the Name and Position of the Croatian Literary Language* in 1967. Tito made every attempt to suppress and erase all such notions, fearing loss of stability and the eventual break-up of the country due to ethnic tensions (see "Croatian Spring").

[57] A Serbian hegemony was imposed after 1918, based on the Serbs' claim that Serbs, Croats, and Slovenes comprised one nation with three names, which should constitute a centralised State. The centralists' slogan was 'One People, One State and One King." The federalist position of the other nationalities upheld the concept of a multinational Sate with a federal structure. The renaming of the kingdom as the Kingdom of Yugoslavia in 1929 marked the victory of the chauvinist centralist forces and the beginning of Serbian royal dictatorship.

were imposed on the minorities and on immigrant society. Both men persecuted those who represented a danger to their position and had their opponents destroyed completely.

General Ne Win's BSPP used Buddhist concepts and described its ideology in a system which is blandly modernist, in striking contrast to the militancy and vivid nationalist symbolism of earlier movements against imperialism in Burma (see Seekins 2000: 39-84). His 'socialism' was actually similar to Japanese National Socialism of the early 1940s, mixed with post-colonial nationalism, attempted vulgar Buddhism, astrology and a brutal war against the insurgents. Burma was led by General Ne Win as a predominantly Buddhist country.[58] Religious repression became another long time centred feature of military rule. Buddhism became so much an integral part of the Burmese ethos that it has become common to say: 'Burma is predominantly a Buddhist country' or 'to be a Burmese is to be a Buddhist'. Theravāda Buddhismhas the greatest influence on Burmese culture and civilisation and played a large part in creating Burma's culture homogeneity.[59] The imposition of General Ne Win's rules reflected Burma's pre-colonial value system. However the Serbian Orthodox Church never has been a pillar of support for any regime of the former Yugoslavia. The Church has been a minor element in Serbian social and political life. Tito was extraordinarily effective in his 35-year struggle to marginalise the Orthodox Church. Throughout the Tito era, it was a major disadvantage to put one's toe inside the church door. Those who wanted to advance in life had to join the Communist Party, in which atheism was obligatory. There is no social structure that was so deeply linked between the religion and Serbia's history, traditions, achievements and sorrows (see Forest, July 1999). On the whole, Tito neither concerned himself with the issues of religion nor of individual Republics (see Cohen *et al.* 1983: 190). Instead, Tito trusted the party chiefs in each locality and republic to deal

---

[58] The first Burmese nationalist movement against the colonial power was inspired by U Ottama, a learned Buddhist monk, influenced by the Congress movement in India, who roused the patriotic fervour of the nation with his spirited agitations for the freedom of Burma. Later, Dr. Ba Maw tried in 1942 to re-establish the relationship between State and *"Sangha"* which existed at the time of the monarchy. After independence, U Nu's victory in the 1960 general election was largely due to his promise to establish Buddhism as the State religion, which was strongly supported by militant monks and the Burman Buddhist majority. His promise created more complexity and conflicts between the Burmese and ethnics, whose religion is Christianity (see Saw Myat 2003: 40-1).

[59] The introduction of Theravāda in the Burmese State by King Anuruddha or Anawrahta (1044-77) was the crucial turning point in Burma's religious history (see Bechert 1984: 147).

with problems in accordance with what they felt would be the best tactical solution or in accordance with their personal preferences.

General Ne Win revolted against the Maoist ideology of China, just as Tito rebelled at Stalin's attempt to enforce Soviet supremacy in the Balkans in 1948 and the Yugoslav Communists blazed a post-war trail of "workers' self-management" at home and "non-alignment" abroad outside the confines of the Warsaw Pact and the Soviet empire in East Europe (see Jukic, n. d.). Tito introduced the world a new theory and discourse "Titoism" and initiated a new ideology and block "a non-alignment block" between the capitalists and communists,[60] and established a foreign policy that profited the people of the former Yugoslavia the most, while General Ne Win's policy of isolation particularly damaged Burma's economy, resulted to become the one of the poorest country in the world. Tito is celebrated as one of the best politician of the Century and succeeded in his foreign policy while General Ne Win led Burma into twenty-six years of surreal isolation.[61]

Tito forces had not only liberated Yugoslavia from the Germans, later his new government had stood up to Stalin (see Glenny 2001: 571). Tito united the former Yugoslavia and unlike General Ne Win, he held the Union together until he passed away. General Ne Win suddenly resigned in July 1988 after a series of continuous demonstrations and protests in late 1987 and 1988, and disappeared from Burma's political scene. There were rumours that he was playing behind the Burmese political scene. In March 2001 he was placed under house arrest following the arrest of certain family members.

On 5 December, 2002, General Ne Win passed away. Though General Ne Win lived throughout his life as a modern king of Burma, no State funeral was held for him. He was buried quietly. Though the images of General Ne Win might be eliminated, and there is no evidence of General Ne Win's successors wanting to revive

---

[60] Under Tito's leadership, Yugoslavia co-founded the Non-Aligned Movement (NAM) with Egypt's Gamal Abdel Nasser, U Nu of Burma, President Sukarno of Indonesia, and India's Jawaharlal Nehru, thus establishing strong ties with other third world countries. On the whole, non-alignment has been a balancing force; however, non-alignment suffers a distortion and does not reflect the strength, which the very number and sincerity of most of its adherents would have imparted to it. Divested of its original meaning and purpose, it can become an instrument of national aggrandisement, subtle weapons for the promotion of a political hegemony by certain powers and the elimination of rivals within their sphere (see Bhutto 1977).

[61] The black market supplied the needs of the people, while the central government slided slowly into bankruptcy. Foreigners were expelled, activists were imprisoned and ethnic trouble was crushed with massive military force.

the old era of former "No. 1" of Burma, one can not deny the fact that his successors continue to practice clearly of his legacies in the way to put Myanmar together, despite General Ne Win's and the BSPP's failures to solve Burma's major problems. It is clear that the current ruling junta, the SPDC, lacks capacity accountability, and its polarisation is not just because of self-infelicity, but also due to General Ne Win's legacies.[62] Thus, there is a tendency for the generals to assume that they know what is best for Myanmar.

Tito died in a clinic centre in Ljubljana, Slovenia, on 4 May 1980, and his funeral drew many world leaders. At the time of his death, speculation began about whether his successors could continue to hold Yugoslavia together. Tito's successors had difficulties dealing with their multi-ethnic countries and were confused about his legacies. Yugoslavia was unable to maintain its unity in the immediate post-Tito era and, due to the old wounds that surfaced, was eventually thrown into the outbreak of civil wars. With the growing ethnic divisions and conflict, Titoism ended and Tito's legacy was dismantled with a series of Yugoslav wars a decade after his death[63].

---

[62] Due to the worsening economy in 1987, General Ne Win criticised government reporting and management practices through the Burma Broadcasting Service's (BBS) Television (which was the only Radio and Television Station and is controlled by the military authority to the present day) and called for opening of foreign exports to private traders. The dictator, while giving his televised speech used words such as 'critic', 'reform', 'need' and 'changes', words that were usually censored in Burma and had probably hinted to the younger generation unintentionally about the need for changes in the country. A few weeks after General Ne Win's speech, the government, without warning, demonetised three units of currency and offered no replacement. The Kyat was demonetisated more than once: in 1965 (50 Kyats notes), in 1985 (100 Kyats notes) and in 1987 (25, 35, 75 Kyats notes). Thus, nearly 70% of the currency in circulation became worthless. The rationalisation behind was to penalise the black marketers; but in fact, it hurt the ordinary people because most citizens held cash and did not use the banks (see The NCGUB 1993: 4). Towards the end of 1987, student protests against the BSPP started, based on the crisis which initially started from the demonetisations, and continued into 1988 when it reached its aim as a countrywide pro-democracy movement which toppled General Ne Win and the BSPP regime.

[63] Tito is buried in his mausoleum in Belgrade called Kuća cveća (*The House of Flowers*). Numerous people visit the place, although it no longer holds a guard of honour. During his life and after his death, several places were named after Tito.

3.2. The Yugoslav Way of Putting-Together Federalism

Tito was the sole support for Yugoslavia's multi-ethnic unity ever since the resistance movement. He led the resistance against Nazi Germany and Italian fascism and helped to oust the monarchy. Tito led a broad coalition made up of Serbs and non-Serbs alike in addition to anti-fascist ideology under the following conditions:

→ *Slovenes,* whose country was split between the Third Reich and Mussolini's Italy and was threatened by Hitler's 'new order';

→ *Serbs* from Croatia, Bosnia and Herzegovina, who were threatened by the *Ustaše* regime, ended up in Tito's partisan ranks;

→ *Croats,* handed themselves over to Tito in large numbers together with their officers, weapons and equipment;

→ Tito's promise of autonomy for Bosnia and Herzegovina was attractive to *Bosnian Muslims,* who needed strong protection against the strongly anti-Muslim *Chetnik*;

→ *Macedonians* were attracted by Tito's promise of a Macedonian Republic within a post-war Yugoslav federation; and

→ The *Kosovo Albanians* joined Tito very late, as communist from Albania holding out the prospect of joining Albania proper (see Cviic 1991: 20-23).

The entire political structure in Yugoslavia was dependent on Tito's belief in his own infallibility. The absence of overt ethnic conflict, so obvious during the war and inter-war period, was taken as evidence for this claim. In order to improve the balance between the aspirations between ethnic groups, Yugoslavia became a federation of six Republics (Serbia, Croatia, Slovenia, Montenegro, Bosnia-Herzegovina and Macedonia) which initially enjoyed very little autonomy but which, over time came to overshadow the central government in Belgrade. Tito implemented Yugoslav federalism, which was characterised by a rapid move toward centralisation of power at the national level, with the Communist Party in total control. The newly elected Constituent Assembly dissolved the monarchy and established the Federal People's Republic of Yugoslavia on 29 November 1945 (see "Yugoslavia: Communist Takeover and Consolidation."), soon after, the borders of each Republic and autonomous region were fixed. A few months later, on 31 January 1946, the federal system was solidified when the Constituent Assembly ratified a Constitution.

Article 1 of the 1946 Constitution defined the principles of the federation:

> The Federal People's Republic of Yugoslavia is a federal people's State of republican form, a community of peoples equal in rights who, on the basis of the right to self-determination, which includes the right to separation, have expressed a will to live together in a federative State (see "Constitution of the Federal People's Republic of Yugoslavia," 1946; Article 1).

The federalism of the former Yugoslavia was born in Jajce in 1943. The Constitution of 1946 exhibited all the main characteristics of a federal State: the supremacy of a Constitution, a clear delineation of powers between the Federal Government[64] and the constituent units, a certain degree of autonomy for the constituent units, mechanisms for resolving constitutional conflicts, and procedures for amending the Constitution (see Kux 1990: 7). The former Yugoslavia's Constitution was drafted so quickly not because it solved the national question using the federative principle but because it was copied almost verbatim from the Soviet Constitution of 1936. Tito was a Croat and he wanted to move away from the national question and get on to the next phase of socialism, a trans-ethnic, if not pan-ethnic, "Yugoslav Socialist Patriotism" (see Cohen *et al.* 1983: 68). Thus Tito's "putting together" federalism focused on a central power with a strong coercive effort to create a single multinational State out of a group of independent States. Unlike the Soviet Union, the Republics could not maintain armies or foreign offices, and the 1946 Yugoslav Constitution firmly stated that self-determination for autonomous regions could not be considered (see Jacobson n. d.). The self-determination issue of the Republics was phrased to make it seem as if they were already independent and voluntarily joined the federation.

Despite the fact that standing up to the most powerful communist power in the world, Tito did not turn to be a democrat. He was undeniably adored by Yugoslavs but he never considered putting his popularity to an electoral test. If he had done so he probably would have won comfortably, because his achievements were real. In a short period after World War II, Tito established a kind of harmony among communities emerging from the imaginable bloodies civil conflict. For the first time Yugoslavia enjoyed peace and economic prosperity under his rule (see Glenny 2001: 574-8). And Yugoslavs possessed greater freedom than the inhabitants of any other Eastern European country.

---

[64] When using "federal government" in the context of this paper, is to mean central government.

In fact, the former Yugoslavia was held together not only by Tito's charisma and political dictatorship but also by a complex balancing act in the international arena and a mixed economy. Yugoslavia's foreign economic relations also operated in three distinct markets: the West, from which borrowed capital and imported advanced technology; and the second world of the USSR and the Council for Mutual Economic Assistance (CMEA), strategic resources in exchange for armament construction projects, and manufactured goods; and the third world (especially oil-rich Iraq and Libya) (see Woodward 1995: 20-27). Western propaganda describing Tito as the most fanatical Stalinist in Eastern Europe ended after Tito's break-up with Stalin in 1948. The majority of Yugoslav population sided with Tito over Stalin. Break-up with the Soviet Union and the renewed relationship with the West ended Yugoslav isolation and began economic decentralisations that led to political decentralisations (see Duncan 1979: 71-5). These decentralizations formed the basis for the Republics to use the federal structure to pose major challenges to the communist system in 1960s. In 1963, the country officially became the Socialist Federal Republic of Yugoslavia.

By 1965, the republics succeeded in regaining all, if not more, of the federal power vested to them in 1946. In the early 1970s, agitation among the nationalities revived, particularly among the Croats. Although controls over intellectual life were stiffened, the autonomy of the six Republics and Serbia's two autonomous provinces increased through the 1970s. A new Constitution, adopted in 1974, further expanded the autonomy of the Republics - Kosovo and Vojvodina - and required a consensus among their governments for the exercise of most remaining federal powers (see Rusinow 2004). National identity and rights were institutionalised by the federal system which granted near statehood to the Republics and multiple rights of national self-determination for individuals (see Woodward 1995: 40-45). Under Tito's leadership the ruling Communist Party was able to resolve two crises including national self-determination in a multinational State and the economic crises of an agrarian economy exposed to world depression (see Hamilton 1968). To conclude, Tito had maintained the stability of the country, not only with his charisma and repression but, firstly, with prosperity which all Yugoslav could enjoy and secondly, with its constitutional order. Tito was a remarkable politician, but he lacked the means to find a long-term solution to the former Yugoslavia's unique constitutional problems (see Glenny 2001: 576). After his death, Yugoslavia moved from federation to confederation. This change would eventually move beyond federalism to be exploited by the Republics in the late 1980s and, together with the economic slow-down which turned to collapse, it led to the civil wars which culminated in independence for the Republics and the dissolution of the former Yugoslavia in the 1990s.

Table 3-1. Chronology of Marshall Tito's Yugoslavia, 1941-1980

April 1941	Yugoslavia is invaded by Axis Forces.
4 July 1941	Tito's public call for armed resistance against Germany.
1942	Tito becomes a prominent leader of the Anti-Fascist Council of National Liberation of Yugoslavia that convenes in Bihać.
1943	Tito establishes the basis for post-war organisation of the country, making it a federation.
4 December 1943	Tito proclaims a provisional democratic Yugoslav government in-exile during the German occupation.
5 April 1945	Tito signs an agreement with the USSR allowing "temporary entry of Soviet troops into Yugoslav territory".
1945	Aided by the Red Army, the partisans win and all Western forces are ordered out of Yugoslav soil.
1945	Tito becomes the Prime Minister and Minister of Foreign Affairs of post-war Yugoslavia. He remains in those offices until 13 January, 1953 when he succeeds Ivan Ribar as President.
7 April 1963	The country changes its official name to *Socialist Federal Republic of Yugoslavia* and *Josip Broz Tito* is named *President for Life.*
1948	Tito is recognised internationally as the first Communist leader who defied Stalin's leadership over the COMinform.
1961	Yugoslavia becomes a founding member of the Non-Aligned Movement.
1972	Tito cracks down the "Croatian Spring" and the Serb liberals' movement severely.
4 May 1980	Tito dies in a clinic centre in Ljubljana, Slovenia.

Source: (see "Josip Broz Tito.")

3.3. The Burmese Way of Setting the Union together

The Panglong Agreement of 1947 was Aung San's task to obtain independence.[65] The purpose of the "Panglong Agreement" was to comply with a condition of the British, who insisted that only with the consent of the people of the frontier areas would agree to give independence to Burma proper and to the frontier areas[66] (see Lwin 1997: 1). Thus, the 1947 Panglong Accord was not one between ethnic groups but between founding nations. The 1947 Union Constitution was written not in line with the letter or spirit of the Panglong Accord signed in February 1947, however, it was understood that it could be amended in the future. Josef Silverstein points out that in the Constitution of 1947, it made no mention of the words "federal" or "federalism", it was clear that the main intention was to become a 'unitary' State (see Silverstein 1977: 54-79), but where the right to secession was granted. Then again, the creation of 'national unity' in Burma was further complicated by the Panglong Agreement and the Constitution of 1947.

In the early 1960s, the constituent States, led by Sao Shwe Thaike, initiated a move to amend the 1947 Union Constitution, to make it "genuinely federal". In response to "Federal Movement", instabilities among the AFPFL leaders, the Communist and ethnic insurgencies, General Ne Win had no choice other than to stage a *coup d'état*. He stated that without a strong military presence, there would be continuous secession attempts and inter-ethnic violence would keep the country away from peace and prosperity. On 02 March 1962, General Ne Win spoke on the radio to announce that:-

> I have to inform you, citizens of the Union that the armed forces have taken over the responsibility and the task of keeping the country's safety, owing to the greatly deteriorating conditions in the Union. [....] We shall do our best to promote the happiness and well being of all the people of the Union (see Maung 1969: 292).

---

[65] The Panglong conference, attended by Aung San and the AFPFL leaders, the entire minority leaders except the Karens started in early February and reached agreement on 12 February, celebrated today as Union Day.

[66] Before giving independence, the British government announced its policy statements in 1947 that they agreed to give independence to Burma proper, but that the frontier areas would still be under British rule for the time being. That British argued that because the frontier areas had never been part of Burma proper and had never actually been administrated by the Burmese, so they could not be considered as part of Burma (see Aung San 1946: 80).

For General Ne Win and the successor ruling generals, the meaning of "federalism" has been equated with 'disintegration of the nation'. This is so despite the continued celebration of 12 February, the day the Panglong Accord was signed, as the Union Day, and despite the rhetoric and slogans about the equality of "national races". The federalism should be equated with secession when the term "Union" in Burmese – *Pyidaung-zu*[67] – is unambiguous. General Ne Win's government initiated a two-track approach to counter the threat of armed struggle and the wider demands from ethnic minorities for increased political rights. On the political front, attempts were made to de-politicise ethnicity by promoting equal rights and equal status for all ethnic groups within a common nation. This policy implied a pledge to protect minority cultural practices, as well as conscious attempts to uplift the remote minority regions, both economically and socially. Conversely, it rejected as illegitimate all demands for political autonomy. The special councils and ministries that existed for the ethnic States in the parliamentary era were abolished (see Ibid). The system as a whole was centralised, in order not to provide ethnic communities with the opportunity and power to manage their own affairs through their own autonomy.

The talks between the RC and all ethnic communist groups in 1963 were facilitated by the Internal Peace Committee headed by the *Thakin Kodaw Hmaing*, but failed. It prompted the *Tatmadaw* to adopt a new counter-insurgency strategy known as the "Four Cuts", designed to undermine popular support for the rebels by depriving them of: Food, Money, Information and Recruits. The map of Burma was divided into three coloured zones: black for entirely insurgent-controlled areas; brown for disputed or temporary cease-fire areas; and white for *Tatmadaw* total controlled areas. The idea was to clear up from black areas, one by one until the whole of Burma was coloured white. Ne Win's idiosyncratic way of socialist policies, while officially aimed at building national unity, served to increase inequality and distrust.

General Ne Win worked hard to make the Burmese Army not only united but obedient to his command. This he achieved by creating a controlling body within the military staffed by absolutely trustworthy men, the Military Intelligence Service (MIS). The role of the MIS keeping a close check on all administrative personnel of the regime, both civilian and military, as well as on the party apparatus and person-

---

[67] *"Pyidaung-zu"* means the coming together of different national States.

nel of several public institutions can not be ignored in any assessment of General Ne Win's overall reach of power monopoly.

In the area of law and order, the performance of the BSPP was to come with a vow to smash the various groups of insurgents within a year. Ethnic insurrections broke out in the Kachin and Shan States after the army coup, continued to deny major areas to government control, including the Burmese part of the Golden Triangle. The Karen insurrection moved to the Thai border where it benefited from the black market trade. The Burma Communist Party (BCP) insurrection migrated from the central Pegu Yoma region to the Northeast border with China, where it retained official support from China.

Under the 1947 constitutional reforms, the map of Burma shows seven divisions which are largely populated by the Burman majority, and seven ethnic minority States, i. e., the Chin, Kachin, Karen, Kayah, Mon, Rakhine (Arakan) and Shan. This gives the deceptive appearance of an easy symmetry to what is undoubtedly one of the most complex ethnic mixes in the world to start with, and over one hundred languages have been identified in Burma (see Smith 1991: 29-30).[68] The State wanted the people who live in Burma to primarily identify themselves as 'Burmese' or 'Myanmar', despite Aung San's question of 'what is a national minority?' However, as the issue of ethnic minorities were considered to be the legacy of British rule by General Ne Win, the policy of "Burmanisation"[69] was implemented.

The goal of "Burmanisation" was presumably to create an ethnically homogeneous nation, whereby all the different 'races' would be assimilated into the Burman mainstream. Politically articulate Burmans find nothing wrong in this. They are proud to be Burman, and can not understand why a Shan, for example, does not want to become a Burman. From the non-Burman perspective, "Burmanisation" represents the 'swallowing up' of their identity, heritage, history, etc., and becoming, in the end, second-class Burmans at best (see Yawnghwe, Chao-Tzang, September 2002: 16). The concept of 'national unity' was in fact the official aspiration of the State, but the frequent practice was not to integrate ethnic minority communities into a new and ethnically blind transcendent identity but to impose 'Burmaness'

---

[68] At the AFPFL Convention, Aung San said that they must set up a Union with properly regulated provisions to safeguard the rights of the national minorities (see Aung San 1946: 71).

[69] It is humiliating to be told that Burman culture, history and values were superior to the mainstream and that the non-Burmans had no choice but to accept things. Burmans, if they aspire to be loyal citizens, wanted to get ahead in life (see Yawnghwe, Chao-Tzang, September 2002: 16).

upon minority peoples. Therefore, while the Burmese language and culture was given superior status all over the country, there was no official space for preserving and developing local languages and cultures of the ethnic minority groups (see Ah 2002: 5). The government's power hinged on the control that the BSPP established over communications. There was still little, if any, communication between the insurgent groups and the people within Burma proper and there was hardly any contact with the outside world (see O'Brien 1991: 98). General Ne Win's concept was based on 'national unity' to assimilate the ethnic minorities within a greater Burman nation. Homogenisation or Burmanisation was General Ne Win's way of putting Burma together.

A new citizenship law was gradually implemented during the 1980s designating as "associate citizens" people whose ancestors were not of the "original races" of Burma. Principal target was the Sino-Burman and Indo-Burman community. Thus, General Ne Win resembles Tito in this sense. Though, Tito himself was a Croat, "Croatian Spring" in early 1970 was a failed attempt at Croatian independence, and their threat to the federation caused Tito to crack down severely in 1972. It is ironically, because General Ne Win himself is a Sino-Burmese, with the original name "Shu Maung" and ambiguous national identity that would have disqualified him from office by the very laws his regime promulgated (see Seekins 2000: 53). Sino- and Indo-Burmans were permitted to vote but could not be elected nor could they attend the higher educational institution such as the Institute of Medical and Technology nor could they hold appointed office above a certain level in the government.

General Ne Win's regime cut off cultural and educational ties with foreign countries. Schools and hospitals run by foreign missionaries were taken over by the State. The Burmese language was implemented throughout the education system. Self-isolation of the country was systematically implemented. Tourist visas were limited to 24 hours (later in the 1970s seven-day visas were introduced), contacts between Burmese living overseas and their friends and relatives at home was actively discouraged (see Ibid 55), foreign newspaper reporters were barred and most foreign assistance was terminated. During U Nu's time of parliamentary democracy, Burma had joined the Tito led "non-aligned movement." However, General Ne Win's bid for total non-alignment proved so extreme that Burma actually left the "Non-Aligned Movement" in 1979 to go it alone. Isolation underlined the lack of development within the country (see O'Brien 1991: 95). The RC abolished independent political parties; independent newspapers were also banned, being replaced by a single paper, *The Working People's Daily*. Any kind of protests were suppressed brutally, students' protests in 1962 against the *Ne Win*'s military putsch were bloodily suppressed and the headquarters of the Students Union in Rangoon where the *Thakin Movement* had been launched decades before was destroyed. A country-wide workers' strike, and the students' demonstration on the funeral day of *U Thant* (a former UN – General Secretary) in 1974, as well as the students demonstration occurred at the *Thakin Kodaw Muaing Monument*, were terminated without any success. General Ne Win and military leaders formed the BSPP in 1964 and nationalized the economy through a plan called the "Burmese Way to Socialism." The economy declined as the consumer goods distribution system became mired in chaos (leading to a booming black market) and agricultural production fell. A new Constitution was put into effect in 1974, transferring power by referendum and single-party election from the military RC to a People's Assembly. The country was renamed as the *Socialist Republic of the Union of Burma*. Though the life-time presidency or chairmanship for General Ne Win was not granted in 1974 Constitution, it was mentioned in Article 11 that the State shall adopt a single-party system. The BSPP would be the sole political party and it would lead the State (see Appendix III).

With the armed forces as its power base and a party apparatus with mass elite communication conveyor belts, General Ne Win had everything locked in for a power monopoly, however, total control of the country was till elusive (see Gyi 1983: 203). In 1981, General Ne Win relinquished the presidency to San Yu, a retired general, but continued as chairman of the ruling BSPP. The BSPP nationalised the banks, factories, industries, wholesale and retail shops, brokerages, organised the demonetisations of large denomination currency notes and the deportation of alien Indian and Chinese nationals was meant to break the backbone of the economic community (see Ibid 201). Demonetisations occurred twice: the 100 Kyats note in 1985, which was reimbursed, but not the 25, 35 and 75 Bank-Notes in 1987. The people movements of late 1987 reached its highest goal in mid-1988, resulting in the resignation of General Ne Win and the regime of BSPP was toppled.

Table 3-2. Chronology of General Ne Win's Reign in Burma, 1941-1988

1941	General Ne Win joins the "Thirty Comrades", led by Aung San.
December 1941	Burma Independence Army (BIA) is established in Bangkok.
1943-45	Burma National Army (BNA): General Aung San, Defence Minster; General Ne Win; Commander-in-Chief.
1944-45	Anti-Fascist Organisation operates underground; later becomes AFPFL.
27 March 1945	BNA rises against the Japanese.
September 1945	The Burma Army is established by the British.
December 1945	Peoples' Volunteer Organisation (PVO) is established.
19 July 1947	Aung San is assassinated.
January 4 1948	Burma Army is commanded by General Smith Dun, a Karen.
1948	Mainstream Communist Party of Burma uprising and PVO insurrection.
January 1949	Karen uprising begins.
1949	General Ne win replaces Smith Dun as Commander-in-Chief.
1950	Kuomintang armed forces enter Shan State.
October 1958 – February 1960	Caretaker Government, headed by *Tatmadaw* Commander-in-Chief General Ne Win.
2 March 1962	Establishment of the "Revolutionary Council (RC)." Student Protests against it are terminated brutally and Students Union was destroyed.
1962 – 1972	RC Period.
1964	50 Value Bank-Notes are demonetised.
1968	Communist Party Burma (CPB) or Burma Communist Party (BCP) is supported by China.
January 1974	One-Party State is established with "Burma Socialist Programme Party" (BSPP), the country is renamed "the Socialist Republic of the Union of Burma" Constitutional period of the BSPP (1974 – 1988), with its ideology "Burmese Way to Socialism."
May-June 1974	Country-wide workers' strike, to increase their salaries, terminates without a success, with causality.
December 1974	Students demonstrate on the funeral day of U Thant (UN – General Secretary), resulting in causality and arrests.
May 1976	The Karen National Union (KNU) was founded in Manerplaw to continue the Karen armed struggle.
1981	Ne Win gave up presidency, but continued to head the party. General San Yu was named President.[70]
November 1985	100 Value Bank-Notes were demonetised.

---

[70] San Yu was President from 1981 to 1988, but his leadership was insignificant inside and outside of Burma, as he held the post of puppet presidency. This is the reason that not much biographical facts about him can be found.

September 1987	25, 35 and 75 Value Bank-Notes were demonetised. Student demonstrations against it took place and many were arrested. Universities were closed and reopened only in 1998 January.
March 1988	A clash between riot police and students from RIT resulted in the death of a student named Phone Maw and several were wounded
March-July 1988	Student unrest occurs on country-wide and suppressed bloodily.
July 1988	General Ne Win resigns.

Source: (see Seekin 2000: xv; Linter 1999: 430-79)

Linking the Differences in the Ruling Regimes:
From the Recent Past to the Present

"It is not the Power that Corrupts, but Fear."
(Aung San Suu Kyi 1991).

This chapter will provide different insights into the complex nature of dictatorship in both the former Yugoslavia and in Myanmar. Thus, the aim of this chapter is to outline and compare the actors of the transition process from both ruling element, late Milošević era in the Federal Republic of Yugoslavia (FRY), and the early and later stages of the Myanmar's regime – at first, the State Law and Order Restoration Council (SLORC) and later the State Peace and Development Council (SPDC). Myanmar is the only State in the Southeast Asian region that has not experienced a change of government, considering that the SPDC, the direct descendant of General Ne Win, continues to dominate the political life in Myanmar even though most of the countries in Southeast Asia, with one exception, have undergone a change of power through elections since 1989. So, as the national ideology of Greater Serbia was sold to the Yugoslav army as the preservation of the former Yugoslavia (the country that had ceased to exist even before the war in Slovenia), Myanmar Army – *Tatmadaw* is security obsessed by the idea that they are given namely: - fear of the disintegration, the balkanisation of Myanmar by ethnic minorities, some of whom demand a federalism, some the right to secession and some self-determination. Thus, the absence of political transition has frequently been sought to be explained by the authoritarian nature of the regimes and their army, and its usage of nationalism to mobilize popular support. Here I shall explain the nature of the regime in Myanmar and compare it to the one of Milošević in the former Yugoslavia.

4.1. Society Under Dictatorships

Both countries have carried in their wake a resurgence of aggressive nationalism, with all its negative attributes of ethnic superiority and xenophobia. Their aggressive nationalism provides a centralising focus for transitional governments seeking to consolidate their claim to political legitimacy. New leadership was introduced to both the former Yugoslavia and Myanmar in the late 1980s: Yugoslavia, a civilian authoritarian regime and Myanmar, a military totalitarian regime. The emergence of new leaderships and their impact on the countries transitions have been different in every sense. Changes of leaderships involve a political transition from one level to other. The key question guiding this part of the thesis on the political transition is in what way the new regimes have changed the political situation in both countries?

To enhance an understanding of transition, the role of the present leadership need to be defined. An authoritarian rule under the leadership of Slobodan Milošević, a non-military person, a Communist Party member, a business man and banker, who transformed the LCY into the Socialist Party of Serbia (Serbian: *Socijalisticka partija Srbije*), regulated the Federal Republic of Yugoslavia (FRY) from the late 1980s to 2000. Since Serbia and Montenegro proclaimed the formation of the FRY in 1992, their common State had a precarious existence. It had been in the midst of the wars that involved ethnic brethren and led to the emergence of the new Balkan States, international economic sanctions, considerable domestic political opposition to Milošević's rule, disagreements between the two federal partners, unrest in the formerly autonomous Yugoslav province of Kosovo that led to NATO's bombing campaign against the country, and to the democratic transition in 2000.

In Myanmar, after General Ne Win's resignation in July 1988, the military rules Myanmar under the leadership of the "State Law and Order Restoration Council (SLORC)" which was later renamed as the better sounding "State Peace and Development Council (SPDC)." In 1989, the name of the country was changed to the "Union of Myanmar" and the capital to "Yangon". The SPDC under General Than Shwe's leadership at actual time-frame, has been going through shuffle after shuffle due to their internal power struggle. Due to the convening of the "National Convention" since 1995 to draw up a State Constitution, the SPDC still rules Myanmar with a lot of uncertainties. In the following chapters, both types of regime will be explained thoroughly.

Figure 4-1. Shift of Politics in The former Yugoslavia and Burma

Time-Frame	Official Name of the Country	Ruling Party or Organisation	President or Leader
1953 - 1963	Federal People's Republic of Yugoslavia	League of Communists of Yugoslavia (LCY)	Josip Broz Tito
1963 - 1980	the Socialist Federal Republic of Yugoslavia (SFR Yugoslavia)	LCY	Josip Broz Tito
1980 – 1991	SFR Yugoslavia	LCY	Presidency was collective
1992 – 2003	Federal Republic of Yugoslavia (FR Yugoslavia)		
1992 - 1993	FR Yugoslavia	Socialist Party of Serbia (SPS)	Dobrica Ćosić
1993	FR Yugoslavia	SPS	Miloš Radulović (acting)
1993 - 1997	FR Yugoslavia	SPS	Zoran Lilić
1997	FR Yugoslavia	SPS	Srđa Božović (acting)
1997 - 2000	FR Yugoslavia	SPS	Slobodan Milošević
2000 - 2003	FR Yugoslavia	Democratic Party of Serbia (DSS)	Vojislav Koštunica
2003 - 2006	State Union of Serbia and Montenegro	The Democratic Party of Socialists of Montenegro (DPS)	Svetozar Marovic

Time-Frame	Official Name of the Country	Ruling Party or Organisation	President or Leader
1962 – 1988	The Socialist Republic of the Union of Burma	The Burma Socialist Programme Party (BSPP)	General New Win Chairman of the BSPP and the President
July 1988		BSPP	General Sein Lwin Chairman of the BSPP and the President
July – August 1988		BSPP	Dr Maung Maung Chairman of the BSPP and the President
September 1988 -1989		The State Law and Order Restoration Council (SLORC)	General Saw Maung Chairman 1988 – 1993
1989 – 1997	The Union of Myanmar	SLORC	General Than Shwe Chairman 1993 – 1997
1997 – present		The State Peace and Development Council (SPDC)	General Than Shwe Chairman

4.1.1. The Former Federal Republic of Yugoslavia under Milošević

Until 1980, the former Yugoslavia had assumed many of the qualities of a modern European State. Later, authoritarian power was held by an elected executive leader and by a dominant political Party through election manipulation. Whether power is held by an individual or collectively, such dictatorships justify their seizure of power in terms of the deposed government's failure to achieve economic growth and alleged corrupt practices.

Miloševic ruled the former Yugoslavia from late 1990 to 2000. The rise of Serbian nationalism was unanimously blamed for everything what happened to the country. Milošević used the Presidency of the Serbian presidium, as a platform to advocate Serbian nationalism and the re-centralization of Party and State institutions. He was the elected President, who had broad authorisation including the right of veto laws, the right to declare by his own decision the 'danger of war', 'a state of emergency' and to decide on the dismissal of the Parliament. In short, his power was immense and, to make things worse, uncontrolled. A disturbed balance between the legislative and executive power made the President of Serbia non-responsible.

Unlike the SPDC, Miloševic did not come from a military background with a military rank and his rule instead emerged via an electoral process. The army was heavily dominated not by an institution but by one person, - Slobodan Milošević, regardless of the office he had been in. However, Miloševic sought an alliance with the federal army of the former Yugoslavia, to create a Greater Serbia (see Woodward 1995: 7). During his rule, relations between the civil and military elites were extremely close, because they had a common interest in maintaining the old-new State. They shared not only the same 'values' but also the military victories and defeats. Milošević manipulated the army and from that moment this definitely became a matter of pure routine (see Vankovska, August 2000). Thus, the scenario of a classical military coup in order to change the authoritarian system of Milošević was an unrealistic one.

The nationalism in the former Yugoslavia arose from ethnic and religious minorities gaining control over its territorial region with the expressed goal of seeking secessionist independence. In Myanmar, five decades of ethnic conflict provided the self-claimed legitimacy to the armed forces to rule the country, even though the ethnic issue was not a major crisis, not least to the extent proclaimed by the military. There are a lot of radical ethnic groups who unknowingly head towards the separation while pronouncing the good of federalism, but the SPDC unknowingly being institutionalised the need to protect the Union more than necessary, a need which is to some extent self-inflicted but can also be seen to be rooted in the British legacy, and that pushed them to the another extreme of the polarity (see Faulder, April 2006). In the former Yugoslavia, the 'Milošević phenomenon' that insist on only one dimension of his appeal is bound to miss the point.

In Yugoslavia, unity and Titoism were for the Party orthodox and army officers, Serbia for the nationalists, reform for the intellectuals, and protection for the Kosovo Serbs (see Vujacic 1995). However, those legacies of the past did not seem to help Milošević to build a State successfully. The federation had emerged from the crisis and operated in the crisis that led to its disintegration.

Milošević's mentor Ivan Stambolć, who was the leader of Serbian section in the LCY, supported Milošević in the election for the new leader, to the dismay of the other leaders in the Party. Milošević became the President of the LCY in 1987. After the death of Tito, Yugoslavia remained a one Party State throughout the 1980s and the League of Communists of Yugoslavia (LCY)[71] remained nominally the primary nongovernmental political institution, with continued heavy influence on matters of political policy at all levels of the federal State.

The Milošević regime was legalised and legitimated its power after Parliamentary and Presidential elections in 1989. Armed with such legitimacy and helped by a rigidly controlled media and powerful instruments of repression, the regime used the spontaneous politicisation of the Serbian people, which was the result of their striving for equality with other Yugoslav nationalities, to secure its own grip on power, becoming more authoritarian in the process. Milošević's charisma achieved its peak in 1989 with the purging of provincial Party leaders in Vojvodina and Kosovo under pressure from the Serbian Party in 1988, which marked a turning point in Serbia's struggle to reassert control over its two provinces. Milošević stripped Kosovo of the autonomy that Tito had conferred on the province in 1974 (see Glenny 2001: 627),

---

[71] Thus, in 1990 the LCY was decentralised in exercising authority, but increasingly elitist in terms of who occupied positions of power in the Party organisations. The 1990 Congress was the first since 1945 to be labelled 'extraordinary' (meaning 'emergency'). It was widely viewed as the Party's 'last chance' for constructive action to improve its sagging national image. Doctrinal reform was the central task of the Fourteenth Congress. The Congress voted to relinquish the LCY's monopoly of political power and allow multi-Party elections, in response to similar moves in neighbouring Communist countries (see "League of Communists of Yugoslavia.").

as the tensions between Serbs and ethnic Albanians in Kosovo province were coupled with fears of secession. Yugoslav army units and police are dispatched to keep order in Kosovo. In 1990, Kosovo's and Vojvodina's autonomy was eliminated.

Milošević transformed the LYC into the Socialist Party of Serbia in July 1990 and adopted a new Serbian Constitution in September 1990, providing for the direct election of a President with increased powers. Milošević essentially portrayed the nationalist and populist movement, a deceptive image of being democratic and pluralist. The League of Communists collapsed in January as other Republic leaders refuse to condone what they perceived as Serbian repression in Kosovo province. The dissolution of the Communist federation left Milošević with no effective federal mandate. Its seemingly democratic nature was central to the Serbian regime's plan to engage in all-out inter-ethnic dispute in the common Yugoslav State instead of effecting structural changes in the society for which the time was ripe. The Serbian Constitution adopted in 1990, which was the normative result of authoritarian and nationalist populism, is a paradigmatic instance of the abuse of law in order to secure the continuity of a political regime.

End of 1990, multi-Party elections in all six Yugoslav Republics were held. The winning parties in all the republics were nationalist in their programmes, appeal and aims. Negotiations among the leaders failed. In December 1990, Slovenia's population voted for independence in a referendum and in 1991, the Republic of Slovenia declared its independence. A bloodless 10-day war followed. Meanwhile, tension and violence between Serbs and Croats mounted.

In 1991, the Croats also declared their independence and the stage were set for war. Only the Macedonians would escape the wars of the 1990s and they seceded from the federation in September 1991. Bosnia and Herzegovina declared its independence in March 1992. The presence of large Serb minorities in Croatia and Bosnia led to wars in each, in which Serbs demanded the same right of self-determination given to their Croat and Muslim neighbours and demanded that their portions of Bosnia and Croatia remain in Yugoslavia. The wars in Slovenia and Croatia were initially fought in the name of forcibly keeping Yugoslavia united. The Serb-Croat conflict was greatly complicated in Bosnia by the presence of the large Muslim (Bosniak) population, which caused it to develop into a three-way conflict that was by far the bloodiest of the Yugoslav wars. After the creation of new independent States in the Balkans, Serbia remained as an only State with an unchanged government, considering that the Socialist Party of Serbia, the direct descendent of the LYC continued to dominate the political life in the Republic.

The rather narrow constitutional framework did not prevented Milošević from continuing in power. There was a significant function internally in-stabilising the political elite centred on him. Milošević was elected President of the Republic by the direct votes of the Serbian citizens. He continued to carry out an authoritarian rule and he was subsequently re-elected President of the Serbian Republic in the direct elections of December 1990 and 1992. There was little opposition to him, which effectively eliminated the ethnic Albanians who boycotted the election.

In the media, more attention has been paid to Milošević's personality than to the social, cultural and political conditions that empowered the man to play a role far more significant than his personal abilities would suggest he was able to perform. Only a few have stressed that Milošević had only been an administrator of the Kosovo myth, a cunning politician who used the historical opportunity to become the leader of his nation (see Vankovska, August 2000). The rise of the myth called 'Milošević' has been facilitated by internal factors as well as by various moves of the international community and media. Taken, together with the economic stagnation suffered after the end of Tito's era, made the individual ethnic groups to revision their past and ethnic identity, old wounds came to the surface. The Serbs led by Slobodan Milošević, Slovene Party leader Milan Kučan,[72] Bosniaks led by Alija Izetbegović,[73] and Croats led by Franco Tuđman,[74] and also the international community all had their part to share in the guilt for these bloodshed wars.

---

[72] Milan Kučanv was the first President of Slovenia (1991-2002). He became the leader of the League of Communists of Slovenia in 1986. He began to support the Slovenian independence after 1989. In 1990, he was elected President of Slovenia, within the old Yugoslav federation under the League of Communists, and also after independence.

[73] Alija Izetbegović (1925-2003) was a President of Bosnia and Herzegovina (1990-1996). He was born in Bosnia, received a secular education and graduated from the Law School in Sarajevo. In 1983, he was sentenced to 14 years in prison for his hostile Muslim propaganda and was released in 1988. The introduction of a multi-Party system in Yugoslavia prompted Izetbegović to establish the Party of Democratic Action (*Stranka Demokratske Akcije*, or SDA) in 1989, which won the largest share of votes. He became co-President of Bosniak-Croat Federation and initially proposed a unitary Bosnian State and a peaceful solution. However, war immediately broke out across the country as Bosnian Serb and Yugoslav Army forces took control of large areas of Bosnia. The Bosnian war was formally ended by the Dayton Peace Accord in November 1995. He died in October 2003. Many aspects of his life remain strongly disputed between all sides in the Bosnian War (see "Alija Izetbegović").

The US, under the Clinton administration, and Western Europe supported Milošević since he was credited in the West negotiating the Dayton Agreement,[75] which ended the war in Bosnia. Milošević was directly supported by the international community. The West ignored the opposition in Serbia, though there were student demonstrations which lasted three months, followed by the election in 1996, which filled the streets of Belgrade daily to protest against Milošević's rule. Instead of supporting the opposition in Serbia, the West opted for Milošević so that he could stay longer in power. Milošević recognised the opposition victories of 1996 only in 1997. The support from the West lasted until the start of a hard-line Serb crackdown on Albanian separatist and terrorist actions in 1998. Hence, NATO air strikes against FRY took place between March to June 1999. Consequently, the Serbian military withdrew from Kosovo. Milošević image was badly damaged despite a substantial rise in popularity after the NATO bombing in 1999. Milošević denied Vojislav Koštunica's victory in the new elections in 2000. However, he was ousted eleven days later in a public revolt orchestrated by the late Serbian Prime Minister Zoran Đinđić in October 2000.[76] Opposition leader Koštunica took office as President on 6 October and authoritarian rule ended in the former Yugoslavia.

---

[74] Franjo Tuđman's (1922-1999) political Party HDZ (*Hrvatska Demokratska Zajednica*, Croatian Democratic Union) won the first post-Communist multi-Party elections in 1990. A year later he proclaimed Croatian independence. In 1971, Tuđman was sentenced to two years in prison for alleged subversive activities during the "Croatian Spring." During these decisive years from 1990 to 1995, Tuđman proved to be a master strategist behind the wars. He was reelected twice and remained in power until his death in late 1999 (see "Franjo Tuđman.")

[75] The Dayton Agreement took placed at Wright-Patterson Air Force Base in Dayton, Ohio to end the war in Bosnia, in particular the future of Bosnia and Herzegovina from 1-21 November 1995. The main participants were Serbian President Slobodan Miloševic, Croatian President Franjo Tuđman, Bosnian President Alija Izetbegović, Chief American negotiator Richard Holbrook and General Wesley Clark (see "Dayton Agreement.")

[76] Zoran Đinđić (1952-2003) was imprisoned for several months for trying to establish a non-Communist student organisation. After being released from jail, he continued his studies in Germany. In 1989, Đinđic returned to Yugoslavia to take up a teaching post at Novi Sad University. Together with other Serb dissidents he founded the Democratic Party. He became the Chairman of the Executive Board of the Party in 1990 and was elected to the Parliament of Serbia in the same year. After a massive series of public protests over rigged elections, Đinđic became the first non-Communist Mayor of Belgrade in 1996. Đinđic played a key role in toppling Miloševic and had a prominent role in the Presidential elections in September 2000. He became Prime Minister of Serbia in 2001. He played a major role in sending Miloševic to the UN War Crimes Tribunal in The Hague. He had constant disagreements with federal President VojislavKoštunica, but he had a close relationship with Montenegrin President Milo Djukanovic. Zoran Đinđić was assassinated in Belgrade on the stairway of the main Serbian government building in March 2003 (see "Dr Zoran Đinđić.")

Table 4-1. Evolution of post-Tito Yugoslavia 1980-2004

15 May 1986	Milošević becomes the President of Serb regional Communist Party.
24 April 1987	First major Serb protests in Kosovo over allege persecution by majority Albanians. Milošević's star rises in Serbia as he defends protesters from Kosovo Albanian police.
October 1987	Milošević purges Serbian Communist Party and media.
January 1988	Milošević's wing in Serbian party ousts State President Ivan Stambolic
December 1990	Result of multi-party elections, Milošević was a re-elected President.
June 1991	Slovenia and Croatia declare independence.
23 December 1991	Bosnia-Herzegovina proclaims independence. President Alija Izetbegovic requests UN peacekeepers for Bosnia.
1992	(1) Macedonia declares independence; (2) Bosnia and Herzegovina declares independence; (3) Serbia and Montenegro form the Federal Republic of Yugoslavia, with Slobodan Milošević as its leader.
November 1995	The Dayton Peace Accord was signed to end the war in Bosnia.
1996	The Kosovo Liberation Army (KLA) begins to attack Serbian policemen.
March 1988	Milošević sends troops to Kosovo to quash unrest in the province.
March 1999	After peace talks fail, NATO threats to launch air strikes on Serbia.
January 2000	In the face of sanctions from the US and other nations, the Serbian economy continues to deteriorate.
September 2000	Opposition leader Koštunica wins elections held 24 September Milošević refuses to release the complete results, demanding a runoff election.
October 2000	A popular uprising led by Zoran Đinđić begins. A general strike is called and one million people flood Belgrade. Milošević's support crumbles, he steps down. Vojislav Koštunica takes office.
April 2001	Milošević is handed over to the United Nations International Criminal Tribunal for the former Yugoslavia in The Hague.
February 2002	Milošević's trial begins at the UN International Criminal Tribunal
2003	Serbia is on its way to consolidated democracy.
March 2006	Milošević died in UN custody.

Source: (see "The Former Yugoslavia: Chronology.").

4.1.2. The Union of Myanmar under the Regime of SPDC

When the democratic transition failed in Myanmar, an authoritarian regime called the State Law and Order Restoration Council (SLORC), which later became a totalitarian regime under different name, seized power to rule for the "failed interim period." After General Ne Win's resignation, the one-man-rule dictatorship in Myanmar was turned into a military dictatorship led by a group of military Generals with totalitarian nature. General Sein Lwin[77] took power for just 18 days before being replaced amid widespread unrest by President Dr Maung Maung, a civilian lawyer and the biographer of General Ne Win.[78] Within weeks, Dr Maung Maung was removed from the position as President, by the military over take led by Sr. General Saw Maung,[79] Commander-in-Chief. In the former Yugoslavia, only Slobodan Milošević appeared on the political stage or instead, it was only he who drew the attention of the media. Nevertheless the regime in Myanmar contained quite a number of key players in the early stages including - the former Chairman of the SLORC, Sr. General Saw Maung; Lieut. General Khin Nyunt, the Chief of the Military Intelligent Bureau (was the powerful Secretary-One of the SLORC) and at later stages of the SPDC, he served as the Prime Minister merely for one and half years; General Than Shwe,[80] the former Chairman of the SLORC and the Chairman

---

[77] General Sein Lwin joined the army in 1943 and General Ne Win's '4th Burma Rifles' in 1944. He was the head of the security force involved in the Rangoon Student Union massacred on 7 July 1962. He was successor to General Ne Win as the Chairman of the BSPP and to General San Yu as President of Burma from 26 July to 12 August 1988 (see The Burma Project 1998: 8).

[78] Dr Maung Maung (1924-1994) served in the army during World War II and attended Officers' Training School, but quit for an academic career after the war. He founded *the Guardian Magazine* in 1954 and *the Guardian Newspaper* in 1956. He was the author of Burma's '*1974 Constitution*' and General Ne Win's biography. He succeeded General Sein Lwin as President of the country and Chairman of the BSPP on 19 August 1988. He conceded past errors, announced the lifting of marital law, which was imposed in August 1988, release detainees and promised a shortened consultation period and multi-Party election. However, as protests and demands for an interim government escalated, a military took over followed on 18 September 1988 (see Ibid).

[79] Sr. General Saw Maung (1928-1997) joined the army in 1949. He was a Minister of Defence under General Sein Lwin. Until his retirement, he ruled Myanmar as a Chairman of SLORC from 1988 to 1992. He resigned due to medical reasons (see "Background Biographies." August 2001).

[80] General Than Shwe is the Chairman of the ruling SPDC and rules the present day Myanmar solely. He graduated from the Officer Training School (9th Batch) in Hmawbi. He was attached to the Psychological Warfare Department in 1958. He rose steadily through the ranks, becoming Commander of the Southwest Region in 1983. He became Vice Chief of Staff with the rank of Brigadier General in 1985. He was promoted to Major General in 1986 and Lieut. General in 1987. He was serving as Chairman of the BSPP's Regional Committee in Irrawaddy Division in 1988 when pro-democracy protests broke out across the country (see Ibid).

of the SPDC; and General Maung Aye, the Vice Chairman of the SPDC; among others.

However, the era of the military rule in Myanmar is as old as its independence. Therefore, it is important to survey the extent of military rule in Myanmar in order to understand the present position of the SPDC: from the time Aung San led BIA, from General Ne Win's "*Tatmadaw*" between 1958 and 1988 to the present ruling junta; - the SPDC that was renamed from the SLORC that ruled from 1988 to 1997.

Being a military regime accountable to no other institution but itself, the SPDC certainly has the competence in the sense of ability, power and authority to set and dictate the rules, but it is very questionable whether it has the competence in the sense of the ability, skill and knowledge needed in order to prepare the ground for meaningful economic progress and to initiate a process of peace and development as its name suggests. The SPDC would answers this question with a most emphatic 'yes' even though the real existing economic and political situation seems to indicate otherwise. Is the SPDC really strong and competent? If it is indeed strong, how strong is it and from which source does it draws its strength? And also, has it got the will to do it?

The last question calls for consideration of two aspects, what is the 'physical' or 'material' strength and what is the 'ideological' strength of the army. So far as the 'material strength' is concerned, the latest assessment by analysts suggests that the ground, naval and air branches of the army, though still beset with serious problems and short comings have, since 1988, gone quite a long way towards developing into strong and effective fighting forces in terms of man-power, equipment, armament and communications. If the analysts are right and the trend continues, it may mean a less permissive stance toward those groups who have 'exchanged arms for peace' and an increase of pressure on forces taking up arms against the SPDC. Another consequence which continues is the abnormally high military expenditure and, given the lack of economic progress, even this means fewer resources for health, education and other civilian purposes. The army will remain an important factor to be reckoned with, which will play a major role in the politics of Myanmar.

The SLORC or the SPDC is not simply a military dictatorship. Rather, it is an army-State. Army officers shadow or control all functions of the State and most everyday activities of social life (see Ash, May 2000). It is the 'ideological' strength of the army that one must seriously turn to for consideration if one wants to understand the SPDC, its logic, its line of argument and its own view of itself. In dealing with the SPDC, it will not suffice to say simply that it is a group of ruthless power hungry generals who usurped power to enrich themselves and to rule the country by any means. Instead, one must look into the history of the army starting at the time of its foundation, its development and the role it played in the Burmese polity. The Burmese army was born under the patronage of the Japanese during World War II and nurtured by them in its early stages in the time of Aung San's life-time. Dr Ba Maw says in his memoirs, *"Breakthrough in Burma: Memoirs of a Revolution"*, that the fascist rule is not the worst thing that the Japanese have done to Myanmar, it is rather the spirit they instilled into the Burmese army, namely, that the armed forces are the masters and not the servants of the people.[81] Robert Taylor writes in *The State of Burma* that after the Japanese granted independence, the army virtually remained a State within the State (see Taylor 1987). The army was able to maintain its role after independence, when the political turmoil and armed conflicts assigned a major role to the armed forces. The idea that the army is the 'life and soul' of the country as Ne Win proclaimed, when the Burmese forces marched into Rangoon after the withdrawal of the British in 1941, was to become deeply rooted in the thinking of the Burmese military. The people generally accepted the special status of the army, which was enhanced by the disunity of the political parties. Certainly, the army grew up as a patriotic force dedicated to the national cause, and was accepted by the Burmese people as such. It has gained the reputation of having liberated the people from the British and Japanese rules and of having saved the country from disintegration after the independence in 1948. Hence, when General Ne Win *coup d'état* took place in 1962; there was hardly any public outcry or protest, except from the students.

The events of 1988 and the following years greatly tarnished the reputation of the army, but it still understands itself as firmly situated in a tradition, which, according to a publication of the Ministry of Information, has "elevated the *Tatmadaw* to be

---

[81] Dr Ba Maw was the Prime Minister of Burma between 1943 and 1945. In 1943, the Japanese permitted the *'Thirty Comrades'* to form a government with the much older Dr Ba Maw as Prime Minister and the young, Aung San as Minister of Defence and Commander of the Burmese army. At first Dr Ba Maw's popularity emerged from the defence lawyer position for *Hsaya San* who led the famous rebellion and was hanged by the British. Hsaya San's rebelling was rooted in the sufferings of the agrarian populations and regarded by the British as a mere peasant's revolt led by a superstitious fanatic who wanted to be a King (see Trager 1976).

the only national force capable of protecting and safeguarding the nation" (see The New Light of Myanmar (ed.) 1989). Whereby, the political parties follow their own interests the army, it is said, acts, as it is its duty to act, in the interest of the whole nation. Consequently, it is quite natural and legitimate, as is unequivocally stated in the publication mentioned above, that "the *Tatmadaw*, the national political force of Myanmar, will endure forever shouldering national responsibilities for so long as such a State as Myanmar exists in the world" (see The Press of the Head Office of the State Law and Order Restoration Council 1996: 45). This theory also immunises the army against any kind of criticism or opposition. Seen in the light of these considerations, it is easy to understand why the regime appears, at least at first sight, as an inert mass incapable of any change. The edifice of self-legitimation built allegedly upon the tradition of the army lacks one essential prop, namely, the legitimation and acceptance of the people. This deficiency undermines the very foundation of the army's ideology, from which the role of the army is derived. For all the rhetoric and trappings of a benevolent ruler, the army has not been able to convince the people that everything it does is in their interest.

The military as a profession has established itself as a monopoly over the political, social and economic aspects of the entire society. In the unique historical context of Myanmar, crossing over from civilian roles to military roles was found to be common. Military Intelligence, says an old joke, is a contradiction in terms, but Myanmar was a country ruled by Military Intelligence. Military Intelligence, in the broader sense, had ruled the country for over four decades. The Military Intelligence, referred to as the MI, was organised as the Directorate of Defence Services Intelligence (DDSI),[82] was the backbone of the military regime (see Ash, May 2000) until 2004 and was considered to be in a permanent power struggle with Battalion forces.

Senior General Saw Maung was replaced by Sr. General than Shwe in 1993. After re-baptising the SLORC as the "State Peace and Development Council (SPDC)" in 1997, Sr. General than Shwe, announced the dissolution of the 21-member Council. Most are Major- and Brig. - Generals, more junior than the old soldiers who made up the now-defunct SLORC; several controversial personalities disappeared from

---

[82] The DDSI is the most powerful intelligence and security organ in Myanmar. All the other agencies are firmly under its control. The DDSI since 1984 has been a function of its Director, Lieut. General Khin Nyunt until 2004.

the political stage. One explanation for the disappearance of famous figures in the junta was their corruption, but the departure of General Myo Nyunt as such, made many observers wonder, since he chaired the National Convention and expelled the NLD's representatives from the Convention in 1995 (see Tesoro *et al.,* November 1997). Later on, this power balance question was intensified by a helicopter crash in early 2001, which led to the death of Lieut. General Tin Oo, who was the Secretary-Two and the number four man in the military government.

Whereas the mode of creation of what is called the second Yugoslavia points to the existence of extremely close relations between the civil and military elites, which at that time found a common interest in maintaining the old-new State, the SPDC rules Myanmar under a purely military confection. The former Yugoslavia's mix of a civil-military relationship existed in Burma under General Ne Win; the Party played the civilian government and the military as a separate institution to protect its power.

The 'old split theory' was based on the assumption of the power struggle between military intelligence and the battalion forces or, in other words, the power struggle between SPDC's Vice-Chairman General Maung Aye, the hardliner, and between Secretary-One, the intelligence Chief Lieut. General Khin Nyunt, the pragmatic man who was appointed as the Prime Minister in August 2003, three months after the *Depeyin* accident.[83] The Prime Minister was seen as a pragmatist who understood the need for political and economic reform, who wanted to engage with the international society and was keen to solve ethnics' problems. Five days after General Khin Nyunt assumed the post of the Prime Minister, he announced a seven-point road map to democracy. The first step was the resumption of the National Convention, which began in January 1993 and adjourned in March 1996, but no timeframe or details on delegates, was provided. General Khin Nyunt, being less of a hard-liner than the other two, was also amenable for the resumption of talks with the opposition, which began in October 2000 but came to a grinding halt later. A series of cease-fire agreements have been agreed under his involvement. He was using a soft line to strengthen the regime duration, as the *Tatmadaw* can not afford to wage wars

---

[83] On Friday, 30 May 2003, while Aung San Suu Kyi and her supporters were on Party organisational trip to the northern part of Myanmar, Depeyin, the government-back thugs had brutally ambushed and killed at least 70 people on the spot. After that assassination attempt, Aung San Suu Kyi was put under house-arrest.

at every frontier at once with current Myanmar's economic stagnations. A sustainable political development is necessary in Myanmar for temporarily for stability.

Unpredictably Prime Minister General Khin Nyunt was purged and put under house-arrest and the SPDC pulled the plug on the National Intelligence Bureau and its existing laws, a move which effectively dismantled the entire military intelligence network.[84] The period under General Khin Nyunt has ended finally forty years of civil war, even though the process of nation building was incomplete. Where previous democratic and military governments failed, his government succeeded and it inherited the problem. We so easily forget these complexities if we are fixated on the more immediate and dramatic issues of Aung San Suu Kyi and her Joan of Arc image (see Faulder, March 2006). The "soft-liner vs. hard-liner" discussions were ended then with the fall of the Prime Minister. The administrative capital was officially moved to a militarised Greenfield site two miles west of Pyinmana in November 2005[85]. Since October 2004, Myanmar has gone through several minor shuffles in the SPDC's administration; however, the country is used to such changes since General Ne Win's era.

---

[84] 'The purged and power cycles' from the Combat and the Intelligence can be listed from 1960 on with Brig Maung Maung and Brig Aung Shwe (now Chairman of the NLD) till 2004, with General Khin Nyunt and several intelligence officers, but dissolving the whole military intelligence network as such by promulgation of Law Repealing National Intelligence Bureau Law and the dissolution of the National Intelligence Bureau, for the first time in Myanmar history.

[85] Pyinmana is a logging town and sugar cane refinery center in Mandalay Division of Myanmar.

Table 4-2. Evolution of Burma: the State of Myanmar: 1988-2004

July 1988	General Ne Win resigns. His succession is General Sein Lwin.
August 1988	General Sein Lwin is replaced by Dr Maung Maung.
18 September 1988	General Saw Maung, Commander-in-Chief, takes power, and the State Law and Order Restoration Council (SLORC) was founded.
November 1988	Many parties are registered for the SLORC promised multi-parties election for a democratic transition, including the National Union Party (NUP) (former BSPP), the National League for Democracy (NLD) of Aung San Suu Kyi, and the Democratic Party for New Society (DPNS) of the students' leader who led the '8.8.88' movement.
March 1989	The first cease-fire agreement took place with a group of insurgent, Myanmar National Democracy Alliance Army (MNDAA- Kokang).
May 1989	The SLORC renames the country as the "Union of Myanmar."
May 1990	Free and Fair Elections are held.
April 1992	The SLORC announces that within six months it will organise a "National Convention" to draft a new Constitution.
January 1993	The National Convention commences, but is suspended after two days.
January 1995	The SLORC take-over Manerplaw, the KNU base.
July 1995	Aung San Suu Kyi is released from house-arrest.
December 1995	The first meeting between the KNU and the SPDC.
March 1996	The SLORC adjourns the National Convention.
December 1996	Student protests in Yangon marked by a crack-down and arrests.
1997	Becomes a member of the Association of Southeast Asia Nations (ASEAN).
November 1997	The SLORC renames itself as the State Peace and Development Council (SPDC) with some changes at top positions.
September 2000	Aung San Suu Kyi is placed in house-arrest, until May 2002.
October	The SPDC starts secret talks with Aung San Suu Kyi.
May 2002	General Ne Win and his daughter Khin Sandar Win were put under house-arrest. Her husband and three sons were sentenced to death.
May 2002	Aung San Suu Kyi was released from House-Arrest.
December 2002	General Ne Win (91) died in Yangon.
May 2003	Aung San Suu Kyi is put under detention after *Depeyin* accident.
August 2003	General Khin Nyunt becomes Prime Minister, proposes to hold a National Convention in 2004 on drafting new Constitution as part of "road map" to democracy.

January 2004	The KNU Leader General Bo Mya's birthday Party is hosted in Yangon.
October 2004	General Khin Nyunt is ousted and his National Intelligence Bureau is dissolved.
November 2004	Many prisoners including Min Ko Naing, a prominent student leader of '8.8.88', the detention of Aung San Suu Kyi is extended.
December 2005	Administrative capital is moved to the middle of Myanmar, near a town called Pyinmana, and named "Nay Pyi Daw."[86]

Source: (see Lintner 1990; Seekin 2000: xv; Linter 1999; and "Research Page.")

---

[86] English Translation: Royal City.

The Quest for Democracy:
Relating the Differences in the Democratic Opposition

*"For the successful restoration of democracy,
we need the consolidation of the 'power of the people'."*
(Kim Dae-jung 1987)[87]

From the later years of the Cold War, strong democratic revolutionary movements seeking the overthrow of authoritarian regimes have arisen in many countries. Such movements have succeeded in some countries, including Serbia in 2000. On the other hand, strong democratic movements which rose up in some other countries were crushed before they could take power, and Myanmar is included in this category. What, then, accounts for the success of democratic revolution in some of these cases and its failure in others? The basic puzzle is how, for instance, in the former Yugoslavia, after a decade of civil wars, the democratic opposition achieved victory. In contrast, in present day Myanmar, after several decades of failed strategies from the opposition, it remains to be seen whether both sides can still come to a compromise. The key question guiding this chapter is in what way have the democratic oppositions in both countries evolved to achieve their goals? To enhance an understanding of transition, I will define the nature of both democratic opposition movements. Thus, the aim of this chapter is two-fold: first, to examine why the opposition in Serbia secured a victory and, second, why the opposition in Myanmar still suffers without any prospect of success and to analyse this failed movement in Myanmar.

---

[87] Kim Dae-jung (born December 3, 1925) is a former South Korean president and the 2000 Nobel Peace Prize recipient. He is the first and only Nobel laureate from Korea. He has been called the Nelson Mandela of Asia for his long-standing opposition to authoritarian rule. Kim Dae-jung was the President (succeeding Kim Young-sam) from 1998 to 2003.

5.1. Democratic Opposition of Serbia: toppling Milošević and his Oligarchy

In this chapter, I shall clarify how Slobodan Milošević and his oligarchy were defeated. In other words, how did the democratic opposition achieve their victory? To answer this question sufficiently, the answer needs to be linked, not only to the traditional opposition, but also to the external involvement and the will of the people, as they decided to be united when the time came to topple the Milošević's regime.

In Serbia, the path of democratisation was very different, even though multi-party elections in both countries were held in 1990[88]. Democratisation was not the result in the former Yugoslavia, even supposing one tends to think of competitive elections in terms of long-functioning, stable democracies, as a way of citizens to choose their government among competing parties and as a set of rules to guarantee the conditions necessary to facilitate choice among a plurality of options, including the right to dissent and the right of defeated parties to compete again (see Woodward 1995: 114-143). However, the country was transformed into a loose confederation[89] of six Republics, which later resulted in a failed State and subsequently emerged to become six independent countries. Serbia united with Montenegro, was left with an option, namely how to deal with Milošević's authoritarian dictatorship. Besides all of these problems, Kosovo was the most critical of the many domestic problems that remained unresolved since the 1980s.

Yugoslavia, as the common State of the Serbian people, began to crumble and the Serbian ethnic question gained pre-eminence. Serbia was no longer politically self-sufficient which suited the Serbian regime well. The opposition was disunited, until the Spring of 1992 marked a change in the consolidation of democratic resistance to the Serbian regime. The prominent opposition leader, the lawyer, Koštunica, was the

---

[88] By 1989, the first political parties were founded and the first multi-party elections were held in 1990. There was a surge in the formation of parties, mostly Republic-based, although until 1990, the sole center of political power was the League of Communists of Yugoslavia (LCY).

[89] A confederation is an association of sovereign States, consisting of countries or businesses *et cetera* that have joined together in order to help each other; for example, the Confederation of British Industry. Confederations are usually created by Treaty but tend to later adopt a Constitution. Confederations tend to be established to deal with critical issues such as defence, foreign affairs, foreign trade, and have a common currency, with the central government being required to provide support for all members (see Ibid). Some nations which originally started out as confederations retained the word in their titles even after officially becoming federations, such as Brazil and Switzerland. The United States of America was a confederation first before becoming a federation with the ratification of the US Constitution.

co-founder of the Democratic Party (Serbian: *Demokratska Stranka* - DS) together with Zoran Đinđic, who had returned from Germany, and with other Serb dissidents. He later established the Democratic Party of Serbia (Serbian: *Demokratska stranka Srbije* - DSS) and formed an alliance with the charismatic Vuk Draskovic's conservative Serbian Renewal Movement (SPO). The Parliamentary opposition parties, notably the SPO and the Democratic Party (DS), the most influential party, were outvoted by the Socialist majority, even though they had supporters in all qualification groups. However, both the regime and the opposition failed to understand that they were reflecting a non-homogenous society.

The Serbian Academy of Sciences and Art (SANU), the Serbian Orthodox Church and other democratic opponents were merged into a coalition as the "Democratic Movement of Serbia (DEPOS)". Milošević's resignation and the dissolution of the Parliament to form a new interim or coalition government was demanded, not only by the democratic opposition and its coalition but, also, by the Serbian Orthodox Church and several Serbian universities. The opposition parties further pressured the regime and stressed the seriousness of the situation but failed to force Milošević to resign and make radical changes in their politics. The conflict between the regime and opposition deepened even further, without giving the authorities a chance either to compromise or make concessions. Nevertheless, in 1996, the elections were held.

The street protests in 1996 and 1997 were sparked by Milošević's refusal to accept the results of the 1996 elections[90]. However, Milošević strategically shifted the focus of political discourse toward violent conflicts in Kosovo and it was extremely effective in marginalising and silencing the democratic opposition and those within Serbia who sought political change. Later, in 1997, Milošević recognised the opposition victories in the November 1996 elections, having contested the result for 11 weeks because he was constitutionally limited to two terms as Serbian President. On 23 July 1997, Milošević assumed the Presidency of the Yugoslav Federation.

Despite the growing anti-Western sentiment during and in the aftermath of the NATO air campaign due to the Kosovo crisis in 1997-8, the unpopularity of Milošević's regime increased. The daily demonstrations calling for Yugoslav President Milošević to resign, over several weeks, had been poorly attended, arising from

---

[90] In 1996, after Milošević ignored an opposition victory in local elections, Đinđic organised three months of daily protest rallies in Belgrade. Milošević eventually relented and Đinđic became the first non-Communist mayor of the city.

the opposition parties' failure to resolve their differences. The main opposition grouping, the "Alliance for Change", held daily protests across the country in an effort to show that the movement was both determined and nationwide (see Oxford Analytica, October 1999). The lack of interest in the street protests was not be interpreted as a vote of confidence in Milošević. Most of the opposition leaders in Serbia have failed to bring about change, over several years, because of following reasons:

1) they could not come to an agreement on the strategy of how to topple the Milošević regime;

2) people were no longer willing to invest their hopes and energy in them;

3) and, for the younger generation, in particular, an increasingly popular strategy was to leave the country, either to study or simply to find work and opportunities for a better life.[91]

The combination of a divided opposition and public apathy undoubtedly lessened the chances of Milošević being replaced. Moreover, Milošević appeared to believe the most immediate threat to his position came from hard-line nationalists, rather than the democratic opposition. He deployed security forces to break up recent protests and arrest opposition leaders. Milošević continued to hold onto power in Serbia successfully. If the determination was there to remove him, it only needed an effort to motivate the public to support the democratic opposition.

Overcoming years of divisions, the Yugoslav opposition formed an 18-Party alliance known as the 'Democratic Opposition of Serbia' with Koštunica as their presidential candidate, who was untainted by allegations of corruption or of being a pro-Western stooge. The opposition was virtually banned from the airwaves and took its campaign directly to the people at street rallies throughout Serbia. International observers were banned from monitoring the elections. However, the opposition claimed victory and Koštunica described the result as a new dawn for Serbia and declared himself the "Peoples' President". Nevertheless, Milošević rejected the claims of a first-round opposition victory in new elections, as in the 1996 elections.

Đinđić, who became involved in politics as a student during the regime of Tito and was one of the founders of the democratic opposition to Milošević, took on the role as the main strategist to organise the mass uprising in Belgrade together with Koštunica and with the non-government sector, led by the student movement - *Otpor*

---

[91] These three reasons are what the opposition in Myanmar is currently facing.

- in October to oust Milošević.[92] Paradoxically, this defeat had been expected more by those who were outside traditional political parties and those who had been devoted to fighting the regime over the previous ten years than it was by the regime's direct political opponents. People seemed to have no aim other than toppling the regime of Milošević.

The independent media in Serbia was able to present the results of the most recent public opinion polls which regularly showed strong public dissatisfaction with the regime in Serbia and that people wanted to see all the regime's opponents united in their opposition. The independent media, after the State's media monopoly was broken by a persistence, not only found ways to survive individually but also established connections among themselves with the people and became stronger, offered information from the large number of individual groups and non-government organisations that made up the "Going Out 2000" coalition, played a major role in toppling Milošević's regime. No part of Serbia was left out of the campaign. Young activists visited the most remote villages and suburbs putting up posters and handing out leaflets in literally every part of the country. It is worth noting the strong voter turnout among the Roma and other ethnic minorities. This show of unity towards the common goal of toppling Milošević and his regime was a new development which would help to ensure the legal and political equality of all citizens in a future Serbia, which is the former Yugoslavia (see Matic, October 2000). It was a political campaign for regime change as well as an outline for future of the country.

Both the election campaign and the protests that toppled Milošević proved that civil society already existed in Serbia, along with other elements including a free press and direct international assistance. Such elements are necessary for a successful transition to democracy, which is missing in Myanmar's case. Though hundreds of thousands of people were involved in the movement against Milošević, the standpoint of its leadership and political perspective of the campaign waged by the 'Democratic Opposition of Serbia (DOS)', which some would have readily labelled "Made in America" as international assistance, for the first time was directed towards helping in carrying out democratic changes.

---

[92] Đinđic later admitted that, at the time, he was playing for the highest stakes. Miloševic made it clear that it was either him or Đinđic. The opposition had no choice but to obey Miloševic otherwise he would have them arrested and killed at the first opportunity. Kostunica stayed away from the mass public protests of late 1996 and early 1997 which helped to force President Miloševic to concede the opposition's unprecedented election victories in Serbia's major towns.

After the collapse of the regime's authority, Koštunica took office as Yugoslav President on 6 October 2000. Đinđić led his party to a landslide victory in the December 2000 Parliamentary elections and in February 2001. Đinđic's fearless leadership was instrumental in ending the regime of Milošević. Đinđic became Prime Minister emerging as the country's second most powerful man. He was the elected Prime Minister in Serbia's first non-Communist government in January 2001 and faced hyper-inflation and a chaotic government system where public sector workers often had to wait several months to be paid. Later, in the second year of transition to democracy, the period was marked by conflict and a power struggle between Đinđic and Koštunica. The 18-party coalition split after Koštunica's party left the coalition and Đinđic outmanoeuvred Koštunica when Yugoslavia was transformed into a new, loose union renamed 'Serbia and Montenegro' and Koštunica was left without an official post. While Koštunica was closely aligned with nationalist forces, Đinđic was generally viewed as the best hope for a technocratic solution to the nation's moribund economy. As Prime Minister, Đinđic reformed the Serbian economy, to the approval of the international community, and was uncompromising in his calls for his country to co-operate with the UN trials of alleged Serbian war criminals.

The political opposition in the former Yugoslavia in the past decade has been marked by two trends of either a high degree of personal continuity or fragmentation and structural discontinuities. All parties have undergone numerous splits, leading to a proliferation of parties in the opposition. This high degree of fragmentation, mostly based on conflicts of personality rather than any political substance, stand in stark contrast to an often-invoked call for unity among the political parties and which makes consolidation a harder task. Koštunica enjoyed popularity, while Đinđic earned grudging respect for his energy, businesslike approach and determination to push through reforms. Koštunica stepped down from politics after Yugoslavia was abolished in February 2003 and Đinđic, who was a strong believer in facing up to what he saw as political realities, was assassinated in March 2003.

The path to democratic transition was successfully taken in the former Yugoslavia. The Serbian opposition and people had managed to unite, at least for one time to topple Milošević's regime. Whether democracy is consolidated in Serbia today or in any of the other six Republics that since 26 May 2006 include Montenegro, which had separated from the former Yugoslavia, seems to be another question and Kosovo's problems remain unsolved.

Figure 5-1. The Democratic Opposition in Serbia

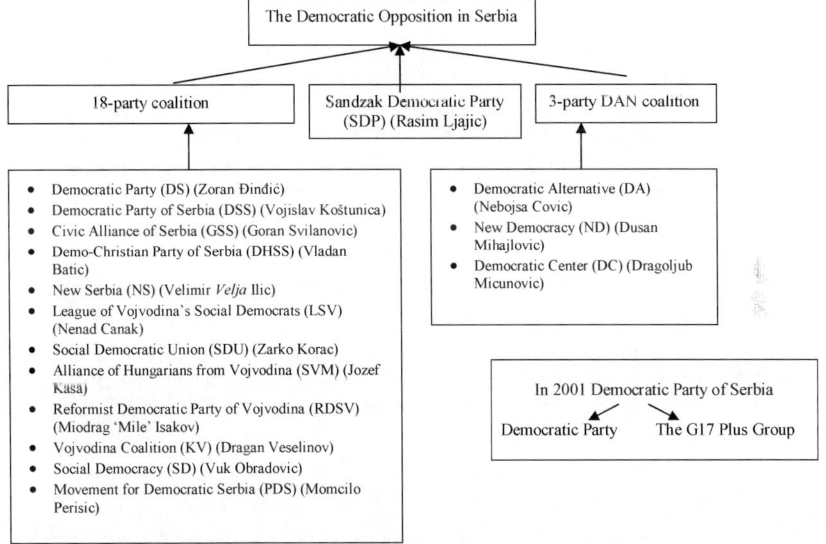

Table 5-1. Progress of the Democratic Opposition of Serbia: 1989-2000

1989	The formation of opposition parties was permitted and the Constitution was changed to allow the secession of States from the Federation.
	Slobodan Milošević eliminates Kosovo's autonomy.
	Democratic League of Kosovo (LDK) led by Dr Ibrahim Rugova was formed.
	A Nationalist Democratic Opposition, Democratic Alliance of Slovenia (DEMOS) was formed under the leadership of Milan Kučan.
	The conservative nationalist Hrvatska Demokratska Zajednica (Croatian Democratic Union) is formed by the leader, ex-Partisan Franjo Tudjman.
	Alija Izetbegović and other Bosniak activists establish the Party of Democratic Action (*Stranka Demokratske Akcije*).
	The Serbian Renewal Movement is founded by Vuk Draskovic and Vojislav Seselj.
	The Democratic Party of Serbia (DDS) was founded.
1990	The League of Communists of Yugoslavia falls apart at its 14th Congress.
June 1990	VMRO-Democratic Party for Macedonian National Unity was founded. The Democratic Party of Socialists (DPS) of Montenegro was founded. The Socialist Party of Serbia (Serbian: *Socijalisticka partija Srbije*) was founded by Milošević.
1991	Croatia is declared independent.
	Slovenia secedes from the former Yugoslavia Federation, along with Croatia.
	Macedonia declares its sovereignty and declares its right to secede.
	The Serbian Radical Party was formed, under the leadership of Vojislav Seselj, with the merger of the Peoples Radical Party and Serbian *Chetniks* Movement.
1992	Bosnia and Herzegovina secedes from Yugoslavia.
	Federal Republic of Yugoslavia is presented as a new State.
	Kosovo Albanians held an underground referendum that voted overwhelmingly for Kosovo's independence, without success.
	The Democratic Movement of Serbia (DEPOS) began and won the battle for a proportional electoral system.
1993	Milošević dissolves the Serb Parliament and calls new elections.
1994	Serb Socialists form a new government with support of New Democracy (formed out of the League of Socialist Youth in 1990).
1995	The Kosovo Liberation Army (KLA) (the UCK in Albanian) first started to claim responsibility for bomb attacks.
	The Dayton Peace Agreement is signed in Paris.
1996	The 'Zajedno' opposition coalition is formed from amongst the Serbian Renewal Movement (Vuk Draskovic), the Democratic Party (Zoran Đinđić) and the Civil Alliance.
1997	Zajedno's gains in local authority elections are recognised. Đinđić becomes Mayor of Belgrade.

1998	Serbian forces begin an offensive against KLA insurgents in Drenica, Kosovo.
1999	NATO begins attacks on Serbia. Massive waves of refugees flow out of Kosovo.
2000	An alliance of political parties in Serbia was formed. Its candidate, Koštunica declared victory over Milošević in September. Later his party, the Democratic Party of Serbia, pulled out of the coalition. The remainder splits into the Democratic Party and the G17 Plus Group.
2001	In April, Milošević was arrested after a 26-hour armed standoff and later sent to The Hague for a war-crimes trial.
2002	The Democratic Party of Serbia (DSS) is the political party founded by a faction of the Democratic Party (DS). The faction was determined to join forces with the Serbian Renewal Movement (SPO) and intellectuals in setting up the Democratic Movement of Serbia (DEPOS).

Sources: (see *Demokratska stranka Srbije*; "Timeline Serbia 1998-1999.")

5.2. Myanmar's Opposition Movement

The democratic opposition in Myanmar, which started clearly in 1988 was initiated by students, reached the status of a nationwide movement, but after more than a decade under continuous repression by the regime, it is weakened and divided and has reached a political deadlock. The democratic opposition is defined as the consequence of the emergence of the leadership of Aung Suu Suu Kyi and her party, the NLD which originated from the movement in 1988. In fact, Myanmar's opposition movement is as old as its military rule,[93] but there is no traditional opposition as was the case in the Republic of Serbia that already existed since 1990. There are different timeframes and actors to be mentioned in order to understand the whole picture. Thus, I am obliged to divide the opposition movement into three parts: first, the movement of '8.8.88'; with the second and third parts subsequent to the "8.8.88" movement - the armed struggle of the 'All Burma Students' Democratic Front (ABSDF)'; and the NLD, led by Aung San Suu Kyi.

5.2.1. From Student Unrest Towards the Country-Wide Movement

In Burma, a common ideology links student movements and popular struggles for freedom. This link was formed through the fight against colonialism and fascism, and strengthened through the national independence movement.[94] Student dissent was a new phenomenon in Serbia when it started in 1996, whereas student dissent in Myanmar dates back to the 1920s. The student movement of 1988 was totally unexpected. It started suddenly and spread quickly and without planning developed into three levels of significance: 1) the starting level in late 1987 at the Rangoon Institute of Technology (RIT); 2) in early March 1988, after the riot around the RIT, and an escalation from June to August 1988; and 3) post-Ne Win dissent and pre-SLORC in early September.

The student unrest in Rangoon started slowly at the end of 1987 because of the currency demonetisations, which later accelerated in March 1988 following the

---

[93] In 1962, student demonstrations against Ne Win military putsch were suppressed. The student unrest after the funeral of U Thant (UN Secretary General), and a country-wide workers strike were terminated without success with high causalities.

[94] Aung San's political career started after his election as President of both the Rangoon University Students Union and the Students Union. Only later he moved from student politics into nationalist politics.

death of a student named *Phone Maw* as a result of the violent reactions of the BSPP's forces. Without plan or design, the movement grew into a mass movement and began agitating. They were clearly also influenced and motivated by student movements elsewhere in the Asia-Pacific.[95] People who had had their frustrations and irritations pent up, found an opportunity to let go. Students were swift in their movements with their youthful energy and dedication. They worked in groups even though they never could unite in one organisation: there were, as usual in similar situations, too many leaders, too many conflicting ideologies and goals (see Maung 1999: 99-100). With the acceleration of the movement, the 'All Burma Federation Students Union (ABFSU)', which was destroyed in 1962 by General Ne Win's forces, was restored in July 1988 to expand protests to include the general public. The movement to defy Ne Win's dictatorship was unprecedented and the results of this courageous confrontation were predictable. The astonishment and jubilation of the entire nation took place when, in a televised address on 23 July 1988, General Ne Win announced his resignation from politics and called for a national referendum on the country's political future. However, he was replaced by General Sein Lwin and a violent crack-down of the demonstrators took place throughout the country. The result of what has become known as the 'Massacre of 8.8.88' was tragic, surpassing even the carnage a year later at China's Tiananmen Square. General Sein Lwin resigned in August 1988 and was replaced by a civilian lawyer, Dr Maung Maung, a close friend and biographer of General Ne Win (see Ibid 3). The demonstrations were snuffed out in September 1988, as the military organised a coup, Dr. Maung Maung was replaced by Sr General Saw Maung and the newly founded "State Law and Order Restoration Council (SLORC)". Dr. Maung Maung writes:

> My story ends on 18 September, when my mandate ended, only partly fulfilled. So ended a cycle of Myanmar history and the life of the Second Constitution, hardly fifteen years old, thus creating a constitutional vacuum. Nature abhors vacuums; so do society and polity as the champions of democracy, the "revolutionaries" were to discover (see Ibid 244).

Some student leaders opted for an armed struggle, but some decided to remain inside the country to carry out their work, to form political parties to enter the elec-

---

[95] The 1980 South Korean Students Democratic Resistance in Kwangju and famous 1986 'People Power I' - the overthrow of the Marcos regime in the Philippines - had possibly alerted Burmese students and motivated them to start questioning authority for the need for political changes in their country, even though any demonstrations against the BSPP were brutally suppressed.

tions. The Democratic Party for New Society (DPNS) was formed by Moe Thee Zun and a number of prominent student leaders.[96] Due to its popularity, the DPNS was soon announced as an illegal organisation and Min Ko Naing,[97] the Chairman of ABFSU, was arrested in March 1989. As the arrests of student leaders had begun, Moe Thee Zun managed to escape to join the ABSDF. Ever since, any kind of underground cell has been intensively prosecuted and uprisings as such were no longer to be seen. However, to the surprise of many people, in December 1996, some 2000 students gathered to protest against an earlier incident in which three of their peers had been roughed up by the police, but it was by far the largest demonstration seen since 1988. Exiled student dissidents spearheaded a campaign, early in 1999, for a mass uprising on 9 September 1999 ('9.9.99') which was intended to replicate the '8.8.88' movement, but it was more of an event abroad. Since then, the student movement in Myanmar remains largely unanimated.

The student movement was able to launch 'people power' and topple General Ne Win and the BSPP regime but failed nevertheless to carry out a meaningful political transition, due to their lack of experience in politics and the absence of traditional opposition in the country since 1962 which could back-up the movement and permit link-ups with other ethnic groups and ethnic politics. Not only are these factors important but there are two others that play a role in destroying the student movement in Myanmar namely: 1) the hardship and repression under the SPDC; and 2) the emergence of the NLD leadership since 1988. Before the NLD leadership existed legitimately, the students were the only political resistance in Burma, owing to its political history. Even since 1990, other opposition sources have had little space to emerge due to two same reasons that are mentioned above.

---

[96] From 1988-1990, Moe Thee Zun was the General Secretary of the ABFSU and Founder and Chairman of the DPNS. Later he was Chairman of the ABSDF, Secretary of the DAB, and Joint-General Secretary of the National Council of the Union of Burma (NCUB) from 1989-1998.

[97] Paw U Tun (al) Min Ko Naing, Chairman of the All Burma Federation of Student Unions (ABFSU), was arrested in March 1989. He was sentenced to 20 years of imprisonment (later commuted to 10 years under a general amnesty) for his anti-government activities. Min Ko Naing was awarded the John Humphrey Freedom Award from Canada in 1999, the Homo Homini Award from the Czech Republic in 2000 and the Student Peace Prize from Norway in 2001. He was released in October 2004 after the ousting of the Prime Minister, General Khin Nyunt. He was released in November 2004 and detained again in September 2006.

5.2.2. To Become The New Armed Forces: the ABSDF

Since the student movement in Myanmar did not accomplish their mission by taking to the streets as in former Serbia, most of the students left for the border areas to pursue an armed struggle.[98] The students, who fled, founded the world's first student army - named ABSDF - at the Thai-Burma border in November 1988. Later, the All Burma Students League (ABSL) was formed in 1994 at the India-Burma border. However, the ABSDF and ABSL have developed differently because of their different geo-political situation.[99] Most borders area of Burma harboured rebel groups composed of different ethnic minorities. The Karen National Union (KNU) was the first ethnic armed organisation to welcome and accommodate the students. As the trust between the ethnic minorities and the Burmans was shaky owing to the civil war of 26 years, trust-building was the first task for the ABSDF to achieve as their leadership consisted mainly of ethnic Burmans. Gradually, the ABSDF managed to form the 'Democratic Alliance of Burma (DAB)' with different armed and un-armed opposition groups at thai-burma border, to overthrow the SPDC and to start the national reconciliation to create a genuine federal union. The ABSDF split into two wings during the period between 1992 and 1996 and has suffered from the conflicts within the leadership that hampered its activities and contributed to the decline in membership.[100] As KNU strong-holds were defeated,[101] the ABSDF became weak. The ABSDF gave up its armed struggle as a strategy in 1997, but retained the right to hold arms for defensive purposes (see Buzzi 2001: 20-21). The ABSDF, however, remains one of the main opposition forces in the movement.

---

[98] Armed resistance in Myanmar began in 1949 with different ethnic minorities groups and the Communist Party of Burma (CPB) that went underground. Students of the 1988 Generation were the last group to join the armed resistance.

[99] The student-led armed struggle was primarily inspired by Aung San's model of the 'Thirty Comrades' and the 'Burma Independence Army (BIA).' As the political structure of world in the present day is something different, the struggle without the assistant went nowhere.

[100] At its height, the ABSDF compressed a force of approximately 10,000 members.

[101] The KNU splits between the Christian leadership and Buddhist units – Democratic Karen Buddhist Army (DKBA) made the movement vulnerable. The SLORC forces successfully stormed Karen resistance headquarters at Manerplaw in 1995 with the help of DKBA.

5.2.3. Aung San Suu Kyi and the National League for Democracy (NLD)

The NLD led by Aung San Suu Kyi unquestionably plays a significant role in Myanmar politics. The existence of Aung San Suu Kyi and the NLD is not inextricably linked. The NLD does not exist without her, t it is not the other way around. Thus, the emergence of Aung San Suu Kyi's leadership and the NLD will be explained in this chapter in two parts.

<u>Aung San Suu Kyi</u> announced her entry into politics by addressing her first speech at *Shwedagon Pagoda* in 1988. Her appearance on the political stage met the excitement and expectations of ordinary people (see Lintner 1990: 109). She serves a role as an uncrowned queen, respectfully referred to even by close acquaintances as 'Daw Suu' and known to millions of Burmese simply as 'the Lady'. She became a legend, because she is the daughter of the father of the nation, Aung San. The '8.8.88' movement lacked leadership and the emergence of women leaders throughout the South and Southeast Asian continent formed the backbone to her instant leadership.[102] In her, the Burmese people possibly have seen another Corazon or Benazir, who unexpectedly swept to power in popular 'people's movements' against equally tyrannical regimes.[103] However, contrary to the others, the military in Burma did not side with Aung San's daughter. She does not become a President or Prime Minister but a prominent opposition leader, inspiration of a nation and international icon, and Nobel Prize winner. Aung San Suu Kyi, who spent her younger years in India, is inspired by Gandhism and engages herself in non-violent struggle, but she fails to believe in mass movement, that which made her a leader. Josef Silverstein states that there is no other person who has achieved her status, love and respect from the people of Myanmar. She is her father's daughter – intelligent, honest, tough and fearless (see Silverstein 1989: 112). Ash argues that Václav Havel, who nominated Aung San Suu Kyi for the Nobel Peace Prize, insists that she had politics thrust upon her, whereas he was a natural politician, yet within that, she has a firm

---

[102] Female leadership is not unusual in Asia region, while having sometimes held most women back at home, have also happily pushed some of them onto the political stage. Women leaders in Asia are often the widows or daughters of assassinated leaders. In this way, Asian dynasties provide transitional leadership as their countries develop their political systems. One may claim that the power of these women is artificial since it is derived from the sympathy that people have for their husbands or fathers. The emergence of female leaderships only began in 1990s.

[103] However, unlike Corazon Aquino, who led the people power movement in the Philippines, Aung San Suu Kyi had no connection to the movement of '8.8.88'.

grasp of what kind of new political system Myanmar needs just a much less clear idea of how to achieve it (see Ash, May 2000).[104] But then again, has anyone else?

The NLD is more than just a political party, because the party has assumed the leading role of a national movement for democracy and internationally its name has become a synonym for the movement itself. The NLD was formed with Aung San Suu Kyi, U Tin Oo[105] and former Brig General Aung Gyi[106] on the 27 September 1988, after the multi-party elections were promised by the army Chief Sr General Saw Maung[107]. Aung San Suu Kyi and other NLD leaders decided to push ahead with the election campaign, which they regarded as the best course. The mass arrest of the NLD's supporters continued once the election-campaign started. Aung San Suu Kyi and U Tin U were both put under house-arrest in July 1989. Despite their absence and the continuous arrest of its supporters, the NLD overwhelmingly won the elections in May 1990. After the landslide victory of Aung San Suu Kyi and the NLD Michael Aris, the late husband of Aung San Suu Kyi, claimed that:

> "the vote was a personal one for her: often the voters knew nothing about their candidate except that they represented Suu" (see Aung San Suu Kyi 1991: xxiv),

---

[104] Dr Maung Maung writes that he might be wrong in advising Aung San Suu Kyi to stay away from the politics. If she had taken his advice, Myanmar would not have any Nobel Laureates; not even U Thant who would dearly loved one for peace, and tried so hard and did much good; [...] The award may, in the course of time, become a heavy cross to bear, and she'll have so much to live up to [...] (see Maung Maung 1999: 274).

[105] General Tin Oo served as the Chief of Staff and the Minister of Defense 1974-1976. In 1976, he was imprisoned for alleged involvement in coup attempt of July 1976 and released in 1980, during an amnesty. In August 1988, he emerged as a prominent opposition leader and became the Vice-Chairman of the NLD and since 19 December 1988 its Chairman (see "Background Biographies."). Since 1988, he is arrested and placed under house-arrest several times. Currently, he is serving house-arrest since the May 2003 Depeyin accident.

[106] General Aung Gyi participated in the independence movement and the anti-Japanese struggle and was a member of Ne Win's 4th Burma Rifles. He played a role in the caretaker government of 1958-60 and was a member of the Revolutionary Council of 1962, serving as Vice-Chief of Staff and Minister of Trade and Industry. He was ousted in 1963 for statements made in Japan about the cause of the coups. He was imprisoned in 1965-68, 1973-74 and between 29 July - 25 August 1988 for initiating the unrest in 1988. His letters critical of the government in 1987-88 were an important opening for opposition to the government. He served as the President of the NLD but resigned on 3 December 1988 to form the Union Nationals Democracy Party on 16 December (see Ibid). He is now inactive in politics.

[107] Merely a few days after the coup, General Saw Maung, Head of the SLORC, announced for the registration of political parties (see Fink 2001: 63).

Some claimed that the votes were anti-military votes. However, with their land-slide victory, the NLD missed a possible turning point in history, to precede the meaningful transition. Timothy Garton Ash argues that:

> "How might peaceful change come about in Myanmar? What chance for a Silken Revolution? One must start by saying that the best chance was probably missed ten years ago In May 1990; the regime was stunned by the NLD's election victory. If, before the eyes of the world's press and television, then present in Rangoon, the NLD had immediately organised a mass march to University Avenue and freed Aung San Suu Kyi from house arrest, the country might look very different today. But the 'uncles' then running the NLD, too fearful of risking violence and perhaps also too trustful of their former army colleagues, failed to seize the moment. This was the turning point at which history failed to turn (see Ash, May 2000).

In contrast, the Serbs democratic opposition took a different path at this point, to pave the way for a democratic transition. The Serbs prominent leaders, Đinđić and Koštunica, called for mass protests to topple Milošević's regime. Yet, in Burma, a few days after the elections, a group of Members of Parliament (MPs) of the NLD, led by Dr Sein Win, Aung San Suu Kyi's cousin, went into exile in order to mobilise international support for the democracy movement. The MPs, with the support from the ABSDF, the KNU and the DAB, formed the National Coalition Government of the Union of Burma (NCGUB) at Manerplaw (the former stronghold of Karen rebels) in December 1990. A decade after its inception in the jungles, very few people know much about the NCGUB and its work. The NCGUB has yet to come out with any concrete political concepts and fails to support the democratic opposition both inside and along the borders. The NCGUB, which now has its headquarters in Washington DC, enjoys little support either at home or abroad (see "Time for Soul Searching," August 2000). Doctor Sein Win led the NCGUB into a 'wait and see' organisation, though its task is to back the NLD from inside Burma.

The NLD has refused to have anything to do with unequal negotiation. They decided to withdraw from SLORC-organised "National Convention" in December 1996 and called for international sanctions. These were the only actions that the NLD took after the release of its leader in 1995. Despite her release, mass arrests intensified on NLD's members and most of them were forced to resign from the party, until the NLD became a 'head' without a 'body' to represent (see Ash, May 2000). The SLORC's constitutional proposals envisage a distinction between 'national' politics, where the 'leading role of the armed forces' would be secured.

The NLD set up the "Committee Representing the People's Parliament (CRPP)" in September 1998, which was a 'showdown with the junta', but the awareness of the CRPP among the Burmese people remains low and even political activists are unclear about its broader agenda (see Min Zin, April-May 2000). The CRPP has so far failed to present a clear-cut strategy to break the present political deadlock.[108] After a short period of freedom since 2002, Aung San Suu Kyi was confined again under house-arrest in May 2003 after the Depeyin accident.

The resignations of the MPs and party members and the closing down of the offices in many townships and districts, by persuasion or threat, will not drive the NLD into oblivion. The very nature of totalitarian rule and its not very sophisticated methods will help the NLD to remain alive in the minds of the Burmese people. It is quite possible that even those who have become somewhat weary with the policies of the NLD will turn to that party again in another free election. Aung San Suu Kyi points out the necessity of concerted efforts by using 'ingenious methods to achieve the objects of our desire' and also to the reciprocity of responsibilities, meaning that the elected representatives have a responsibility to act on behalf of the people in their interests. The people who elected them have a responsibility to support them. Implicitly, this seems to go for the NLD in general also. She stated that 'one hopes, of course, that objects of our desire will thus finally be achieved' because 'if we are united, we will attain democracy very quickly.' This dictum sounds very convincing but it is not impertinent to ask what the chances are of this possibility becoming a reality, or if it will remain only latent unless steps according to the practical ethics of responsibility are incorporated into the policy of the opposition. However one may wish or strive for, a mass uprising in the form of 'We, the People' demonstrations in East Germany in 1989 or of 'the People Power' series of actions in the Philippines to end the authoritarian regime is unlikely to happen in Myanmar today.

From the beginning, the NLD missed a chance to recognise the role of the military in political transition, failed to lead its people and the pro-democracy movement effectively. The NLD has been not aware that implementing a democratically elected civilian government is totally impossible under the current policy of the

---

[108] The CRPP consists of the representatives of the Parliament that won the vast majority of seats in the 1990 democratic election. The Committee acts as an Executive Committee of the Parliament, most of whose members are in detention or in exile. The CRPP had proxies from 251 of the surviving MPs, who have given the Committee the mandate to convene the full Parliament to act on their behalf in the meantime.

SPDC leadership. The regime has no willingness to establish democracy or meet the NLD's demands for the absolute transfer of power, which is a zero-sum game. In this case, any kind of political transition by any standard is hard to achieve.

Figure 5-2. The Democratic Opposition in the Union of Myanmar

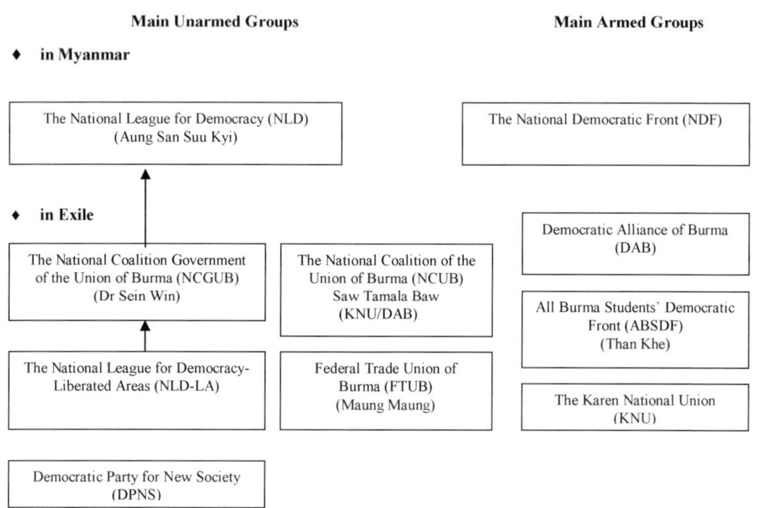

Table 5-2. Progress of the Democratic Opposition of Myanmar: 1988-2004

5 September 1987	25, 35 and 75 Notes were demonetised. Student demonstrations took place and many were arrested. Universities and schools were closed and re-opened in January 1998.
12 March 1988	A clash between riot police and students from RIT resulted in the death of Phone Maw.
13-18 March	The military bloodily clamped down on the student protests and many were arrested. Universities and schools countrywide were closed down.
26 August	Aung San Suu Kyi entered politics addressing her first speech in front of the Shwedagone Pagoda, before more than 100,000 people.
28 August	The All Burma Federation of Students Union (ABFSU) was founded. Min Ko Naing became the Chairman and Moe Thee Zun the General Secretary.
August	Former Prime Minster U Nu came back to the political stage.
2 September	Lawyers called the abolition of Constitution 1974 and nine survivors of the legendary "Thirty Comrades" asked the army to support the nationwide uprising.
9 September	U Nu set up a counter government and charged himself as a Prime Minister and U Tin U as Minister of Defence but, 5 days later, U Nu cancelled this counter-government, as he did not get enough support.
12 September	Aung San Suu Kyi, Tin U and Aung Gyi called for the creation of a transitional government and Dr Maung Maung rejected it.
19 September	The SLORC directed the massacre of hundreds of people in Rangoon and dissolved the existing organs of State power; the next day it set up its own government. 2,500 students escaped to Thailand and India.
23 September	Students started their military training under the KNU.
24 September	The National League for Democracy (NLD) was founded.
November	All Burma Students Democratic Front (ABSDF) was founded at Manerplaw.
December	Aung Gyi decided to split from the NLD to set up his own organisation, the oddly-named Union Nationals Democracy Party (UNDP).
20 July 1989	Aung San Suu Kyi and U Tin Oo were placed under house-arrest.
27 May 1990	General election. NLD wins overwhelmingly but the result was not acknowledged.
December	In Manerplaw, the National Coalition Government of the Union of Burma (NCGUB) was formed. The Prime-Minster is Dr Sein Win.
November 1991	Re-opening of the Universities and Schools countrywide.
10 December	Aung San Suu Kyi wins the Nobel Prize for Peace.
23 April 1992	General Saw Maung is replaced by General Than Shwe.
January 1993	The National Convention is announced by SLORC.
January 1995	Burmese Military over-ran the KNU's stronghold at Manerplaw.
July	Aung San Suu Kyi was released from house-arrest.

August	Universities and Schools were re-opened.
January 1996	Khun Sa, an opium warlord, surrendered to the SLORC.
June	The weekly meetings at Aung San Suu Kyi's residence were banned.
December	NLD decided to withdraw from the SLORC's National Convention. Students showed solidarity by demonstrating for a fair National Convention. The universities were closed down.
August	Aung San Suu Kyi spends 13 days in a roadside protest, in her fourth attempt to travel to Bassein.
September	The Committee to Represent the People's Parliament (CRPP) was formed.
9 September 1999	Exiled dissidents spearheaded a campaign beginning early in the year for a mass uprising on 9 September 1999 (9.9.99).
August	After 9 days of another roadside protest, Aung San Suu Kyi was placed under house-arrest.
May	Aung San Suu Kyi was released after 19 months of house-arrest.
October	Aung San Suu Kyi reportedly starts to meet with SPDC members. The content of the discussions is unknown.
15 June 2003	Aung San Suu Kyi makes her first visit outside of Yangon.
30 May 2003	The *Depeyin* accident. Aung San Suu Kyi and U Tin Oo are taken into 'protective custody' and are placed under house-arrest.
November 2004	SPDC began releasing thousands of prisoners who may have been wrongly imprisoned by a recently disbanded military intelligence unit (including former student leader Min Ko Naing).

Source: (see "Timeline Myanmar [formerly Burma]."; "Research Page.")

The Politics of Ethnicity

*"Yet if every ethnic, religious or linguistic group claimed Statehood,
there would be no limit to fragmentation and peace, security and
economic well-being for all would become ever more difficult to achieve."*
(Boutros Boutros-Ghali, 1992)[109]

I am encouraged to write this chapter for the basic understanding of the derivation and to gain some insights into the alternative paths which may have led towards the resolution of the political conflict in Myanmar. Ethnic conflict refers to a very specific phenomenon and encompasses all forms of small and large scale acts of violence between and among different ethnic groups in which ethnicity plays a causal role in the conflict and one's ethnicity is circumscribed by historical discourses (see Sambanis 2001; and Lake *et al.* 1996). In this chapter, I shall provide details of memories of the shared political history that link the civil wars and the politics of ethnicity that has created them in both States, the past and, also, the present, because there is little doubt that the third wave of 'democratisation' since the 1990s has seen an increase rather than decrease in the visibility of ethnic politics and conflicts. Simply, democratisation poses the issue of the definition of the people and citizenship, the boundaries and the organisational structure of the State and thereby destabilise the existing multi-ethnic State (see Smith, Anthony D *et al.* 1996: 336-9). Decentralisation and democratisation, in practice, have been successful in curbing ethnic conflicts in some multi-ethnic States, for example, in Belgium, India, and Spain, but not in some others such as in Nigeria or in the former Yugoslavia. Hence, there is usually more interest in decentralisation than in federalism because it entails a level of political autonomy, even sovereignty. In this section, I shall also address a major question, whether federalism can be the answer for the ethnic conflict in Myanmar?

---

[109] Boutros Boutros-Ghali CC is an Egyptian diplomat and the sixth Secretary-General of the United Nations, serving between January 1992 and December 1996.

6.1. The Burden of the Past

In the case of the former Yugoslavia and Myanmar, it seems that everything can be proved through history. They share resemblances at this point and are not alone in this matter as nowhere in the world is likely to make an end to its turbulent history. Ones ethnic identity is circumscribed by historical discourses. In the former Yugoslavia, wars were the legacy not only of traditional ethnic and territorial problems in the Balkans but also of their shared past and of the Yugoslav Federation constructed by Tito which involved a whole series of compromises aimed at making sure that no single constituent Republic dominated the State (see Economides *et al.* 1996: 63). However, the civil wars that waged since 1948 in Myanmar are not just contemporary conflicts but are rooted in history. The ethnic characteristics of Burma were formed during the pre-colonial period of the Burmese Kingdoms, ethnicity that was accentuated during the colonial time and the political stage that was set-up during the anti-colonial fighting before the profound conflict occurred after the country's independence from the British in 1948. Hence, the question of Yugoslav nation-building is developed into two stages, but that of Myanmar in three, because Yugoslavia lacked any colonial experience.

- Firstly, in history, the first Yugoslavia, which was a kingdom formed in 1918 as the Kingdom of Serbs, Croats and Slovenes, which was later re-named the Kingdom of Yugoslavia on 6 January 1929. However, in the revised and expanded version of the Burman Kingdom, the Burman power elite had long forcibly integrated the Mons, Shan and Arakanese kingdoms and this was known to be the period of sustained innovation. There were sentimental ties between the Ava polity and the related 'Burmese' or 'Myanma' identity that did not achieve the full national liberation and unification of the respective peoples of Myanmar. The present conflict and civil war in Myanmar are seen as the continuation of the national struggles of the past, as the clash of nationals and national Kingdoms, as Burman oppression rooted in history.[110]

---

[110] A unified nationalist Kingdom existed since the 11th Century, unified by the conquest or sword of nationalistic ethnic- Burman Kings. In the mid-nineteenth century, Ava began to come into being almost exclusively as the *Myanmar Naing-ngan*, the 'Burmese Kingdom'. A Myanma identity is like all identities, a partial one. It is tied to language, religion, political institutions and a shared written history, but the one throughout the core area of Ava Kingdom. Hence, certainly there was a sense of a Myanma identity in opposition to other 'ethnic' identities, one based on an idea of shared culture and ancestry of the Myanma as 'race' or *lu-myo* that perceived to be tied by blood (see Thant Myint-U 2001:88).

100

- Secondly, Burma under the British Empire developed a strong patriotic sentiment centred on the rump Ava polity and memories of a conquering past. New boundaries were drawn by the colonial power. Thus, the territorial limits of the country, the notion of who is Burmese and who is not, key social and political structures, all find their origins in the events surrounding the fall of Mandalay (see Thant Myint-U 2001: 9-11), which brought to an end the Myanma centralised administration.

- Thirdly, the former Yugoslavia existed under that name until it was invaded on 6 April 1941 by the Axis powers. A Socialist State was established immediately after World War II on 29 November 1945 as the *Democratic Federation of Yugoslavia (DFY)*[111] which, in 1946, became the *Federal People's Republic of Yugoslavia (FPRY)* and on 7 April 1963 the *Socialist Federal Republic of Yugoslavia (SFRY)*[112]. Yugoslavia a passed dramatic transformation from 1945-1974, which included four Constitutions[113]. Among those, the 1974 Constitution was the most important turning point in the former Yugoslavian history. Those changes in the former Yugoslavia's Constitution remained in place until 15 January 1992 by which time four of its six constituent Republics - Slovenia, Croatia, Macedonia and Bosnia and Herzegovina - had seceded. As for Burma, during the period of anti-colonial fighting, the new multi-ethnic modern Burman State which had previously never existed was invented, when

---

[111] After the Great War (1914-18), more than 300,000 Serbs were living in Croatia and about 100,000 Croatians were in Serbia. In Bosnia-Herzegovina, large communities of Serbs and Croatians were living with Bosnians. More than 200,000 Albanians from Kosovo were in Serbia. In Bosnia, none of the ethnic groups' reached an absolute majority (see Senigalliesi, n. d.). A National Council of Slovenes, Croats, and Serbs became the *de facto* government of the region. This prompted the National Council to seal a quick final agreement with Serbia, over the objections of the Croatian Peasant Party, without obtaining guarantees of regional autonomy. Leaders in Bosnia and Herzegovina and Vojvodina favoured union; on 24 November 1918, the Montenegrins deposed the Negus Dynasty and declared solidarity with Serbia. On 1 December 1918, Prince Regent Aleksandra Karadjordjevic and delegates from the National Council, Vojvodina, Bosnia and Herzegovina, and Montenegro announced the founding of the Kingdom of the Serbs, Croats, and Slovenes to be ruled by Aleksandra (see Library of Congress, n. d.).

[112] Yugoslavia, meaning "land of the South Slavs", was a multinational State, a single country inhabited by several different communities of people who believe they share a common ethnic origin, culture, historical tradition, and language (see Rusinow, n. d.).

[113] The Constitution of the Socialist Federal Republic of Yugoslavia (SFRY) and its predecessor, the Federal People's Republic of Yugoslavia (FPRY) was developed after World War II as follows: Constitution of FPRY, adopted on 31 January 1946, Constitutional Law of the FPRY adopted on 13 January 1953, Constitution of SFRY, adopted on 7 April 1963 and Constitution of SFRY adopted on 21 February 1974.

Aung San's task was to garner support from the frontier areas to achieve his legitimacy and right to speak for the whole of Burma (both Burma proper and frontiers) independence. On 12 February 1947, Aung San's version of "imagined Burma" was endorsed by some representatives of ethnic groups. Aung San used the recognition of the self-determination rights to get agreement with the Kachin and the Shan. However, after independence in 1948, barely 14 months later, Myanmar was thrown into civil war, as it was sealed by the harmful practice of Burman nationalists trying to "engineer" the nation to serve the goals of Burman domination and expansion. Post 1988, this concept supposedly repeated as Burma was renamed the 'Union of Myanmar', which was later confirmed when the administrative capital was moved to Pyinmana in the middle of Burma which the leader, Gen Than Shwe, dubbed Naypyidaw, or Royal City.

6.1.1. The Shadows of the British Raj

Under the Burmese Kingdoms, the Myanmar territories had differed to the one under British rule and to the one in its current form.[114] The present day Burmese State, arranged in 1948, represents the restoration of what had already been achieved in the past; an integrated national, Pax Birmanica, which was destroyed by the British, when they imposed colonial rule. With transforming territories, ethnic consciousness became unquestionably sharper in colonial time.

Nation-building was never a British objective. Under British control, diverse peoples far from Rangoon were brought under at least nominal central administration. Burma, which was annex into the British Empire – not as a sovereign nation but as a province of India (see Smith, Martin 2002: 6). Burma was under "British India: Coat of Arms" from 1824 until 1937, and the British intentionally kept the frontier areas separated from the administration of mainland. Consequently, most of the ethnic

---

[114] Some archaeological findings reveal that parts of Burma were inhabited some five thousand years ago. Several Kingdoms were established throughout the country from the 1st Century to the 10th Century A.D. Burma history dates back to the early 11th Century, when King Anawrahta unified the country and founded the first Burmese Empire in Pagan. The Began Empire encompassed the areas of the present-day Burma and the entire Mon area Valley in Thailand that lasted two centuries. The second Burmese Empire was founded in the mid 16th Century by King Bayinnaung (1551-1581). King Alaungpaya founded the last Burmese Dynasty in 1752 and it was during the zenith of this Empire that the British came. Myanmar has experienced a long history of migration and conflict among various ethnic groups along fluid frontiers, which were finally fixed only during British imperial rule from 1820s to 1948 (see Yawnghwe, Chao-Tzang, September 2002: 12).

minorities inhabit areas along the country's mountainous frontiers. The British administration and local integration were divided into parts due to the wars: (a) 1824 (b) 1854-56 (c) 1886-1942 and (d) 1945-47.[115] The first areas occupied by the British were the Arakan and Tenasserim areas. In this early period the British used the Karens in their wars against the Burmese. The 1886-7 uprising in Lower Burma as well as the intensified resistance in Upper Burma made the British decides not to recruit Burmese into either the Indian Army or military police. Then the British began the new recruits among the Karen as well as from the Kachins and Chins. Local leaders in the Chin and Kachin hills organised fairly extensive resistance to British overtures in the aftermath of the 1885–86 war.[116] Eventually, the British were able to convince most Chin and Kachin leaders to accept British authority in return for a promise not to interfere with local politics, customs and not to undermine the local chiefs' taxation powers with their subjects.

The Baptist missionaries had success in converting Karens to Christianity and in teaching them English. The Karen served the British. Karen troops even participated in suppressing the Hsaya San peasant rebellion of 1930–32, the 1936 student strike and the 1938 general strike. These deployments were considered evidence of collaboration on the part of Karen, other minority troops and of British attempts to divide and rule Burma (see Callahan 2002: 1-24). Burmese ethnic nationalism was to fill the vacuum to the control over it. The descendants of the Burman court elite teamed up with the Arakanese and Mon, and built a strategic alliance with the left-leaning forces to imagine a new modern Burmese nation and formulated and propagated a new form of nationalism and the radicalised Shan Kings (*Saw Bwa)* who were not part of the traditional feudal power structure. Furthermore, the British were determined to impose a centralised bureaucracy; hence, the *Saw Bwa* could maintain a large degree of autonomy and local power (see Thant Myint-U 2001: 212). In fact, the fall of Mandalay mean that the Burman, Mon and Arakan were reintegrated back into Ava Kingdom, built their unity again, and together formed a new pattern of 'Burma' with the fashionable 'Rangoon.' The age of Kingdom was formed into a

---

[115] Burma became a British crown colony after three Anglo-Burmese Wars in 1824, 1852 and 1885.

[116] The British army in Upper Burma numbered around 7000, with 3000 British and 4000 Indian troops. In addition there were over 10,000 military police, nearly all Indian, with some Karens but almost no Burmese, as well as over 7000 civil police, predominantly Burmese, with some Karen and Indians (see *Government of Burma, Economic and Social Board* 1957: 5).

Nation. During the anti-colonial fighting, Burma was re-strengthened with its old Ava's memories and renewed Burmese nationalism. Directly upon its independence, owing to the ethnic politics that was built in the colonial period, Burma lapsed into civil wars. Burma, by 1948, faced a weak pre-condition upon which to build an independent nation.

6.2. The Constitutional Problems

The ethnic conflicts in the former Yugoslavia and in Myanmar resulted from constitutional failures. The former Yugoslavia's integration process commenced with decentralisations in 1970s and the amendments of 1974 Constitution in Burma, the present day Myanmar, suffered from the Constitution of 1947 which was drawn up quite quickly.

Under Tito's rule, throughout the 1960s and 1970s, the trend in the SFRY was towards the further decentralisation of power to the governments of each of the Republics and this was entrenched in the final Constitution in 1974. While the society of the former Yugoslavia was largely free of ethnic tensions, the restructuring from federation to confederation, starting with the Constitution of 1974, led to the empowerment of ethnic and national elites (see Blagojevic 1999). The six Republics were to be autonomous and partially self-governing. Five of them were designated as the "homelands" of the nations that the Yugoslav government officially recognised namely the Croats, Macedonian Slavs Serbs, Montenegrins and Slovenes. The sixth Republic, Bosnia and Herzegovina, despite the presence of significant numbers of Croats, Serbs and Muslims, no one ethnic group was in the majority and, thus, there was no recognised Bosnian "nation" until the 1974 Constitution was promulgated, whereby the Muslim population of Bosnia and Herzegovina gained recognition as one of the peoples of the SFRY.[117] In the 1980s, after the death of Tito and economic decline, this badly defined confederation resulted in the emergence of new States.

The Burmese ethnic question was renewed when Aung San's task was to unite the minorities for Burma's Independence. His version of Burma had never existed be-

---

[117] Yugoslavia's "nationalities" were the Albanians, Bulgars, Czechoslovak, Hungarians, Italians, Romanians, Ruthenians, Slovaks, Turks, and Ukrainians. Other ethnic groups also present included the Austrians, Germans, Greeks, Gypsies, Jews, Poles, Russians, and Vlachs (a Romanian group).

fore, which was agreed during the Panglong Agreement. The death of Aung San disorientated the Shan and Frontier leaders, who trusted him not only because he was a man of his word but because he could get things done. The 1947 Constitution, which was the consequence of the Panglong Agreement, was made in a very short period in the aftermath of independence, and was followed by unavoidable political crises and civil wars lasting fifty years. From 1948 to 1988, Burma went through different transitions which included two Constitutions; the 1947 'independence Constitution' and the 1974 'one party' Constitution (overturned and initiated by Gen Ne Win).

6.2.1. The 1974 Constitution of Yugoslavia

The text of the Constitution of 1974 was long and dogmatic. The first basic Principle listed in the Constitution begins with the formulation "the nations of Yugoslavia, proceeding from the right of every nation to self-determination, including the right of secession..." nevertheless the application of this principle was limited by the fact that no mechanism existed in the Constitution to allow for secession (see Rich, n. d.). The idea of self-management applied in all State institutions. However, this Constitution did not answer basic questions and define institutions which lawmakers mentioned including minorities, ethnic nations, self-determination and secession. The definitions of Republics and autonomous regions were made in the Constitution and its institutions by their wish: Slovenians and Croatians thought that the right to self-determination was connected with the term "people" and, further, with the territory where those people lived. On the other hand, Serbian opinion was that the right to self-determination belonged to the ethnic nations, and proved that this was not connected with territory. Albanians used the term secession in terms of unifying the State with Albania.

In addition, two autonomous provinces were set up within the Republic of Serbia: Kosovo, which had an Albanian majority, and Vojvodina, which itself was multinational. These two provinces had more limited powers than did the Republics (see Rusinow, n. d.). Albanians were not recognised as a "nation" under the 1974 Constitution because, according to the Yugoslav government, their traditional homeland was outside Yugoslavia. However, in general, Albanian culture was practised more openly in Yugoslavia than in Albania, where the remains of Stalinist suppression limited many aspects of self-expression. Within Serbia, Kosovo and Vojvodina were given considerable autonomy including control of their educational systems, judiciary, and police; nowhere else in Europe were such far-ranging concessions to national rights granted in a region considered so potentially separatist. The decentralising effect of the 1974 Constitution further reduced the oppression of Albanians in the province. The 1974 Constitution rekindled the Serbian drive for dominance by limiting Serbian control of Kosovo and Vojvodina, constituent provinces with large non-Slav ethnic groups. This was a serious obstacle to Serbian control over Kosovo in the face of a strong Albanian separatist movement in the province. Therefore, the recapture of the Serbian provinces became the chief political goal of all Serbian leaders after 1974. This system maintained a semblance of unity during most of Tito's four decades of unquestioned rule, but the autonomy granted to Kosovo in the 1974 Constitution was virtually revoked in 1990s.

Contrary to Burma's 1947 constitutional implementation, Tito's Yugoslavia went better and further in their implementations. The former Yugoslavia's 1974 Constitution also dealt with the sensitive matter of its national minorities, such as language and religion, not only concentrating on how the power had to be shared and on the parliament. The Constitution guaranteed members of the various nationalities the right to use their own language and alphabet, including the right to use it in public affairs and before government agencies. The nationalities also received the option of education in their native language through high school or vocational school. Children attending such schools were required to study one of the three official Yugoslav languages. In the 1970s, the government eliminated the requirement that schoolchildren study a second official Yugoslav language; this change caused a steep drop in the number of Slovenian and Albanian students who learned Serbo-Croatian and threatened to isolate some Slovenian and Albanian communities.

The 1974 Constitution also provided that Tito should be succeeded by a collective federal presidency. In his later years, Tito began restructuring his government to prepare it for the post-Tito era[118]. The last decade of the Tito regime paved the way for a power-sharing government-by-consensus that he saw as the best hope of bind-

---

[118] There were, in fact, two versions of the Presidency. The first one was the President of State, which belonged to Tito for duration of his life. Also he was the President of the Presidency, although, according to the Constitution, Tito, as a State President, could not be part of that body. That problem was solved with Tito's leading post under the League of Communists of Yugoslavia (LCY), as the Communist Party had been renamed in 1952. Due to the Constitution, the President of the League was President of the Presidency. The Chair of the Presidency of the League was abolished after Tito, and none could thereafter be President of the Presidency (see Popovic, n. d.)

ing the Federation after his regime ended (see Popovic, n. d.). The 1974 Constitution gave substantial new powers to the Republics, which obtained veto power over federal legislation. This tactic also kept Tito's potential rivals within small local fiefdoms, denying them national status. Both the government and the ruling LCY became increasingly stratified between federal and regional organisations; by Tito's later years, the locus of political power was already diffused. It can be concluded that the Constitution of 1974 was a main cause for the dilution of second Yugoslavia in 1990.

6.2.2. Panglong Agreement and the Independent Constitution of 1947

The Panglong Agreement of 12 February 1947, which was endorsed by 23 representatives from the Shan State, the Kachin and Chin Hills, agreed to form an interim government (see Appendix I). Only the representatives of the Chin, Shan and Kachin had attended and signed the Accord. The Karen only attended the conference as observers. Parallel to the Panglong Conference, a Karen Congress was held in Yangon to examine the "Aung San – Attlee Agreement," and shortly afterwards the KNU sent a message to the British Prime Minister about their rejection of that Agreement and their wish to remain as part of the Empire. However the British failed to reply to the memorandum as Burma was never a priority in British imperial policy (see Callahan 2002). The Karenni government also decided not to join the Frontier Areas because by joining it might lose its independence and sovereignty. During the Panglong Conference, the right to secession was agreed upon principally, but it was also agreed that later it had to be decided at the People's Parliament.[119] Thus, the politics of Myanmar's 'national unity' is complex and is further complicated by the founding document of the Union of Burma; the Panglong Accord.[120]

---

[119] In February 1946, the Shan *Sawbwas* (princes) invited Karenni *Sawphyas* to attend the First Panglong Conference, which was to be held in Shan State. The Karenni *Sawphyas* refused to attend the conference because Karenni was an independent country and they feared that they would risk losing their independence.

[120] Based upon the representatives of both States inside Burma the government should be responsible for State affairs absolutely, and the self-determined Kachin State is acknowledged, and both States should have a right to secession after Burma's independence. Ethnic groups including the Arakan, Karen, Karenni, Kuki, Naga, Pa-O, Palaung, Rohingya, Wa, *et cetera*, did not sign the agreement because they either were not being invited or they doubted the sincerity of the majority Burman ethnic group. Unsatisfied with that agreement, the ethnic groups like the Karens decided to pursue an armed struggle.

In accordance with the terms of the Aung San-Attlee Agreement, elections for a Constituent Assembly were held in April 1947. Before Aung San's death, the AFPFL held a preliminary convention in May to draft a Constitution after which several were prepared. The Constitution was finalised in September 1947. The agenda of the AFPFL Convention included a major address by Aung San during which he outlined his views on crucial issues at the heart of the constitutional draft, in particular the form of State to be adopted, namely a 'union.'[121] The term "federal", in his view, was redundant or unnecessary once one understood that a Union State was not a unitary State. Aung San referred to Stalin's definition of what constituted a national minority and argued that a Union State should include appropriate provisions that recognised seven autonomous States (for the seven main ethnic minorities) as well as autonomous areas within these States for smaller 'national minorities' of various population strengths (see Smith, Alan 2003: 6).[122] Silverstein argues that the term "federation" and "federal" did not appear in the English version of the draft Constitution of 1947.

The highest status of the Constitution of 1947 which passed through then national Assembly, was that of the 'Union State' which is given to a people who possess a "unity of language", different from Burmese; a unity of culture; a community of historical tradition; a community of economic interests; a measure of economic self-sufficiency; a fairly large population; a defined geographical area with a character of its own; and the desire to maintain its distinct identity as a separate unit (see Maung Maung 1959: 169). The creation of 'national unity' was a daunting task for the Burmese State from the day Myanmar gained independence in 1948, as the State wanted the people who live in Myanmar to primarily identify themselves as 'Burmese' or 'Myanmar.'

The Union of Burma was formed with five Union States: the State of Burmans, the Shan State, the Kayah State, the Kachin Hills and the Chin Hills, which would be divided into three, namely the Union Republic, the Autonomous Republic and the

---

[121] Aung San dismissed questions as to whether the constitutional form should be recognised as 'Federal Union' on the grounds that the Burmese term for "Union" (*Pyidaung-zu*) was clearly different from "Unitary".

[122] Yet the term "Union" itself implied a Federal State on the pattern of the Soviet Union, for example clause 13 of the Soviet Constitution stated that "The Union of Soviet Socialist Republics is a Federal State, formed on the basis of a voluntary union of equal Soviet Socialist Republics." The AFPFL draft Constitution there was no similar statement (see *The 1947 Constitution and the Nationalities. Vol. II.* 1999: 69).

National Area[123]. In spite of the broad language of the Constitution, only two States – the Shan and the Kayah – were eligible to secede. Chapter XII of the Constitution dealt with the right of secession that would be granted to the Shan and Kayah States ten years from the date on which the State concerned came into the Union of Burma, if so desired by the States within the Union.[124]

Two others – the Kachin and the Karen – are explicitly denied the right, while the remaining two States – the Special Chin Division and Burma proper – are usually considered outside of the discussion (see Silverstein 1958: 43-57). The Constitution provides that the Union and the States share judicial powers. However, the Act had not been fully implemented in the Shan States by the end of 1956. With some modifications, the structure of the Shan State is reproduced in the Kayah State. The Kachin State Government, while outwardly similar to the structure in the Shan State, also has its variations which result largely from the ethnic composition of the population. The members of the Constituent Assembly were unable to get the Karens to agree on the size, location and political organisation of their State.

The creation of an Arakan and Mon State would mean, in effect, the creation of sub-administrative units and not separate political entities. Their area became a Special Division of Burma proper (see Silverstein 1960: 260-280). The Arakanese submitted a proposal on 29 October 1948, to have the Arakan Division transformed into a Region, rather than a State in order not to weaken the Union and to avoid encouraging separatist tendencies. Mon made the suggestion that to have a Mon State that would comprise the Tenaserim, Pegu and Irrawaddy Divisions, practically, the whole of lower Burma. They based their claim on the fact that they had a separate history, traditions, language and culture and those descendants of the original Mons who still lived in the above named areas. The Mon and Karen asked for a united Karen-Mon State, as outlined in a declaration signed by two Mons; Mon U Po Ho of the United Mon Association and Nai Hla Maung, of the Mon United Front and three Karens; Saw Ba U Gyi, Saw Tha Din and J. Tung Aung, all of the KNU. They lived

---

[123] The terms 'Union Republic', 'Autonomous Republic' and 'National Area' were borrowed from the Soviets. 1. a defined geographical area. 2. a unity language different from Myanmar. 3. a unity of culture. 4. a community of historical tradition. 5. a community of economic interests and a measure of economic self-sufficiency. 6. a fairly large population. and 7. a desire to maintain its distinct identity as a separated united of the union (see Ibid 71).

[124] Sections 223 to 229 inclusive elaborate the details of the principle of State succession which has come into full play in the emergence of the Union of Burma as a sovereign independent State (see Maung Maung 1959: 211).

in harmony in the past, with the Karen serving the armies of the ancient Mon Kings and studying the literature and relations of the Mon people. However, if the Union decided to go ahead with plans for a separate Karen State it was 'most likely to stir up strife and ill-will between the Karens and Mons.'

Nonetheless, the choice of *Pyidaung-zu that* was made in May 1947 was unitary in nature. Strangely, despite forming the federation without a federal nature, the Constitution included the right to secession for its States. The ten years was a hard journey for the Union. The first stage after x independence had ended at 1958 and another period then began. At the beginning, in 1959, Dr Maung Maung writes that "yet, if our generations should fail and fall under totalitarian forces or into totalitarian thinking and practices, this is not the end of the beginning, but the beginning of the end" (see Maung Maung 1959: 216).

6.3. Wars of Ethno-Federal States

Ethnicity in the former Yugoslavia provides both nationalist and non-nationalist elites, as well as their individual leaders, with an instrument that can be utilised and manipulated for any number of ends (see Bozic 1999: 123). Theoretically, the ethno-federal State of the former Yugoslavia collapsed because its core ethnic regions became very costly for central leaders to continue suppressing in the event that core regional leaders would directly challenge central authority, making a federal crackdown was not successful (see Hale 2003: 7). In fact, there are two basic elements that led to the bloody wars: a declining economy and decentralisation and, generally[125], there is more than one analytical explanation of the disintegration of Tito's Yugoslavia after his death in 1980: including a rotating government with representatives from each of the Republics: -

1st the *first and foremost widespread explanation* is connected to *the economic, political, and social crises of the 1980s* which are the increase in social poverty,

---

[125] By the 1990s Yugoslavia had become an international metaphor for ethnic strife and political fragmentation. The metaphor was based on four major political problems that remained unsolved in Yugoslavia that led back to old nationalism themes: (1) economic decay that had occurred in the 1980s; (2) finding and institutionalising procedures for compromise among regions with increasingly diverse political and economic interests; (3) forging useful political relations with Western nations willing to provide economic aid, and making foreign policy adjustments to harmonise with new political conditions in Europe; and (4) negating the divisive influence of the rotation system to ensure selection of national leaders competent to focus attention on solving all-Yugoslav issues.

unemployment, the 'melting' of the middle class, the concentration and strengthening of the power of the elite and the political transformation from Communist to post-Communist society (see Ibid).

2nd *An Increase of authoritarianism, nationalism, and aggressiveness* became a rule, while the living standards of most Yugoslavs plunged dramatically and painfully. Tito's successors were the leaders of Republics with conflicting economic and national interests and could not agree on effective remedies for the economic crisis. Politicians within each Republic blamed other Republics rather than admit that they could not handle the situation.

3rd Connection of *political elites and their manipulation* of the masses with the help of *nationalistic programmes*[126] while they prepared for multi-party elections to look forward to the democratic society.

4th *An overnight invention of the 'other'* that did not exist before with justification of animosity, discrimination and aggression toward the 'other' from 'oneself'.

5th The *role of media* includes the promulgation of ethnic conflict and war, even though on its own it does not create sufficient pre-conditions for war to occur (see Ibid).

6th The final explanation is that foreign elements engaged in various international conspiracies and were driven by renewed imperial aspirations.

However, there are different explanations to the conflicts in Myanmar, which are put in four main narratives that can identify the cause of these wars as follows:

1st Victimisation (we are the only victims)

2nd Hierarchisation of victimisation (we are the greater victims)

3rd Justification of revenge (we are getting back at them for what they did to us)

4th "Preventative aggression" (if we do not do it to them, they will do it to us).

Myanmar's ethnic conflicts actually started four decades ahead of those of the former Yugoslavia. It is not always a well-known fact that Burma has a rich ethnic diversity and that its political problems are actually deeply rooted in country's ethnic issues. There were many unsolved or badly solved questions in Myanmar's history

---

[126] Any nationalistic ideology offers simple answers to complex questions. It offers 'warmth' as well as the feeling of security to those of who are already accustomed to their anonymity within the collective.

which sharply contrasts depending on the different version; that is, the Myanma version versus the other versions of various mono-ethnic groups; namely, the Karens, the Shan, the Chin, the Karenni, the Mon and the Arakanese and the list goes on. Thus, ethnic conflicts in Myanmar since its independence are still an issue to be solved before the country's national reconciliation and transition can be attained.

6.3.1. Yugoslavia's National Minorities and the Emergence of New States

For the majority of citizens in Yugoslav they did not expect those bloody wars. An individual born after World War II, regardless of ethnic origin, until the end of the 1980s, could live the whole of his or her life without experiencing ethnic or religious discrimination or prejudice. This was especially true in urban settings, of which Sarajevo was a prime example. Post-factum explanations of those tragic wars start with the self-validating assumption that they were logical, determined and therefore explicable but, for the vast majority of people living in the former Yugoslavia, wars were not expected, not logical and not justified. The 1980s in Yugoslavia was also a decade singularly lacking in strong political leadership in the Tito tradition, even at the regional level. The process was expressed by a kind of 'empty hatred'. However, at the end of the 1980s, hatred existed, prompted by harsh economic realities.

The political system of the former Yugoslavia was marked by a differentiation of its nationalities despite the federal Constitution. The inferior status of Serbia, as Yugoslavia's largest federal unit and the Serbs as its largest nationality, became one of the basic principles of the federal system established between 1971 and 1974. For more than seven decades, Yugoslavs had lived together in several quasi-States[127].

Most of Yugoslavia's six Republics and two provinces showed significant ethnic diversity. Only Serbia proper, Slovenia and Montenegro were largely homogeneous. Muslim Slavs, Serbs and Croats made up the population of Bosnia and Herzegovina, but no single group predominated. Kosovo was predominantly Albanian. The share of a Republic's population that belonged to that Republic's dominant national group generally declined over time (see Curtis, December 1990). During the era of Tito, a

---

[127] The reasons for it were 1) the disintegration of the Eastern Block; 2) the institutional completion and the political expansion of the European Union; 3) the collapse of Yugoslavia and the political turmoil that has developed since then in the Balkans and 4) US hegemony and the precipitation of economic globalisation.

lot of mixed marriages (in particular in Bosnia) were made and in a majority of the population the new generation came from mixed marriages.

The main factor which produced wars in the former Yugoslavia was the national political elites. The LCY fell apart in January 1990. During election time, the political elites found in a nationalist ideology the best instrument to strengthen the legitimacy of their national politics; hence they worked to arouse the suppressed national feeling in order to utilise it in their struggle for power on a national and regional level. The winning parties in all the Republics were nationalist in their programmes, appeal and aims. They included the Communists in Serbia (who renamed their organisation the Socialist Party of Serbia - SPS) and in Montenegro and the leading Muslim, Serb and Croat parties in Bosnia. Negotiations among the post-Communist Republic leaders from December 1990 to June 1991 failed to produce a formula to preserve Yugoslavia in some form. The new governments in Slovenia, where a seven-party coalition took office, and in Croatia, led by President Franjo Tuđman and his nationalist Croatian Democratic Union (*Hrvatska Demokratska Zajednica* - HDZ), argued for a loose association among effectively sovereign States. The Serbs and Montenegrins insisted on a highly centralised "modern federation" (see Ibid).

The survival of Yugoslavia became increasingly doubtful. To serve such a purpose populist and separatist movements were inspired and their conviction supported the idea that the "nation" was being jeopardised by the other peoples living in Yugoslavia. That had resulted in an increase in ethnic distance, especially in relation to Albanians, Bosnian Muslims and Croats. The impetus to nationalist attitudes was given by the fact that majority of the newly constituted parties were established on national basis and accepted the slogan "national liberation comes first - democracy later" (see Golubovi, n. d.). The four Republics had decided to secede and, after free and fair elections in 1990, had to live with the consequences. Presidents Alija Izetbegović of Bosnia and Kiro Gligorov of Macedonia were equally fearful of either a violent break-up of Yugoslavia or of Serb domination of a federation with a stronger central government. In vain, they continued to seek a compromise. The Titoist vision continued to command strong support as late as May–June 1990 (see Glenny 1995: 58). It witnessed the failed process of transition from a totalitarian (or authoritarian) system into a democratic one. The autonomy which was implemented in the Constitution of 1974 became a step closer towards a new State in 1990s.

Meanwhile, tension and violence between Serbs and Croats mounted in Krajina, a rural part of Croatia with a Serb majority in many districts. The mounting crisis became acute in June 1991 when the Republics of Slovenia and Croatia declared their independence from the tottering federation. Fighting between secessionist forces and the Serb-dominated Yugoslav military (supported by Serbian militias operating inside Croatia) erupted immediately. Although the conflict slowly subsided in Croatia (after the Serbs seized large chunks of territory) and the contending parties reached a cease-fire agreement enforced by UN peace-keeping units, an even more ferocious struggle began when the Republic of Bosnia and Herzegovina declared its independence in February 1992. Serbian-led forces soon seized more than two-thirds of Bosnia's territory and besieged the capital of Sarajevo.

An exception was the situation in Kosovo. After the end of Tito's era, ethnic Albanians in Kosovo stated to agitate and the internal division worsened everywhere. Milošević's role in the Yugoslav wars is one of the focal point of every academic or political analysis produced over the last decade. Only a few have stressed that he has been an administrator of the Kosovo myth (see Vankovska, August 2000). The province of Kosovo was put under virtual military occupation by Yugoslav and Serbian military and police, but what was significant is the almost total lack of violent conflict in Kosovo between ethnic Albanians and Serbs at an individual level. There was also a complete lack of organised or sustained violence along these lines and the "mobilisations" of Serbs that took place in the early to mid-1980s were organised by the Serbian regime, secret police and their allies among nationalist intellectuals (see Gagnon 1996). In the first months after the NATO-led Kosovo Force (KFOR) entered Kosovo in June 1999 and the Kosovo Albanian refugees returned to their homes, the minority Serbs and Gypsies became the victims of Albanian revenge attacks. The few Serbs who have remained in Kosovo live in scattered enclaves under the protection of KFOR troops. Nevertheless, KFOR has been unable to stop the violence from spilling over Kosovo's borders into Macedonia and into Serbia's Presevo Valley region, which has a sizeable ethnic Albanian minority (see Greenberg 2001). Uncertainty over Kosovo's future remains a destabilising factor in the Balkans and should be explained by following steps:

- Question arose before other Serbian ethnic issues as Milošević had first abolished their autonomy that had been granted to them in 1974. With the changes of the Constitution in 1989, Kosovo lost all the attributes of a State. Both provinces were reduced to a rank of politically and territorially autonomous regions with limited competence. The Serbian regime responded to Kosovo's problems with its authoritarian nature. Thus, the Kosovo Albanian opposition used the repression in Kosovo to present its demand for Kosovo's secession from Serbia. Beginning in 1995, the Kosovo Liberation Army (KLA) started to claim responsibilities for the terrorism that took place in Serbia.

- The fall of the Milošcvić regime also removed another argument in favour of the independence of Kosovo. The resolution of the Kosovo conflict when Milošević was in power would have served the interests of democratic development in Serbia, as it would have removed a major burden for the new democratic forces, while the historical responsibility of that loss would have been placed on Milošević (see Yannis 2001: 59). Instead, the independence of Kosovo became a burden, while many Serbs shared the view that it was in the interest of both Serbs and Kosovo Albanians to try to find a pragmatic solution to living together in Kosovo.

- Coming to power under the weight of troubles left over from the Kosovo war, the late Prime Minister Zoran Đinđic faced the dual challenges of tempering ethnic Albanians' breakaway ambitions with negotiating the dissolution of Yugoslavia into a loose Union between Serbia and Montenegro which ceased to exist in 2003.

In 2003, Đinđic said that Kosovo was a national and security problem which must be resolved and proposed the Kosovo Federation, with equal rights (see "Đinđic Proposes Kosovo Federation," February 2003).[128] Shortly after that, Đinđic was assassinated[129]. After the assassination of Đinđic, Kosovo was not a priority for Serbia for some time until August 2003. The 'Declaration on Kosovo' maintains that as far as Belgrade is concerned, Kosovo will only have an autonomous status within Serbia, and specifies when the Serbian army and displaced Serb civilians are allowed to return. Time seems to be running out in Kosovo. The deadly rioting in March 2004 proved that Kosovo Albanians are frustrated with their unresolved status, the eco-

---

[128] "Serbs would accept this kind of Kosovo, with a status greater than autonomy but less than a federal unit such as Serbia and Montenegro," said Đinđic (see "Đinđic Proposes Kosovo Federation," February 2003).

[129] The assassination of Serbia's Prime Minister does not seem to be in the national interest of Kosovo's Albanians.

nomic situation and the problems of dealing with the past. The future status of Kosovo remains an unresolved problem. So long as the problems are not solved, Serbia's democracy will remain to be consolidated.

In 2002, the Serbian and Montenegrin components of Yugoslavia began negotiations to forge a looser relationship. In 2003, the country was transformed into a loose federation of two Republics called Serbia and Montenegro. The Constitutional Charter of Serbia and Montenegro includes a provision that allows either Republic to hold a referendum after three years that would allow for their independence from the State Union. In 2006, Montenegro held a referendum which advocated terminating the union with Serbia.

6.3.2. *Myanmar's On-Going Fragmentation*

The 1947 Constitution though rooted in a strong democratic tradition, suffered from shortcomings, notably in the area of ethnic rights and granted its national minorities the right to secession after ten years. This engendered considerable dissatisfaction among sections of the ethnic population after the decade was over, when the constitutional rights were due to be fulfilled. In 1962, the Burmese military, then headed by General Ne Win, staged a *coup d'etat* which effectively tolled the death-knell of the 1947 Constitution.

Historically, Myanmar has undergone wars between the Mons and the Burmese and between the Arakanese and the Burmese, but not really with the other ethnic groups. The first Karen insurgencies started the moment Burma attained independence, because they did not accept the Burmese Government or, rather, a Government dominated by Burmese. The truth is that the tales sprang more from wishful thinking than facts, or from the psychological need of the Karen, Kachin, Shan, and others, to soften the pain of being abandoned by an esteemed and trusted 'friend', the British. In reality, the British could not give enough attention to the fate of the frontier people since there were enough problems elsewhere in the British Empire. Consequently, when Burmese nationalists in turn became *protégés* of another imperial power, the Japanese, the Karen were severely repressed. The feelings of apprehension and foreboding felt by the Karen at the prospect of life under Burmese domination was shared in varying degrees by other ethnic groups as well (see Yawnghwe, Chao-Tzang 1987: 85-95). Burma's ethnic nationalities, who belong to the regular British troops - Kachin, Karens, Chins and Burma Gurkhas - stood at their posts under the new Burma. However, the Burmese government reformed a new Burmese army as they had seen the minorities' troops as a potential danger towards the country's disintegration.

The Karen National Defence Organisation (KNDO) insurgency began as 'The People Volunteer Organisation (PVO)'[130] and the Communist rising of the Communist Party Burma (CPB) or Burma Communist Party (BCP),[131] which was led by Thakhin Than Tun, who went underground in 1949, which was barely 14-months after independence and waged an armed revolt against U Nu's government. The KNDO, who should have been staunchly anti-Communist by their Karen temperament and Christian faith, sided with CPB in places, and also with the mutineers and the PVO insurgents. The Mon National Defence Organisation (MNDO) followed the KNDO into revolt in 1949.

Hence, the definition of 'National Unity' was closely related by the Burman leaders to the survival of the new State and later the definition seems to be mixed up with the Burmese fears that resulted from the KNDO insurrection in Rangoon, the 'Battle of Insein'. The several splits in U Nu's AFPFL government, the unrest of different ethnic rebel organisations and the CPB throughout the country after independence were the reason for everything. General Ne Win's military coup "Caretaker Government" was later named the "Revolutionary Council", in 1958, and for dissolving the democratic parliament of 1958, abolishing the Constitution of 1947, the founding of the BSPP and promulgating the Constitution of 1974, which divided Myanmar into 14 administrative official units, which included the seven divisions and seven named ethnic States. The number of ethnic insurgencies increased dramatically under the BSPP. This was mainly because people were not allowed to ex-

---

[130] The People's Voluntary Organisation (PVO), which was founded and led by Gen Aung San also split into "the PVO Yellow faction" led by Bohmu Aung and "the PVO White faction" led by Bo Po Kun.

[131] The Burma Communist Party (BCP) led by Thakhin Than Tun was expelled from the AFPFL; the "Red Socialist" party led by Widura Thakhin Chit Maung and Thakhin Lwin quit the Socialist Party, which was led by U Ba Swe, U Kyaw Nyein and Bogyoke Aung Gyi; Thakhin Soe also split from the Burma Communist Party, which was led by Thakhin Than Tun, Thakhin Thein Pe (U Thein Pe Myint), and himself and formed the "Red Flag Communist Party (Burma Communist Party)". Later, the AFPFL, which was in power again split into two – "the AFPFL Clean faction" led by U Nu and Thakhin Tin and "the AFPFL Stable faction" led by U Ba Swe and U Kyaw Nyein in 1957-58. Again, in 1960-61, the ruling Pyidaungsu Party (Pa-hta-sa Party), which reorganised the AFPFL-Clean Party led by U Nu and Thakhin Tin, separated into "the U Group", "the Bo Group" and "the Thakhin Group."

press their dissatisfaction through acceptable political channels rather than because of obvious ethnic hatred. The only way they could express their dissatisfaction was by taking up arms. Armed struggles, as events in 1988 demonstrated again, were a consistent and often spontaneous way of expressing political opposition.

6.4. Myanma Question for Federalism in 1990s – 2000s

The issue of ethnic conflict has attracted the attention of both observers and protagonists, localities and the international community only since the 1990s, which followed the collapse of Gen Ne Win's BSPP regime by the eruption of the 1988 uprising. This attention also heightened following 1) the flames of ethnic upsurge in different parts of the world with the third wave of democratisation, 2) the successful implementation of self-determination and secession in the former Soviet Union, Yugoslavia, Czechoslovakia and 3) the formation of the "New World Order" by the end of 'bloc-politics' that led to a reassessment of moral values, involving accommodation of self-determination.

However, the ethnic problems in Myanmar cannot be compared to the wars in former Yugoslavia which was provoked ethnically, or the conflict which was rooted in racism in South Africa[132] or in the US during the days of Martin Luther King Jr. [133] The Burman domination or Burmanisation is more implemented towards the regime apparatus than to the daily social life among different groups. There are more prejudices among each other rather than racism[134]. Ethnic conflicts in Myanmar are, like any other ethnic conflicts, focused on elite level, where most of them demand self-determination and the right of secession. Myanmar's ethnic community is composed of three elements: 1) the United Nationalities Alliance (UNA), representing sixty-five ethnic nationality candidates elected in 1990, which has always worked closely with the NLD; 2) Some twenty armed ethnic organisations which have agreed ceasefires with Yangon since 1989, some of whom retain their arms and

---

[132] To be an African in South African means that one is politicised from the moment of one's birth, whether one acknowledges it or not [. . .]. His life is circumscribed by racist laws and regulations that cripple his growth, dim his potential and stunt his life (see Mandela 1996: 100).

[133] In those days in the USA, Blacks Americans were confined to positions of second-class citizenship by restrictive laws and customs. To break these laws meant subjugation and humiliation by the police and the legal system.

[134] A great deal of emphasis has been placed by foreign analysts and Non-Governmental Organisations (NGOs) on the rebellion against the regime led by ethnic minorities.

sometime still control extensive blocks territory; and 3) the insurgent groups still at war with the government, most of which are members of the NDF, though their military strength has declined significantly in recent years (see South 2002).

Myanmar's insurgency is unlike a revolution because insurgency is not a sudden, limited and short-lived outburst but, rather, a planned and protracted struggle that keeps on slowly and steadily developing its own operational dynamics (see Anand 1985: 1-31). The insurgent groups in Myanmar possess only some of these characteristics such as favourable homeland, indigenous masses, indigenous resources (which is not the case for the Chin and Karen), but they lack charismatic leadership, compelling incompatibilities, permissive system, popular cause, attainable goals, consolidatory aims, motivating ideology, absence of mass mobilisation, unique organisation, lacking of important facts, for instance, and outside patronage. The absence of all these important facts above, make their struggles intangible, non-variegated and unsuccessful. There are no charismatic ethnic leaders to come up for the ethnic unity[135] and to collect the united voice and demands. The disunity between the minorities' insurgencies makes their struggle far more complicated, unproductive and ineffective.

Some of Myanmar's ethnic minorities, while losing the battle against the current regime, or remaining at the *status-quo*, went for ceasefire, and some wait for the ceasefire talks with the junta, preparing their State constitutions. Though the ethnic and different insurgencies have agreed to unite under umbrella organisations such as the National Democratic Front (NDF), the Democratic Alliance of Burma (DAB) and the National Council of the Union of Burma (NCUB), most of them have already undergone a ceasefire with the regime separately in the 1990s or chosen complete surrender. The ceasefires have not been comprehensive as many of the armies were allowed to retain their arms and a portion of their territory, and were even granted business concessions by Yangon. The regime, however, steadfastly refused to discuss politics with these groups but asked for complete surrender in order to participate in the political process, which is effectively a non-starter due to the regime's total lock on power. The regime's attempt to write a Constitution cementing

---

[135] If non-Burmese national organisations, the Nationalities Liberation United Front (NLUF) composed of the SSA/SSAP, KNU, KniNPP (Karenni National Progress Party), Kachin Independence Army (KIA) the Padaung, Mon, and Arakan were united in the past, the Burmese Army would have no choice but to perhaps ask for American assistance who were helping them under the name of War on Opium (see Yawnghwe, Chao-Tzang 1987).

its leadership in any future political system resulted in the NLD walking out of the constitutional convention in 1995 (see Aung Naing Oo 2002). After purging the Prime Minister General Khin Nyunt, the SPDC continues with the trend of the Road Map and of the National Convention in order to draft the State Constitution. In the search of a common future through a Constitution is just one matter among exile groups and federalism was the most debated issue. Ethnic minorities and certain pro-democracy opposition groups, seek to establish a Federal Constitution assuming their right in the shaping of a federal Burma (see Smith, Alan 1997: 253). For the majority of ethnic Burmans, there is no 'Burman' identity as such that they know of and no effort is made to ensure Burman's representation, politically or as an ethnic group. For them, Myanmar is a nation-State and political organisations established by Burmans are usually presented as 'all Myanmar' in nature and they take it for granted and overlook present day problems and problems of the future of their country. The Burmans, who are looking forward to multi-party democracy, see Myanmar politics as fought out between parties, seeking support some locally, some nation-wide, rather than a contest of ethnic electorates (see Smith, Alan, July 2003). Every non-Burman is concerned with federalism and the power-holders are striving for their legitimacy (see Son, June 2003). The ethnic leaders believe that the permanent solution in Myanmar is federalism or a decentralised structure for establishing a viable civil society, the Central Government as well as the local governments should be totally secular *et cetera*. (see Tharckabaw 2005).

The federalism and tri-parties talks have long been a suggestion of the minorities'. The reason for the SPDC to object to federalism is that it would bring decentralisation of both power and of power structures. In a federal union, power is no longer in the centre, nor can it be monopolised by one element of the State. To the non-Burman, federalism does not mean anything, unless the right to self-determination, including the right to secession, is part of it (see Khin Maung Win, December 2001). Clubbing the two concepts of federation and secession, which are contradictory in term, is inaccurate, as no Federal Constitution in the world contains a provision of secession. A federation does not permit separation. The classic example is the case of the United States of America. Abraham Lincoln succinctly said that "The Union is One and Indivisible" (see Sen, December 2001). Hence, in the parameter of federation, secession has no legitimacy. The movement for the right of secession in Myanmar has reached a no-win situation. The right of secession in Myanmar must be viewed as an unrealised and vague power which is more useful as potential then as reality (see Silverstein 1958: 43-57). In the end, the right must be viewed in two ways: constitutionally, it is not exercisable while one demands for the federation; politically, it is also not. So long as the state has the right in reserve, it will continue to give the people a feeling of having a potential choice of either remaining in or leaving the Union. It will be a difficult task to build a nation without the national unity as some would like to keep one of their feet out of the union before starting its building.

The criticisms towards the omission of "federalism" in the Constitution of 1947 or not implementing it in regard to the political system of Burma in the early 1950s is not fairly done, because Burma in the 1950s was a very new nation which had just come out of the colonial education and administration of almost one hundred and fifty years. The real meaning of 'genuine federalism or union' not was to be understood and accepted immediately by its constitutional fathers and the people of Burma, as in many other countries in the post-World War II era. For example 'Genuine Federalism' requires not only a strict separation of power between the Federal and State governments but also requires the individual members of the Union to compete for the favours of its citizens.[136] Yet the "Federal Movement" initiated by Sao Shwe Thaik and other Shan leaders was immature and young at that time (see Yawnghwe, Chao-Tzang, September 2002). The minority leaders began to clamour for more rights, for privileges which they claimed in the name of 'pure federalism', though the Constitution of 1947 provided for the secession of the Shan and Kayah States, after a trial period of ten years, if the people of the State expressed their clear desire to secede (see Maung Maung 1969: 291-2).[137]

The political problems in Myanmar today can only be resolved by meticulous application of the Rule of Law in all spheres of the political, economic and social life of the people. These new ideas can flow unless and until the ruling SPDC, the opposition and the ethnic majorities will be free from prejudice and mistrust.

---

[136] The USA and the Federal Republic of Germany are mentioned as examples of federalism, because the federal structures in those countries could be considered to be truly federal. However, a survey carried out in Germany in 1952 showed that only twenty five per cent of the population were in favour of a federal structure. Indeed, it was only by 1983 that this figure had risen to seventy-five per cent (see German Embassy, n. d.).

[137] Ethno-political groups whose leaders demand independence or sovereignty usually are willing to settle for a more limited form of autonomy which is not necessarily territorial (see Bächler 1997:12).

Federalism is Not the Answer

For the case of Myanmar, some sensitive minorities and complex opposition groups started to suggest the principle of federalism as a compromise, although some still demand the right of secession or of self-determination or of more autonomy.

The principle of federalism is one of the key elements of debates and discussions about democratisation, decentralisation, individual rights protection and minority community guarantees. The federalist ferment is very much a searching reaction against the era of highly centralised nation States which so often proved to be internally oppressive and externally aggressive.

Federalism has, for many decades, been seen as an answer to the challenges posed by multi-ethnic societies the world over. In some cases, the idea has worked, while in others it manifestly has not. Where it has failed, the reasons have often lain as much with human deficiencies as with systemic shortcomings (see Iyer, April 2002). In Europe, there are success stories of federalism as well as examples of failures. The Federal Republic of Germany; Belgium has become officially federal; Spain's post-fascist State is quasi-federal; and Austria sustains its federal system remaining a robust federation with a newly revised Constitution. Switzerland, Canada, Belgium, Spain, and India are all characterised by linguistic, ethnic and other forms of fragmentation, but their federal systems offer them the means for managing some of the leading problems associated with extensive pluralism. These successes are countered partly, however, with the failure or potential failure of several other European federations. Thus, Czechoslovakia is now two countries, Slovakia and the Czech Republic. Yugoslavia experienced traumatic disintegration into a shadow of its former self and, with a new federal arrangement, Bosnia-Herzegovina, having been carved out of the former Yugoslav territory is now under western military guarantees. These three cases Czechoslovakia, Soviet Russia and Yugoslavia, however, were federal only in form, not in reality. In Asia, India has sustained its federal 'Union of States' for more than 50 years, but Pakistan, again experiencing military rule, has had considerable difficulty building federalism and democracy. Malaysia, one of the few federations to expel a member (Singapore in 1965), remains highly centralised and troubled by ethnic conflict. However, Stepan reminded that there are potential dangers as well as potential advantages in federalism in a democratic context: while the majority of democratic countries in the world today are unitary, all the multinational democracies are federal (see Stepan, November 1998). Federalism is the idea of a group or body of members that are bound together (Latin: *foedus*, covenant) with a governing representative head[138]. The representative head can be a king or a general assembly. In politics, federalism is the political philosophy that underlies a system of government in which sovereignty is constitutionally divided between a central governing authority and constituent political units (like States or provinces), creating what is often called a federation. In theology, federalism is a synonym for basic Covenant Theology.

The argument for federalism may, however, have a quite different meaning. It may express the theory of "grass-roots" democracy, the view that small-scale units alone permit the practice of democracy and that, consequently, the value of small units must be preserved even in large States so that mass participation in politics will remain a political practice (see Neumann 2005: 207-220). Arguments in favour of federalism have to do with diversity of needs, closeness to the people, experimentation and innovation. Arguments against federalism involve national standards, popular control and the need for uniformity (see Greenberg 2003: 81). Federalism is, of course, also one aspect of the broader question of self-determination. A secessionist or separatist movement means the group of people geographically concentrated in a portion of the State territory and demanding complete separation or secession. Separatist movements are more inclined to armed struggle, a situation which may be explained by their purpose (complete separation from the State)[139]. An autonomy movement involves not just protest against certain State policies but also a demand of ethnic groups for a greater extent of control over the governance of their affairs, that is, autonomy from the central government that the autonomy will enable the group to formulate and implement certain policies which may be contrary to certain national policies, but responsive to its peculiarities (see Muslim 2004: 1-12). The

---

[138] Federalism describes the relationship between the first representative man, Adam, and those born of the flesh (i.e. all naturally-born mankind), and likewise between the second and last representative man, Christ, and those who are in addition born of the Spirit (i.e. all spiritually-born mankind; see John 3:1-8 and Romans 8:1-17). This doctrine is most clearly described in Romans 5:12-21 and in Corinthians 15:20-28, 42-49. In theology, the two parties (i.e. the representative head and the represented members) do not share sovereignty.

[139] The ethnic group is generally understood as: 1. sharing fundamental cultural values, realised in overt unity in cultural forms, 2. making up a field of communication and interaction, and 3. has a membership which identifies itself, and is identified by others, as constituting a category distinguishable from other categories of the same other (see Barth 1996: 296).

right to self-determination is similar to an autonomy movement, demanding the right of peoples to determine their own destiny. In particular, the right allows a people to choose its own political status and to determine its own form of economic, cultural and social development, free from outside interference (see Wansai 1998). The ethnic preference falsification and untypical nature of federalism were significant in the former Yugoslavia where public behaviour underestimated (overrated) the importance of ethno-national identities before the 1980s. In the early 1980s, the psychological impact of Tito's death, the decline of Socialism and widespread unemployment triggered ethnification that laid the foundation for the country's disintegration. The disintegration of the former Yugoslavia has taken place against the backdrop of bloody conflict, as people keep searching for newer and better ways to accommodate long-suppressed ethnic and live in some kind of relative harmony.

Ethno-federalism is frequently recommended for countries torn by ethnic conflict such as in rebuilding post-Taliban Afghanistan and post-Saddam Iraq, although some scholars have argued that ethno-federal arrangements generally do not work well in Africa (see Mozaffar *et al.* 1999; and Wamala 1994) because this institutional arrangement, they concur, has had the effect of strengthening ethnic difference and providing resources for political entrepreneurs to play the "nationality card," thereby promoting secessionist activity (see Snyder 2000). Specifically, ethno-federal States are more likely to collapse when they contain a *core ethnic region*, a single ethnic federal region that enjoys dramatic superiority in population. Such regions tend (a) to promote the rise of "dual power" situations that are frequently found to lie at the heart of State breakdown and revolution; (b) to reduce the capacity of central governments to credibly commit to the security of ethnic minority regions; and (c) to facilitate the collective imagining of a core-group nation State separate from the Union State. The successful secession of a single ethnic region does not constitute ethno-federal *collapse* unless it is part of a wave of multiple successful secessions from the same country or is the only ethnic minority region in that country. Thus, one can typically say that the former Yugoslavia collapsed because it faced multiple secessions that effectively undermined its authority (see Hale, February 2003). Privately, ethnic activities in Myanmar are undertaken to meet intrinsic needs, mainly the cultivation of a positive self-image. In public, however, ethnic activity is also undertaken to co-ordinate with group members to obtain economic, social and political benefits. Anthony Smith, in *Theories of Nationalism,* proposes a continuum for nationalist movements, with ethnic movements based on a "high degree of cultural distinctiveness" at one end of the spectrum and territorial movements "bound only by aspirations and a common territorial-cum-political base" at the other.

Acknowledging that many nationalist movements are characterised by both ethnic and territorial components, Smith adds a third category of nationalist movements - also the one in the former Yugoslavia and in Myanmar - that lies between ethnic and territorial varieties, which he terms "mixed".

In the case of Yugoslavia, the eruption of nationalist passions seems at this moment to have been contained by the intervention of another federal polity. Yugoslavia failed to demonstrate the efficacy of federal solutions to bridge the kind of severe ethnic hostilities that the peoples of Yugoslavia have shown toward one another for centuries. As Yugoslavia cannot work out a successful federal solution, it is hard to demonstrate federalism as a shining example for other intense inter-ethnic conflicts, perhaps even including our own, the case of Myanmar.

Let us understand what federalism is. It is a combination of self-rule and shared rule, a set of co-operative arrangements allowing the preservation of the autonomy of the partners within a constitutional framework that protects both. To succeed, federal solutions require a will to federate a spirit of comity, of give and take, on the part of the parties to them, for whatever reason, not necessarily out of love for one another but perhaps out of necessity (see Elazar, "Will Federalism Preserve Yugoslavia?"). Federalism and right to secession, federalism and the right for self-determination do not go along together. The principle of federalism is incompatible with the idea that the government of a province can unilaterally declare independence, that is, appropriate the powers of the federal government, without the latter having the right to make sure this is what the province's population clearly wants, or without having any say on how this transfer of power would be decided on and implemented. Just as the federal government could not abolish the government of a province, a provincial government cannot appropriate the constitutional responsibilities of the federal government in that province.

Theoretically, there are five approaches that have been adopted to reconcile ethnic diversity and common citizenship: 1) a 'neutral' or 'difference-bind' State; 2) Jocobin republicanism (nation-building from above); 3) Civil society (nation-building from below); 4) Consociationalism; and 5) Federalism/ decentralisation.

The 'neutral' or 'difference-bind' States neither promote nor discourage cultural affiliations and practices. The State cannot avoid implicitly or explicitly supporting some cultures over others. The State must make decisions about the language of public administration, public health care, schools, public media and road signs and so on. The group that manages to get its language adopted as a State language in this way can gain enormous benefits. The 'difference-blindness' recognises and benefits some groups but inevitably ignores or disadvantages the others.

The 'Jocobin republicanism,' the French model of citizenship, in which all citizens are expected to assimilate to a particular national language, republican political heritage and secular culture, has been pursued in Francophone Africa, yet the level of identification with the State remains very low, the strategy has simply not worked and, in many cases had backfired, by fuelling fear and resentment amongst groups who feel excluded.

The 'Civil Society' model, nation-building from below, simply relocates the problems, rather than providing a means of resolving it.

The 'Consociationalism' model is applied in countries where ethnic groups are not territorially concentrated and where federalism is obviously not a solution to the issue of ethnicity. Like federalism, this model has been successfully adopted in some Western States, such as the Netherlands, Austria and Belgium.

Then it comes the 'Multination Federalism' model which supposes to solve the political issues in multi-ethnic States. There are some successful stories and some failed examples regarding federalism. The failures are not peculiar to the general failure of the federal constitutions (for example, the former Yugoslavia, the Soviet Union and Czechoslovakia) or the general failure of democratic governance on the continent (for example Nigeria).

Still, in all the history of federalism, no federal system that has survived for at least fifteen years has abandoned federalism of its own volition. Federal systems have been destroyed by outside conquest or transformed by the decision of their own citizenry to shift to some other form of federal arrangement, as was the case with the Americans in 1787, the Swiss Confederation in 1848, or the Germans who transformed a loose federation into a centralised federation in 1871 and underwent subsequent transformations after World Wars I and II in response to military defeat.

Federalism can take on a form where the groups are more or less territorially concentrated, which it is not the case in Myanmar. Federalism might exacerbate the problem of the exclusion of Myanmar's sub-ethnic groups, in the Shan State as a prime example, and of its internal migrants. Sub-units such as the Pao or Palong who would feel membership to a particular group will agitate for preference over mere 'citizens' from elsewhere in the State.

The constitutional draft of the Democratic Alliance of Burma (DAB) restricts members of the armed forces, at any time, from interfering in political matters, involving themselves in business and from declaring a state of emergency, a military administration or martial law (see Silverstein 1997: 266). It seems that the opposition finds the ways to exclude the SPDC in every way, even though the SPDC's suggested Constitution, the outcome of the National Convention, demands a 25% role for the military in politics and gives autonomous status to its sevens States.

While federalism is still widely conceived of as a symmetric structure embracing an entire country, autonomy is a relative concept defining a degree of power and independence of a region or group. Autonomy is, therefore, a trait of asymmetry in State power. It seems that the SPDC wants to start with a bit of decentralisation to try and find out whether the country can handle it. Decentralised systems of government in most cases have three different levels of government including a national level, an intermediate level and a local level,[140] even though political decentralisation increases ethnic conflict and secessionism, when the ethnicity is not territorially-concentrated. The SPDC seems to have more of an interest in the decentralisation of centralised systems than in federalism. The reason is simple. Federalism entails a level of political autonomy, even sovereignty, for constituent communities that rest uneasily, even threateningly, with traditional or elite conceptions of national unity. Federalism involves a polycentric non-centralised arrangement in which neither the constituent governments nor the general government can unilaterally alter the constitutional distribution of power. Nonetheless, the SPDC's National Convention lacking endorsement from any source is having difficulties in trying to establish any political transition in Myanmar.

Myanmar's multi-ethnicity seems to be enhanced by historical and institutional legacies, that have prevented clear-cut ethno-political mobilisation and polarisation. For the case of Myanmar, the idea of multi-nation State may instead be implemented

---

[140] Political decentralisation is a system of government in which there is a vertical division of power among multiple levels of government with independent decision-making power over at least one issue area (see Riker 1964; and Rodden 2004).

through some form of consociationalism. In a consociational regime, the State may be unitary and centralised but there are guarantees that all ethnic groups will share power at central level. It helps to provide a sense of security amongst the members of the various groups and help them develop some sense of identification with and loyalty to the State. It is not possible to imply federalism where the ethnic groups are divided, not territorially concentrated and sub-ethnic groups exist within the structure. In the framework of federalism, if the sub-ethnic groups are not given control over territory, a secession movement or irredentism can be raised and can lead to disintegration.

The State should simply ignore the differences of ethno-cultural diversity and allow people to develop and express their cultural practices and identities in private, home, church or private associations, so long as each one respects the right of the others. The sharing of a common language and national culture has helped strengthen democratic trust and solidarity across ethnic, religious and regional lines within the country. However, the forming of a unified nation State is hardly possible as limitations exist in both top-town and down-top nation-building in deeply divided societies. In a multi-nation federal system, the country is divided into several sub-units whose borders are drawn. This then suggests that the remedy to the crisis in Myanmar is not to change the form of government from unitary to federal which is not realistic at this time since the end of the transition is too near for such a significant overhaul of the political system.

Influences of the International Community

"Sanctions centralised the management of the economy. That obviously strengthens the State, but they damage the democratic opposition"[141]
(Zoran Đinđic 1998)[142]

In the promotion of ethnic hostility and conflict-making, there is unavoidably a vague and porous boundary between the political manipulation of conflict in the specific interests of concrete social actors including the involvement of international community, the promotion of conflict by the media and its justification by "scientific" interpretation and prediction. Hegemonic actors invoke the name of the international community, such as, Intergovernmental Organisations (IGOs) and International Financial Institutions (IFIs), to intervene in order to: (1) uphold State integrity/ sovereignty; (2) promote/ enforce human rights practices; and (3) forestall/ contain the negative and dysfunctional aspects of globalisation processes in developing countries. Nevertheless, unlike in Myanmar, the international community had been involved in Yugoslavia's wars to a much greater degree and this intervention had also played a role in the country's disintegration. In this chapter, I would highlight the impact of international involvement in political transitions. To elucidate how the international community and its engagement master political transitions, I will elaborate it in three parts: international interventions and the disappointment of the high hopes in its success in the former Yugoslavia, sanction regimes and their failure in both States, and the impact of the geopolitical situation that jeopardises the international community's involvement in Myanmar.

---

[141] Bandow, October 1998, Vol. 48, No. 10.

[142] Zoran Đinđić was Serbian Prime Minister, long-time opposition politician and a philosopher by profession.

7.1. International Involvement in the SFR of Yugoslavia for Human Rights

During the Cold War era, the rights of ethnic groups to self-determination or to secession were not major concerns either of Western governments or of international organisations. Western and Eastern Europe looked forward to building 'the new common European home' at the end of the Cold War and believed that the end of the Cold War signalled an era marked by stability and peace. Hence, the war in Yugoslavia produced a rude 'reality check' (see Carpenter 1992). Arising from its unfamiliarity with the Balkans, the West was surprised by the return of the Bosnian question and of the violence between the Serbs and Croats; the international actors were completely unprepared. Yugoslavia was a crucial test to the international system after the Cold War. The crisis and the intervention in Yugoslavia were brutally complex, and the UN and the regional powers utterly inexperienced and unprepared for dealing with those problems of peace and order in the post-Cold War era. Hence, the interference in the former Yugoslavian conflict has been premature as well as unrewarding. The strategy of imposing sanctions and isolation proved wrong in the case of the former Yugoslavia because international assistance also played an important role for the transition society in developing democratic forces and in carrying out change.

Yugoslavia demonstrates the limits of sanctions. The sanctions against Serbia and Montenegro, that is, against the FR of Yugoslavia, were imposed on 31 May 1992 through UN Security Council Resolution 757. The Security Council instructed all UN members to impose a total economic blockade on the FR of Yugoslavia and to sever all scientific, cultural and sporting ties with the country. Foreign diplomatic missions in Yugoslavia were told to reduce their activities. The United States and Western allies isolated the Serb State during the lengthy Bosnian war, without success. They imposed bans on air travel, investment and trade. The bottom line here is that internal economic conditions have deteriorated in Yugoslavia and the response of the West has been, in many ways, to worsen economic conditions through debt payment requirements and through UN economic sanctions that began in 1992. All of these have made the situation worse. The sanctions did not change Belgrade's policy or Milošević but, rather, benefited Milošević's family and friends, who sent their money abroad. This economic elite even used the sanctions to justify that conduct. Indeed, economic war from the West largely eliminated the indispensable constituency for liberalisation, as the middle class was completely destroyed. Milošević's path to power was paved with the destruction of the middle class (see Bandow, October 1998). Thus, impoverishing the people for the actions of their rulers has been simply bad politics. The conflict between the regime and the opposition deepened even further, without giving the authorities a chance to compromise or to make concessions. Social and political tensions heightened, as UN sanctions continued to bite. This increased the power of nationalist and fascist forces, ushering in dictatorship and an unlimited period of isolation of the FR of Yugoslavia.

Diplomatic recognition of Slovenia and Croatia, extended by the EU Member States, intensified the conflict among Serbs, Croats and Muslims in Bosnia and increased the pressure on Western States to find a peaceful solution to it. The internationalisation of the Serbian question in Croatia was the result of the inability of any of the parties to the conflict to find a solution by its own means. The 'back-to-war' option would mean catastrophe for both warring parties, while the Serbian question would be resolved only by eliminating it altogether, that is the annihilation of the largest part of the Serb minority, Croatian society would lapse into total militarisation, permanent ethnic homogenisation and all-out violation of human rights and political freedoms. In the case of Croatia, Tudjman and his colleagues felt strongly enough to give the Serb minority in Krajina only the flimsiest of guarantees for their civil and political rights - guarantees that the Croats proceeded to violate. In this campaign, the Croats were the beneficiaries of an extensive build-up of arms, mostly surplus equipment from former Warsaw Pact countries, imported in violation of the UN mandated arms embargo, almost certainly with the help of Western intelligence agencies.

The international community betrayed legal principles when it failed to proclaim the unilateral decisions of Slovenia and Croatia to declare themselves independent as acts of secession and to take all the legal consequences of these acts into consideration when proposing solutions to the Yugoslav crisis. Instead, it legalised secession by accepting the legally unwarranted view of the EC Arbitration Commission that Yugoslavia was undergoing a process of disintegration. Germany and the Vatican even announced that they would recognise Slovenia and Croatia prior to the publication of the Commission's recommendations. By legalising secession, the international community betrayed the main principles of the UN

Charter and of the Final Act of the CSCE, and their interpretation of rights to secession and self-determination clashed with the principle of the international law, according to which the territorial integrity of States is inviolable.

Even though it was the former Yugoslavia's constitutive nationalities that had formed a common State at one point in the past, the international community now recognised the right to self-determination to the Republics, that is, the territories. Of all the former Yugoslav Republics, in 1918, only Serbia and Montenegro were internationally recognised States in their own right, prior to the creation of common Yugoslav State. The secessionist Republics were quickly granted recognition by the international community, in clear breach of the principle of the inviolability of international borders of sovereign countries and without fulfilling the criteria that a given State has to meet to be recognised internationally. Later, in Serbia, following international involvement, Milošević was transferred to The Hague.

By granting the right of self-determination to Yugoslavia's federal units, the international community overlooked the fact that, except in the case of Slovenia, the population of the former Yugoslav Republics was ethnically heterogeneous. Thus, Yugoslavia's constitutive nationalities, many of whose members lived outside their mother Republics, were placed in an inferior position. The people of these nationalities who remained outside their mother Republics were denied the right to self-determination and were reduced to a state of a national minority.

The UN Security Council decided to take the radical step of branding the Serbian and Montenegrin authorities as the most responsible for the armed hostilities in Bosnia. UN sanctions were one-sided because there were many actors and parties to share the responsibilities in the Bosnia war. The international community exerted a powerful influence on developments in Bosnia and Herzegovina in 1992, which also coincided with the start of the Yugoslav crisis. The recommendation of the arbitration commission of the conference on Yugoslavia was, the Serbian people in Bosnia should have the status of a national minority, or ethnic group in this Republic and that a referendum of citizens is the precondition for the recognition of Bosnia as an independent and sovereign State. The Serbian and Montenegrin authorities would have to meet all the demands concerning Bosnia that the Security Council made, in order that all the sanctions would be lifted, however, the problem involved not only Serbs, but also Bosnians and Croats. Bosnia even became a member of the UN through a summary procedure while civil war was being waged on its territory.

Sarajevo has no mystical significance, nor does the Balkans have inherent strategic or geopolitical importance. A crisis in the Balkans led to the first World War not because of the region's intrinsic value but because the major European powers foolishly identified their own vital interests with the outcome of its parochial conflicts. As the RAND Corporation's Benjamin Schwarz correctly observes, "the fuse for that war was lit in Sarajevo not because ethnic conflict existed in what is now Yugoslavia but because great powers meddled in those conflicts" (see Schwarz 1992: B-5). That ought to be a pertinent lesson for today's advocates of US interventionism.

It was certainly possible that the fighting in Croatia and Bosnia may have spread to other parts of the Balkans. The desire of ethnic Albanians in Serbia's Kosovo province to cast off Serbian domination and territorial disputes involving another Yugoslav Republic, Macedonia, are the two most probable catalysts. It is a hypocrisy that a US, NATO or UN occupation force would induce the warring factions to settle their disputes peacefully (see Carpenter 1992). There has been little reason to believe that outside intervention would resolve the Yugoslavian tragedy, however, in 1995, with the US-led military intervention, a massive NATO bombing campaign in response to the killings at Srebrenica, targeting Serbian artillery positions throughout Bosnia, brought an end to the wars with the Dayton Peace Accord.

The international community has not recognised the FR of Yugoslavia as the legal successor to the former Yugoslavia, although the FRY consists of Serbia and Montenegro, the only two Republics which advocated Yugoslavia's survival and which had invested their own statehood in the common Yugoslav State. In other words, they formed the nucleus of the former Yugoslavia; in much the same way as Russia was the core of the former Soviet Union. The continuity should not be affected even when a country loses some of its territory, for example, Holland after Belgium's secession, Sweden after Norway's secession or Great Britain after it lost its colonies.

The ordinary people of the FR of Yugoslavia felt the consequences of the devastating economic crisis. The falling behind was accompanied by an irremediable brain drain. The non-selective nature of the sanctions also hit those who could have become a democratic alternative to the current regime. No further development in any area was possible. It is obvious that the international community had applied a double standard in dealing with the former Yugoslavia.

1. The insistence on the territorial integrity of the former Yugoslavia was abandoned with little resistance, while the territorial integrity of one of its federal units, Bosnia-Herzegovina, has been defended by all available means, including political and military pressure and economic sanctions.

2. The international community insists on the legitimacy of the rump Presidency of Bosnia, but it refused to recognise the incomplete Presidency of the SFRY.

3. Despite the UN Resolutions 713 and 724, arms deliveries to Croatia did not stop.

4. The Croatian army in the Bosnia-Croatia War was condemned, but no sanctions were imposed on Croatia, only on Serbia, because the JNA (Yugoslav Peoples Army) had left part of its armaments to the Bosnian Serbs.

5. The UN Security Council ignored the report of the UN Secretary-General which condemned all the parties to the conflict in Bosnia.

6. The US government warned that no agreement reached by two sides at the expense of the third would be recognised. However, the negotiation between the Croats and Muslims had been going on for months at the expense of the Bosnian Serbs.

7. Peace negotiations broke off after two incidents in which civilians were killed in downtown Sarajevo, but the Serbian side was unanimously condemned despite the absence of any hard evidence.

8. There was a focus on humanitarian aid to Sarajevo, but the delivery for the largely Serbian population in other parts of Bosnia had long been blocked, resulting in an even larger number of casualties.

Afterwards, another military intervention, described as a "humanitarian intervention" by NATO, affected the Kosovo crisis. This was because solutions for Kosovo were hard to come by, other than launching a new economic war against Yugoslavia. The sanctions had no discernible impact on Belgrade's policy. In the Kosovo conflict, three sides were clearly involved: the Serbs, the Kosovo Albanians and NATO. What NATO embarked upon with its war against Yugoslavia has been labelled "humanitarian intervention", that is, intervention motivated by humanitarian concerns? US President, Bill Clinton, justified the NATO action as a "moral imperative" to end the killing of ethnic-Albanian civilians (see Schwarz *et al.* 1999).

In the aftermath of the NATO bombing campaign against Yugoslavia, instability continued to plague the country. All the areas of the former Yugoslavia faced increasing instability. However, the Clinton administration made one miscalculation after another in dealing with the Kosovo crisis. The NATO alliance was not prepared for many eventualities, including for the refugee problem. The sense of responsibility had failed (see Layne 1999). The two and a half months long air campaign against Yugoslavia ended without a clear answer to any one of the serious questions that had arisen before it started (see Vankovska, July 2000). This military intervention ended the war in Kosovo that still surfaces on the international law discussion table regarding the legality and desirability of interventions to counter atrocities which had not diminished. The assassinated Prime Minister Zoran Đinđić had suggested the need to promote a rational definition of the Kosovo problem and to gradually suppress emotional and irrational definitions; to encourage the readiness for engagement in resolving of any given part of the problem; spreading the sense of reality, that is, suppressing exaggerated expectations.

However, until the present day, the Kosovo problem remains unsolved and Albanian politicians are seeking a way out of their six-year limbo as an UN-administered province of Serbia. In 2001, Milošević was delivered to The Hague for trial on the charge of "Crimes against Humanity" and became the first Head of State to face an international court for war crimes committed while in office. Belgrade had no choice but to deliver Milošević to the International Criminal Tribunal in The Hague. The United States and its European allies withheld aid that Belgrade so badly needed until it complied with their demand. The general perception is either that Milošević was extradited because of the inability of the domestic legal system to manage high profile humanitarian law cases or that he was 'sold' for international aid. Thus, the conditions under which Milošević was delivered to the Tribunal only serve to raise doubts both about the legality of the procedure and the motivations of the political actors who carried it out.

A further obstacle to the perceived legitimacy of the Tribunal has been the lack of clarity in domestic public opinion regarding what the trial is about (see Gordy 2003). Many in Belgrade have argued that, for all the horrible things that Milošević was supposed to have done, he is a Serbian citizen who must be protected by the Constitution. If a trial had to be held, they wanted it held in a local court in accordance with the law of the land. To send him to The Hague has not only brought shame on the man and his regime but, also, on the entire nation. It will leave a stigma that will be hard to erase for years to come. Prosecutors also planned to charge him with war crimes committed in Bosnia and Croatia. After Milošević's unexpected death in custody, there may be already many lessons to be learnt from the way the international community or, more precisely, the West, pressured Belgrade. Sanctions have failed to mitigate the political chaos; economic mismanagement, corruption and incompetence have injured Yugoslav society as a whole. Sanctions were one of the reasons for Yugoslavia's disintegration. In that sense, they weakened the Yugoslav State.

Interventionist politics cast into doubt settled legal principles concerning the former Yugoslavia where the finding of an international tribunal, to the effect that the country had been subjected to dissolution rather than secession, has been hotly contested. In the opinion of one of the critics,

> "The response of the international community to the events of Yugoslavia has done much to weaken the principle of territorial integrity and to encourage the notion that self-determination can be achieved through secession from an independent and sovereign State (see Musgrave 1997: 192).

There is more than one explanation for Yugoslavia's disintegration and the nature of that disintegration. Hence, we are to conclude that among one of them is that they were mainly caused by foreign factors engaged in various international conspiracies and driven by renewed imperial aspirations (see Institute for European Studies 1993: 2)[143]. There is no full account of the theories trying to weigh the importance of international factors against that of external influences.

---

[143] This chapter is produced according to the best comprehensive discussion of that process which can be found in Ronen, Dov. "The Origins of Ethnic Conflict: Lessons from Yugoslavia." *Research School of Pacific Studies: Working Paper No.155*. Canberra: The Australia National University Press, November 1994, and Institute for European Studies. "Inter-Ethnic Conflict and War in the Former Yugoslavia." *Research School of Pacific Studies: Working Paper No.140*. Canberra: The Australia National University Press, November 1993.

7.2. The International Community and Myanmar

Self-imposed isolation under Gen Ne Win's BSPP regime had kept Burma out of reach from the international community. However, after the collapse of the BSPP, the newly opened up "Union of Myanmar" has faced "international sanctions" called for by its democratic opposition leader, Aung San Suu Kyi who has enjoyed the dubious distinction of being the only Nobel Laureate to be under arrest.

Myanmar's regime is among the worlds most incompetent, its people among Asia's poorest, its record on human rights is at the bottom of the pile. More recently, the United States appeared to be the leading force behind a UN Security Council Resolution imposing on Myanmar comprehensive economic sanctions, including a ban on air travel, the freezing of assets abroad, a visa-ban and an arms embargo[144]. However, the sanctions policy and Western pressure, ostracism and tough talking have clearly all failed to make the slightest dent in the regime's behaviour. Equally, the East's engagement policy is not working in Myanmar either: the admission to ASEAN, the premier regional club, and regular dialogue on everything from trade to cultural exchanges. None of this has wrung the slightest concession out of the Generals and while China, for one, may not mind too much about this, others do. The SPDC's National Convention was to start the first step of its "Seven Step Road Map to Democracy," has been running for thirteen years but which again paused at the end of January 2006, frustrates other ASEAN governments, but nothing else. The engagement policy, however, remains active and, by passing up its chairmanship of ASEAN, Myanmar has shown that it has opted for its domestic politics, which do not allow foreigners or journalists to enter the country for its transparency.

One problem with both approaches is that the two tend to cancel each other out. Western sanctions can hardly be expected to succeed if the regional powers especially Myanmar's immediate neighbours - China and India - simply ignore them. One also has to note that one is dealing with a country and it's self-imposed isolation of 26 years. Diehard opponents of the regime, who insist on the regime's unconditional surrender, have got precisely nowhere which such a policy over the past 15 years. Thus, the policy of sanctions needs re-thinking.

---

[144] The United States has refused, among other things, to recognise the new name 'Myanmar', but it has maintained limited diplomatic and economic ties as well as counter-narcotics cooperation with Rangoon (see Hader 1998).

However, weakening the regime economically coupled diplomatic and political pressure does little to strengthen the people's struggle for freedom, in concrete terms. The real problem is that the movement to replace the regime with a more enlightened government has not been built up to the degree necessary to *either* force the Generals to find a negotiated settlement with the National League for Democracy and other opposition forces *or* to force it out of power through the coordinated efforts of a "people's power" uprising, international sanctions and armed resistance.

Present sanctions and pressure policies toward Myanmar is not bringing about any meaningful change in the human rights practices of the regime and probably actually make a bad situation even worse. Furthermore, it isolates the international community from Myanmar (see Hauswedell, December 2005). Sanctions strengthen the hand of the ruling authorities by creating a scapegoat for their own internal policy failures and narrowing the opportunity of private individuals in Myanmar to expand their economic, social and cultural contacts with the citizens of the West (see Hader 1998). Sanctions help create the mass of unfulfilled young people with untapped talent living on the margin of existence. It can be seen that the regime profits from the sanctions in the short term (see Will 2003: 17). There is no doubt that ordinary Burmese have an interest in improving the government's disastrous economic management, checking the alarming spread of HIV/AIDS and putting an end to Myanmar's endless guerrilla wars, in addition to political reforms.

Condoleezza Rice, the US Secretary of State, has identified Myanmar as an "outpost of tyranny" where the US must help bring freedom[145] (see "Rice names 'outposts of tyranny." January 2005). On the one hand, the EU has consistently favoured limited sanctions against the SPDC and has supported UN agencies and NGOs that are involved in human rights issues, counter-narcotics trade and with the HIV/AIDS crises and, on the other hand, the EU has exercised constant pressure on ASEAN regarding Myanmar. Within the EU, policies towards Myanmar are not uniform. In 2005, it was proposed that the existing EU policy framework, which was established in the late 1980s and early 1990s at a time when Myanmar was widely perceived to have entered a "democratic transition zone," required a fundamental rethinking (see Taylor *et al.* 2005). In the case of Myanmar, the UN has not been

---

[145] They are Cuba, Iran, North Korea, Zimbabwe, Burma and Belarus.

successful to bring about on-going confidence-building talks between the military junta and the democratic opposition.

Furthermore, the sanctions have had deleterious social effects on an already poor country with the status of Least Developed Countries (LDC). The sanctions have given the military the chance to expand the State's coercive capacities as a matter of survival and, thereby, weaken the intellectual strength and the capacity for civil society to develop.

A more fundamental problem is that no one really takes Myanmar seriously enough. Most countries, whatever their attitude toward the regime, treat Myanmar as a backwater rather than a pressing strategic concern. That is a mistake. For one thing, one has to take following facts into account: Myanmar is the world's second-largest producer of heroin. It cheerfully exports drugs, refugees and disease to its neighbours and beyond. Its many rebellions regularly spill over into Thailand, India and Bangladesh. It hosts China's only military base on the Indian Ocean, has big reserves of natural gas, which it already sells to Thailand and also to both China and India, and, thus, plays a crucial part in the growing rivalry between Asia's two raising regional powers. Myanmar links both China and India who have recently been developing rapidly and now span a broad spectrum, ranging from the economic to wider political, diplomatic and military relationships. Professor Pinheiro's[146] carefully sets out in measured tones his concerns with the human rights situation and makes eighteen specific and uncontroversial recommendations in his Report which was submitted in accordance with the Commission Resolution dated 25 July 2005 (see Pinheiro 2005). He mentioned in a HardTalk interview in BBC that:

> "China, India and Thailand [...] I think that they have the key to change in Myanmar, I think that in their own way, in their own style they have some qualities to convince the Myanmar authorities that, for instance, the road map cannot be stuck and waiting for ever [...]"[147]

In 1995, led by the retired Anglican Archbishop Desmond Tutu of South Africa and former Czech President Vaclav Havel - the Czech playwright who helped to end the era of Soviet domination - activists are calling on the UN Security Council to adopt a resolution that would pave the way for non-military intervention in

---

[146] Professor Paulo Sérgio Pinheiro, UN Special Rapporteur of the Commission on Human Rights.

[147] Professor Paulo Sérgio Pinheiro, on BBC "HardTalk", 1 September 2005, http://news.bbc.co.uk/1/hi/ programmes/hardtalk/4216736.stm

Myanmar. They brand Myanmar's military regime as a "threat to peace," and a global coalition of human rights advocates is urging the United Nations to intervene in the South-East Asian nation to restore democracy, deliver humanitarian aid and win the release of political prisoners. Tutu and Havel called on the Security Council to pass a resolution requiring Myanmar to work with the UN to achieve national reconciliation and restore a democratically elected government (see Paddock 2005). The recommendation in the Report is that the UN Security Council should adopt a Resolution "on the situation in Burma in accordance with its authority under Chapter VII of the UN Charter (Article 41) and past Security Council precedents" (see Tutu *et al.* 2005). Due to the Tutu-Havel Report called "Threat to the Peace: a Call for the UN Security Council to Act in Burma," there has been a sense of paranoid evident among the SPDC. However, the Security Council itself is not a legitimate institution in the context of the needs of the present day. If the Security Council really looks at Myanmar and the Generals who continue to be intransigent, what steps would be contemplated? More punitive measures? More sanctions? (see Faulder, March 2006). Yet it is unlikely that under any circumstances, that the international community led by Washington would consider a military or any other kind of intervention in Myanmar, either as a unilateral mission or as a multilateral enterprise through NATO or the UN.

There are no US security interests at stake that even remotely reach the threshold of importance needed to justify the costs and risks. The US Is neither keen to risk its relationship with China in particular and India in general nor is America eager to make constructive involvements to interfere in the Myanmar issue as they did in Vietnam. American involvement in the intractable, parochial conflicts of Myanmar would be an exercise in foreign policy masochism. It is difficult to make even a plausible case for intervention on national interest grounds. Myanmar does not have any valuable commodity, such as oil. Consequently, it is not possible to foment fears of supply cut-offs or economic "strangleholds," as the Bush administration did so effectively to generate support for its Persian Gulf crusade. Myanmar is not poised to become armed with nuclear weapons as Iraq supposedly was. Hence, Myanmar cannot be portrayed as a surrogate of America's superpower enemy. The undemocratic countries of Africa, the Middle East and mainland Asia were less susceptible to American influence. In 1988, for instance, the demonstrators for democracy in Burma hailed the US for its denunciations of government repression and "seized on every scrap of hope that the US would intervene". At one point, they were swept with enthusiasm by a report that the US Navy was sailing into Burmese waters. On occasion, in support of democracy, the US Navy has sailed into the waters of the Dominican Republic, Haiti, Panama and Grenada. It might conceivably at some point sail into Cuban waters on such a mission. Myanmar, however, was at the utmost outer reaches of American interests.

Despite the position of the NLD, saying that they have not asked the West to impose sanctions against Myanmar[148], the pro-democracy activists aboard continue their call for sanctions. Myanmar's political activists in exile do not do anything to alleviate the plight of the people inside the country and yet withhold endorsement for those who do. The sanctions policy against Myanmar never had any chance of working because of the refusal mainly of ASEAN and China. Indeed, one lesson of the history of economic sanctions is that, once launched, they are very difficult to terminate, with domestic politics militating against an administration's attempt to "back down". Hence, one can expect a self-perpetuating cycle of Myanmar sanctions, with the inevitable refusal of Yangon to implement political reform. In the final analysis, the sanction policy toward Myanmar is an irresponsible moral posturing. Supporters of sanctions want to feel good that they are doing something to improve political and economic conditions in Burma by forcing someone else, and the people of Myanmar, to bear the costs.

Hence, the world needs to recognise that there is little hope of influencing the regime unless a more coherent policy can be found, even if that has to mean easing up on the Generals in some limited respects. The West and East should co-operate with one another. They might also try harder to persuade their allies in Asia that a better government in Myanmar is in everyone's interests, or a more committed engagement from the US, as witnessed in Vietnam with same concrete deals. The UN playing a more active part, instead of begging the regime to admit its Special Envoy, might "facilitate" a non-existent dialogue between the SPDC and the NLD movement. The real achievement would be to marry the Western and Eastern approaches.

---

[148] "Interviewed with U Lwin (NLD)." By Min Zin, Radio Free Asia. 2 June 2006.

Conclusion

The human mind and customs cannot change overnight and to build a completely new system of values and to accept it just requires some time.
(Václav Havel 1994)[149]

The origin of this thesis lies in a basic puzzle about continuity and change in political transition in multinational States, the case of the former Yugoslavia, and the present day Myanmar. However, in the former Yugoslavia, the present day Serbia and Montenegro, first turned into a failed State with the first wave of transition during the 1990s and, later in 2000, faced a period of late transition. In 2000, Serbia's political clashes undertaken prior to the transfer of power from the old regime can be contrasted with the event of "8.8.88" in Myanmar. The overall objective is to answer the major question of whether the present day Myanmar will follow the former Yugoslavia's fate; and by doing so it advances the transition research where ethnicity has a role. The present analysis comes at the time now when Myanmar is moving to another crucial stage of its transition process while the former Yugoslavia's problems are considered history. The inductive and deductive aspects interplay between theoretical and analytical concepts. The chapter concludes with four parts: a discussion of the implications for transition theories and research, an empirical section that answer the major question of the dissertation, the part of international involvement and the outcome of the political transitions in both countries.

---

[149] Václav Havel became famous as the leader of the Velvet Revolution. During the 1970s and 1980s, Havel was repeatedly arrested and he served several years in prison for his dissident activities (1977, 1978-79, 1979-83, 1989). In the 1980s, Havel became the undisputed unofficial leader of the Czechoslovak human rights movement. In December 1989, he was elected President of Czechoslovakia and, later on, of the new Czech Republic. He was awarded numerous international prizes and honorary doctorates.

8.1. The Failure of Transition Theories

In chapter two, transition theories were presented and throughout this study I have theoretically defined the various elements of the theories. Ever since real Socialism began to crumble in most of the Central and Eastern European countries during the 1990s, the issues of transition from non-democratic regimes into a democratic order has recaptured the centre stage in the political sciences (see Pavlovic, June 1999). The lip service paid to building a political system based on the values of Western European political philosophy marked the beginning of the so-called third wave of democratisation (see Huntington 1991). The most thorough research in this area has been conducted by Linz and Stepan and published as *Problems of Democratic Transition and Consolidation* in 1996. Transition theories are used by political scientists to explain post-authoritarian democratisation processes. In a nutshell, theorists claim that transition to democratic system and its consolidation depend on certain groups of conditions and the character of the people at the helm at the point when transition commences. Developed in the context of Southern European and Latin American experiences, such theories were "transplanted", often inappropriately, to analyse political processes in the former Yugoslavia and formerly Soviet States in the 1990s. In due course, transition theories "migrated" also into South-East Asia. However, there are questions of the shortcomings of the theories and some argue against their uncritical use in the political transitions of multi-ethnic States. It is clear that the cases of multi-ethnic States cannot be explained by existing transition theories. Both the former Yugoslavia and Myanmar do not exactly fall within the frame-work of current transition theories which are used in this work, and up to now, they had not been covered in the transition literature. Apart from the spate of historical and journalistic studies on the break-up of Yugoslav and Myanmar political scenes (bad Junta vs. good Aung San Suu Kyi), no serious political study has so far appeared which would explain the failure of Yugoslavia, or its seceded Republics, or how to democratise Myanmar. The absence of such a study cannot be accounted for by the presumed claim that the former Yugoslavia and Myanmar do not constitute valid subjects of analysis for transition theory. On the contrary, transition theory lacks the analytical tools to successfully account for such cases. This is outlined in the Table below. The research has been completed and the cases are analysed, however, the outcome of this endeavour is that current theories of regime transitions do not cover the political transition in multi-ethnic States.

To elaborate theoretically and empirically on the concept of meaning, I have first made an analytical distinction between the facts and the structure, with a linkage between meaning and political transition. The absence of political transition or failed transition has frequently been sought to be explained by the authoritarian nature of the regime and its ruthless usage of nationalism to mobilise popular support. New ideologies of political nationalism required all the members of a 'nation State' to be united and homogenous and this produced some new conflicts in most States which were, after all, composed of several ethnic communities (see McNeill 1986: ch.2). In this chapter, it will be argued that nationalism has played no role in delaying democratisation, even though nationalism as such has been powerful in bringing about a change of power in the former Yugoslavia.

Much of the literature on political transition centres on the type of the regime and how they assume their political power. The focus is often on the insertion of institutional mechanisms into relatively stable political systems rather than on the ethnic dynamics involved in a transitional society. The study of transition shares some of the key assumptions of neo-institutionalism, namely, a definition of institution which goes beyond the formal set-up and focuses on the interplay of structures and actors as part of a dynamic process. On the one hand, institutions act as constraints; on the other hand, they help to structure incentives and political behaviour (see O'Donnell 1996: 96-98). A close examination of the failings of Linz and Stepan's analysis and, thus, the failings of the general transition theory, leads to the conclusion that it is precisely a more accurately defined relationship between actors and structure. The problem of accounting for unsuccessful transitions is brought about by a theoretical framework that leaves unresolved the distinction between the actor and the structure, as explained by Linz and Stepan. All these approaches and theories are unable to account for the way in which the former Yugoslavia and Myanmar developed; despite a not insignificant advantage at the beginning of transition, Yugoslavia turned into a kind of Sultanic regime in the second half of the 1990s and later into the status of a failed State; whereas Burma turned into a non-hierarchical military regime led by the SPDC. Reformulations and new research in transition theories are required, as ethnic relations are included in the multi-national States and their political transitions.

The meaning of the political transition in this study has therefore played a central, critical role in the analysis, with an emphasis on how it is perceived, interpreted and understood. The table below illustrates for the better understand of the argument.

Table 8-1. Alternative Governance Scenarios in the 1990s

Type of Regime	Characteristics of Political Power	Examples
Traditional Strongman	By force of arms, centralised around a dominant individual, often elevated by a cult personality	Libya, Cuba, Iraq, Syria, North Korea, Zaire
Military Junta	By revolt against a previously elected government or prior military regime, power held by junta, legitimacy based upon claims of ending former corrupt regime, governing by decree with limited political rights, often promises for future democratic election	Nigeria, Algeria, Haiti, Fiji, Ghana, Myanmar [Burma], Pakistan **Future Possibilities:** Thailand, Somalia, Jordan
Oligarchy of Ruling Families	By an elected member of one of the ruling houses, to act as guarantor of continued rule and wealth, legitimacy based upon protection of national identity, limited participation in politics	Saudi Arabia, United Arab Emirates **Future Possibilities:** Mainland China, Vietnam, Nicaragua
Fascist Nationalism	By either seizure or elections, the governing body seeks its legitimacy through a common message of nationalism, intolerance and xenophobia proto- democratic in that there is limited popular participation in politics for most citizens, excepting religious and ethnic minorities	Romania, Serbia, Croatia **Future Possibilities:** Vietnam, Russia, Bulgaria
Dissent Nationalism	Succession from a federal or multi-ethnic State in an attempt to guarantee a "national" identity which is the basis of the governing body's legitimacy, if the "new" State is successful, it would quickly become a fascist national regime with limited popular participation in politics for "national" citizens and, if unsuccessful, it would be placed under a military junta with restricted political rights for all residents	Czechoslovakia (Slovakia) **Future Possibilities:** Moldova
Monarchical Rule	By a hereditary leader: legitimacy based on symbol of national identity and nation-building - limited popular participation in politics	Brunei, Oman, Swaziland, Morocco, Jordan **Future Possibilities:** Romania, Hungary, Brazil, Serbia

Type of Regime	Characteristics of Political Power	Examples
Religious Fundamentalism	By force; religious fundamentalist movements seek power through the ballot box: legitimacy based upon strict adherence to religious tradition, limited participation in politics	Iran, Sudan **Future Possibilities:** Algeria, Tajikistan, Tunisia, Morocco, Libya, Egypt, Mauritania, Kenya
Authoritarian Technocratic Rule	By political power centralised in one-party or dominant party control, legitimacy based upon policies of strong economic growth and/or capacity to control ethnic conflicts: limited popular participation in politics	Singapore, South Korea, Taiwan, Peru, Chile, Malaysia, Senegal, Kenya, Indonesia **Future Possibilities:** South Africa
Dominant Political Party Rule	Although maintaining a multi-party political system, government is dominated by a single major party which controls elections - legitimacy based upon regular elections and wide popular participation in politics	Japan, Mexico, Zimbabwe, India **Future Possibilities:** South Africa

Source (see Henderson, September 1992)

8.2. Balkanisation in Myanmar?

The stories of the former Yugoslavia suggest that balkanisation and nationalism has created new nation States, however, the scenario in Myanmar has continues to unfold and stability in the country remain precarious. Balkanisation has come to refer to any region in the world faced with internal turmoil and schisms. Even though the Soviet Union dissolved into fifteen countries, balkanisation finds its roots in the former Yugoslavia. Certainly, the very words, balkanisation and the Balkans, conjure up images of violence, destruction, genocide and dissension.

That both Yugoslavia and Myanmar fell into nationalist regimes was not solely due to ethnic conflict or even a history of animosity, for that matter. Rather, the disintegration of political and civil order, in conjunction with economic problems, together contributed to their problems. On the one hand, "balkanisation" is a term that has emerged in response to small-scale independence movements and the increasing trend of mini-nationalisms (or micro-nationalisms), as they occur along ethnic, cultural and religious fault lines, and it has also expanded to connote a varied tableau of scenarios involving disintegration. Thus, balkanisation could occur during the period of civil wars. At that stage of Burma's history, the country was headed towards disintegration. However, balkanisation scenarios have been obliterated since 1958 with the coup by General Ne Win and the period of his "caretaker army government". On the other hand, Balkanisation generally describes the process of geopolitical fragmentation and is used to depict any kind of political dissolution across the world. For this reason, Myanmar and its political situations in the present days can be comparable to the case of the former Yugoslavia, as its fragmentations of both societies are very much alike. Myanmar nowadays suffers from unfathomable political and social situations that fragment the country into an unrecoverable and dreadful state of affairs. Civil unrest, ethnic, linguistic, cultural and religious tensions, factionalism and separatism have conjointly created a new texture of political friction and anxiety in contemporary Myanmar society. Stated differently, micro-nationalism or ethnic, linguistic, cultural and religious separatism, and geopolitical tensions are the problems of Myanmar today. Hence, in its political transition, Myanmar does not become a failed State, but it becomes and remains as a weak State.

8.3. Limitations in International Involvement

There is a limit in what international society can do for a country's crisis. The need for intervention by an external great power is the exception, not the rule. Even though Myanmar is compared to the former Yugoslavia, because of its intra-state ethnic conflicts, the international community does not adopt the same policy to respond to it. The fighting in Yugoslavia has been characterised by ethnic wars and, yet, the international community has taken very different approaches on the Myanmar case, intervening extensively in the former example through embargoes and military force, and taking a largely hands-off approach to the latter conflict as an "internal political affair" not as "ethnic issue". This apparent inconsistency in approach by the international community provides an effective context in which to address the question of what role can and should the international community play in Myanmar. Several forms of international involvement have existed in the case of the former Yugoslavia and it seems needless to mention that the international community has played a great role in the former Yugoslavia's political transition. However, no active international measure can be promoted in Myanmar because of its geopolitical situation. Many democracies implemented sanctions against the military government in Myanmar. With their backs to the wall, Aung San Suu Kyi and the NLD have called for international economic sanctions against the SPDC, following a strategy reminiscent of the ANC during its struggle against apartheid in South Africa. The NLD believes that international sanctions will deprive the SPDC and its cronies of opportunities to enrich themselves and will contribute to pressure for an unconditional, tripartite dialogue between the SPDC, the NLD and the leaders of the ethnic nationalities. Despite suggestions to the contrary, there appears to be a greater consensus on key issues such as when, on 30th May 2003, NLD leaders and supporters were attacked at night in a remote area near Depeyin in Sagaing Division, Upper Myanmar. Since that incident, Aung San Suu Kyi and U Tin Oo, NLD Vice Chairman, have been detained and as recently as May 2006, the SPDC has threatened to dissolve the NLD, accusing it of having links to illegal organisations. Western sanctions and pressure have no leverage in Myanmar's political affairs just as in Cuba, Haiti or Iraq - where sanctions have served to gravely worsen an already bad situation.

8.4. The Outcome of the Political Transition

Due to its different historical legacies, dissimilar political culture, altered cultural, religious and linguistic factors, and unrelated geopolitical situations, the outcome of the political transition in both countries is diverse. The former Yugoslavia underwent a twofold transformation and political transition which resulted in several new States in the Balkans and the former Yugoslavia – in the present day, the State Union of Serbia and Montenegro's consolidation has yet to be achieved.

While "transition" and "consolidation' are generally seen as distinguishable phases of overall democratisation process, they should be qualitatively distinguished and not necessarily in terms of chronology. They are not strictly divisible as successive phases although, invariably, consolidation is completed after transition if not long afterwards, since it is a much longer part of the process.

During the rule of Yugoslavia by Tito in the Communist years, measures taken to decentralise the country's decision making processes (rather than democratise the country) ultimately led to the collapse. The federalism of the former Yugoslavia was an untypical one and based on one-party rule. That is to say, decentralisation of its federal system bred ethnic nationalism and fuelled identity politics, while the lack of real democratisation efforts accelerated the increasing climate of fragmentation. This is a phenomenon that scholars and statesmen need to examine various strategies for ethnic conflict regulation from partition to federalism, in the hope of peaceful accommodation of the different demands of ethnics and national States. In Burma, for the period of General Ne Win's rule, the country was entirely centralised and isolated and the country was driven into complete poverty. Former Yugoslavia was rather prosperous under Marshall Tito, had the benefit of good relationships with many countries and its citizens enjoyed access to wealth and freedom to a certain extent.

The resolution of the complicated problems connected with the dissolution of Yugoslavia and the development of the emerging successor societies and nation States, took a long time, despite its tradition of a decade-long traditional political opposition. The political transition in the Federal Republic of Yugoslavia had begun in the 1990s. The first wave of political and economic transition in Serbia was initiated during the federal government of Ante Marković, when the country was already coming towards the end of the existence of the former SFR Yugoslavia, at the same time as in other Republics, the present independent States. However, democratic transition in Serbia had been blocked by the Milosevic regime, which created an atmosphere of fragmentation and fear in the country. Serbia and Montenegro suffered from the wars and the political transition which was extremely painful. It was further aggravated by their international economic and political isolation (with UN sanctions lasting from 1992 until 1995), by their extremely high inflation, by NATO bombardment in 1999 and by economic mismanagement and disinvestment. The idea that quick changes for the better are possible is an illusion, owing more to propaganda on the part of some of the new regimes than to real opportunities. A few months after the NATO bombing, Milosevic's regime was toppled by hundreds of thousands of angry protestors from all over Serbia flocking to the capital and demanding that Milosevic accept his defeat in the Presidential elections and resign. The battle against Milosevic had at least temporarily united the 19 political parties that supported the opposition's candidate, Vojislav Kostunica, even though the problems facing the opposition in Yugoslavia were tremendous (see Kramer, October 2000). The unity was made easier as they shared a common language and cultural background. The political forces that united against the despot then had to start working together. New common themes had to be made to keep them united and a solution for the future of the Federation of Yugoslavia as an entity needed to be found.

Despite the daunting and depressing situation at the end of 2000, when the new leadership took over, high expectations were raised for the country, that it would step away from its recent past and move towards economic growth and social recovery. But months after Vojislav Koštunica's new Presidency, violent clashes underscored the continuing volatility of the region, particularly in Kosovo, and divisions between the democratic oppositions have not been resolved in the new nation-building process. Nevertheless, it can be said that second wave of transition in the former Yugoslavia was led by Vojislav Koštunica, Zoran Đinđić, Miroljub Labus and others.

However, one can claim that the transition in Serbia, so far, has been quite unsuccessful and is, consequently, still towards the beginning. The mainspring of transition in Serbia is not within the country but outside it. There is no original, internal driving force for transition since there is no consensus among political forces on whether transition is necessary, that it is, in fact, a desirable outcome. Therefore, transition in Serbia is mostly unfolding under the influence of international factors, that is, the international community, with the IMF in the greater extent (see "Four Years of Transition in Serbia", 2005).

After the creation of the third Yugoslavia and its implications for preventing political change, the different crises have played a role in hindering democratic consolidation. The building of a (new) State and the search for (new or innovated) national identity makes the former Yugoslavia's transition much more complicated. This is particularly true for Serbia, which came out of the 1990s as a defeated side in the war for Yugoslav heritage and, thus, faced the problems of the determination of the new State (the issues of Montenegro and Kosovo and the formulation of a new national strategy). Its economic transition is perceived as a more complex and less certain process than political transitions while the social aspect is, generally speaking, quite disregarded.

Almost five years after the democratic changes, Serbia and Montenegro have not managed to get the common State to function. In order to understand the process of transition in Serbia one must identify the initial advantages that the country had in that process as well as the most significant difficulties which place limits upon it. The transition in Serbia began in 2000. In other words, transition in Serbia was ten years too late. During those ten years the transition States, excluding Serbia, had gained experience on various aspects of transition.

The new Yugoslavia consists of only two thirds of the population belonging to the two dominant nations, Serbs and Montenegrins, possessing a large minority which could hardly be described as South Slavs and which never enjoyed the full support of the political elite, especially among the opposition and national minorities. The territorial construction of the State has also been strongly influenced by the political and military developments of the past years. Today, the likelihood of Kosovo returning to the institutional framework of Serbia or Yugoslavia beyond a symbolic mechanism is extremely unlikely. Kosovo might opt to belong to some common confederal or federal arrangement with Serbia but, for all purposes, Kosovo has to be excluded from the territorial conception of Serbia. And, ever since, the Federal Republic of Yugoslavia has remained a transitory construction. On 21 May 2006, Montenegro will hold a referendum to determine whether or not to terminate the Union with Serbia. Hence, the case of Serbia and Montenegro remains even more complex than could be perceived with a superficial glance. Nearly a decade after the collapse of the second Yugoslavia, Serbia has still not found a territorial and political system, which is perceived as a lasting and satisfactory solution and remains as a weak State.

Even though the democratic consolidation is understood, it is not only a much lengthier process but is also one with wider and usually deeper effects, I shall however draw the conclusion that the former Yugoslavia has embarked on and even makes it through a process of democratic transition but then it seems to fail the tests of democratic consolidation. It is because of the country's continuation of social and economic decay that there are threats to democracy in the country. If a transitional government is unable to achieve a level of economic production sufficient for local needs, popular support for it will ebb, and with it support for the democratic political system as a whole. While the transitional leadership may attempt to reconstruct social patterns previously suppressed by the old regime, it will be unlikely to halt the rise in crime and public disorder resulting from a collapsing economy and a deposed police force.

To conclude the case of the former Yugoslavia case:

1. The first and most widespread explanation is connected to the economic, political and social crisis of the eighties. The process of political transformation from Communist society had created the weak State, and then the disappearance of the middle class with the increase of poverty and unemployment and emerging of the power of the elite had continued to increase authoritarianism, nationalism and aggressiveness that led to the wars and disintegration of Yugoslavia.

2. The second explanation is connected to political elites and their manipulation of the masses with the help of nationalistic programmes.

3. The third explanation is linked to abuse of the media, nationally and internationally.

4. The fourth and the last of explanation place the influence of the international community to the foreground. It has two elements: first, some kind of 'conspiracy' which has 'correction of history' as a goal and, secondly, the global pre-structuring of the world as a consequence of changes in power within the centre as well as on the periphery (see Blagojevic, September 1999).

For Burma, political transition began in 1988. The misrule and despotism of Ne Win, the SLORC and, later, the SPDC *clique* has destroyed not only all forms of cohesion (political, social and economic) in Burma, but also the institutional framework and channels for interaction and political communication. In order to live on, a military coup occurred in 1988 and, subsequently the regime of SLORC tried to continue to exist, by changing its name to the SPDC, shuffling its own people from power every now and then. The survival of the regime remained problematic even after a change of power and thus it continues to have a long-term impact on the political development of Myanmar. Finally, the opposition, including Aung San Suu Kyi and the NLD itself, remains as a possible cause in preventing a change of power in Myanmar. However, in Myanmar both the ruling party and the opposition ignore the fact that society is highly polarised and that what is needed is a historic compromise between all the parties. The SPDC legitimised its power with force of arms, and the opposition also receives messages from only one section of the society, acting as if it represented the entire electorate. This probably accounts for the failure of the opposition to turn the democratic potential of the people power movement to its own advantage. Unfortunately, many opposition leaders failed to comprehend the deeper meaning of the "8.8.88" event.

National reconciliation is at the core of Myanmar's problems as well as being an integral part of the solution. The task of reconciliation and reconstruction in a new Myanmar seems certainly not an easy one, as it means arriving at a political settlement, which resolves the conflict between the Burman majority and diverse ethnic nationalities. For the ruling SPDC junta, Aung San Suu Kyi, her NLD and the 1990 election are irrelevant matters in Myanmar politics for the process of national reconciliation to move forward. In the meantime, the SPDC keeps mentioning that the *Tatmadaw* has saved the country from "the kind of anarchy experienced in the former Soviet Union, Yugoslavia and Indonesia" (see Yawnghwe, Chao-Tzang, October 2002: 6). According to the SPDC, a period of transition towards a multiparty democratic society should occur in a disciplined way, presided over by the SPDC in fulfilment of its historical task. Here is a semantic gap. The NLD seems to be rejecting the very idea of a transitional period under army rule, deeming it to be a contradiction in itself. According to this theory, democracy can only develop under its own conditions and consequently an undemocratic authoritarian regime has to be removed as a pre-condition for any progress. This is a controversial issue not only of theoretical interest but also in terms of practical policies relating to Myanmar.

The NLD and its most avid supporters are not only equally emphatic in saying no to this claim they go a step further and, proceeding from the so-called hostage theory, assert that progress under an authoritarian rule is a sheer impossibility. Their policy of boycott and isolation is based on this understanding. The SPDC regards this as defamatory to their intentions and to the positive steps they are taking and also as obstructionism with the aim of sabotaging the process towards peace and development. This is the reason they give for the measures that are taken against the opposition groups. Myanmar seems to have arrived at an impasse between two forces of quite different natures; one which is strong in terms of power but lacks legitimation and the other which has the legitimation of the voters but is weak. The heart of the Myanmar problem is that Aung San Suu Kyi has all the legitimacy and the SPDC has all the power. If the NLD had a little more real power and the SPDC had a little more legitimacy, a negotiated transition would be easier to imagine (see Ash, May 2000). Meanwhile, General Than Shwe, the Chair of the SPDC and his wife, Kyaing Kyaing, have adopted the airs of ancient Burmese royalty, taking elaborate titles and performing temple rites once reserved for kings and queens, under the guidance of astrologers. He is definitely not going to deal with Aung San Suu Kyi. Sheridan writes that she made a grave miscalculation by not making a compromise with Khin Nyunt while he held power. Now the SPDC will make her irrelevant (see Sheridan, May 2006). If the situation persists or escalates it would be the people who must bear the consequences. However, as paradoxical as it may sound, the situation contains elements which, under certain circumstances, can be conducive to arriving at a solution to the deadlock. Some would object to the description of the situation as a deadlock and maintain that it is the wish to cling onto power and uncompromising stance of the SPDC, which stands in the way towards progress. In a way they are right of course. However, this kind of analysis is too narrow in the sense that it leaves hardly any room for any possibility of an understanding, which seems to be the only means of a solution for the benefit of the people.

The Serbs problem is that the intellectuals have been involved too much with too little room for classic politicians meaning that the conflict would inevitably be to the detriment of Serbia, since too much political energy was spent on unproductive activities, such as the fierce fight for power. In Myanmar, neither an intellectuals nor classic politicians force exists to deal with its political complexity. In Serbia, there was a group of second-line intellectuals whose leaders toppled Milosevic's regime, whereas the second-line leadership is also missing in Myanmar. The vertical approaches from both the ruling party and the opposition can not meet anywhere for compromise and the horizontal forces are absent. Even though the Union of Serbia and Montenegro, with a late transition, suffered from a decade of wars and NATO bombing, the country and its people are not really left behind. The people of Myanmar are forty years behind its South-East Asian neighbours. The ability to catch up is a very big question. The continuing marginalisation of the people of Myanmar has to do with the lack of assistance and the fact that the government has not been willing to make the adjustments themselves (see Faulder, March 2006).

Addressing the ethnic question in Myanmar, by the early 1990s, the junta appeared to be winning militarily. However, the time and costs involved were debilitating, so the SLORC switched tactics in 1992 by offering 'peace' talks with selected minority groups and arranging deals in which they laid down their arms in return for guarantees of specific economic benefits. As a result, those who wanted to keep on fighting were further isolated and ethnic groups were split from the remnants of the democratic movement. With this policy, the SPDC feels that it has gained the upper hand over the ethnic groups. The ethnic groups remain diverse and are not capable of achieving any political goal but, nevertheless, ethnic armed groups will further contribute to the country's fragmentation.

In the former Yugoslavia, ethnic groups shared the same language, cultural background and religion. In Burma, as ethnic groups cannot aspire to their own nation State, so too States cannot attempt to integrate by diffusing a particular ethnic group's language and culture throughout the territory of the State. Ethnic conflicts in Burma arose in post-colonial pan-ethnic nation building whereas the ethnic conflicts broke out only at the end of the Tito era in ex-Yugoslavia.

At the heart of ethnic politics in the former Yugoslavia is the use of historical and cultural resources of past and present in a struggle for control of the future and definition of the terms of social changes whereas, in Myanmar, there have been contradictions mainly between the process of ethnic contraction, patronage politics, legacies of historical anti-colonial nationalist movements and post-colonial projects of nation-building.

The accommodation of human diversity in Myanmar remains the leading challenge for federalism. In Myanmar, these attempts still continue, as they have done over the decades, towards accommodating ethnic and other differences through such mechanisms as federalism, autonomy and the like. Just over a decade ago, one commentator spoke of "a federal revolution sweeping the world" (see Elazar 1991: 7). It is a moot question whether that claim can be made today when the world is facing at one time the contradictory pressures of globalisation and of fragmentation. However, the ethnicity-focused conflict politics in present day Myanmar does not offer much hope for those who wish to seek for reconciliation; reconsolidation and reconstruction of a modern nation.

According to the Myanmar opposition, multination federalism is one possible outcome, where State nation-building is based on the language, culture or religion of the dominant ethnic group, territorially concentrated minorities may mobilised as ethno-nationalists to gain some form of autonomy and self-government which, in turn, leads to demands by internal minorities for protection of their rights from self-governing minorities, even though federalism can only work out well where boundaries are drawn in a way that the national minority forms a local majority. The former Yugoslavia came to the tragic end of successive ethnic wars and genocide because of its constitutional failure. In Myanmar, the ethnic groups are simply too intermixed to create sub-units where the minority form a clear majority and even where there are minority dominant regions there are always 'internal minorities'. In this case, federalism can not be enough to accommodate such diversity; it must be supplemented with non-territorialised forms of protection of civil, political, social and cultural rights. In a country like Burma, where ethnic groups are not territorially concentrated, federalism is not a solution to its problems. In this case, the idea of a multinational regime should take place as the State should be unitary and centralised, but guarantee that all the ethnic groups will share the power at the central level (see Berman, Bruce *et al.* 2004: 10-21). Though such resistance to federalism can itself be a subterfuge for resisting democratisation, the possibility of the disintegration of a formally centralised State is always present, especially where constituent racial, ethnic, religious or linguistic communities have experienced severe oppression or genocide assaults. Even a minimum level of trust needed for federalisation may not be present. Any nationalist leaders will, thus, often decry federalism and reject it as a subterfuge for secession or route to disintegration. The efforts to hold onto centralised power and impose unity can exacerbate disintegration or destroy both federalism and democracy. Increasingly, there is a trend on the part of international law to overcome some of the problems of ethnic self-determination by classifying ethnic groups as "minorities" and attempting to guarantee such groups cultural, linguistic and religious freedoms on a universal basis.

One inversion is that Myanmar's so-called democratic opposition falls short of recognising the role of military or the ruling party in political transition - the *Tatmadaw*. Whether we like it or not, it is evident that there will have to be a role for the *Tatmadaw,* to construct a new political order in which the military's special position and influence will be as assured as in Thailand, South Korea, Taiwan or Indonesia. As a matter of fact, the *Tatmadaw* has no other alternative but to play an active, even a leading, role in constructing a new and democratic political order. The next inversion is contained in so-called democratic elections. Aung San Suu Kyi, the NLD and their supporters still hold to the results of the election held in 1990, which usually exists in the relation of conquerors and the conquered. Both conflict resolution and democratisation studies emphasise the role of institutions, suggesting that in post-conflict transitions the role of an interim government and the construction of democratic institutions, such as political parties and effective electoral commissions, will be critical to both the security and political agendas.

Although officially proclaimed as a higher level of democracy in relation to the one-party regime, in reality they contribute to narrowing the limits of democracy, that is, to extensive strengthening of autocracy. Democratic regimes express total intolerance for accepting and recognising the rights of minorities in places where minorities represented a very significant proportion of the population. Minorities are, thus, in the name of 'democracy' *de facto* excluded from power and their rights were narrowed down and finally annulled.

For the SPDC and the NLD, together with other champions of the Myanmar cause, the words "democracy" and "transition" have different meanings. The NLD understands democracy as parliamentary democracy in the style of Western provenance; democracy for the SPDC will be disciplined, with all its consequences. The SPDC calls the present time a transitional period in the sense that peace and stability and economic development will be achieved under their leadership, so that a multi-party democracy can flourish at an appropriate future time.

What they overlook is that democracy will not and can not suddenly prevail by a mere act of declaration or even an election. How might peaceful change come about in Burma? What chance for a Silken Revolution? One must start by saying that the best chance was probably missed ten years ago and the last chances have been passing in early 2000. Aung San Suu Kyi and the NLD have missed the time to take any chances and the window of opportunity that had been given to them and, by repeating these mistakes, Aung San Suu Kyi's leadership has failed to turn the tide of history when it was a time to turn. The SPDC-led National Convention and its draft Constitution proposal, even though it might be too liberal for such a multi-national State in the opinion of many constitutionalists, the NLD fails to consider it and, perhaps, to take a chance for the sake of the country. On the one hand, Aung San Suu Kyi and the NLD dream of having a political transition in the style of the French revolution but, on the other hand, they neglect to deal with the power of the people. Aung San Suu Kyi unlike the second-line leaders in the former Yugoslavia, she and her party – the NLD - and their methods have not succeeded in empowering the people to participate in the process of transition and express the concept of a people-centred society because they are detached from the grassroots. The people had done their part for history in 1988, but its leadership has not succeeded in attaining the political tasks that were handed to them. Only when these political realities become accepted by the political elites in Myanmar, can the ethnic or federal question be put to rest and room made for the political transition. To conclude the case of Myanmar, I will also explain it in four facts:

1. The first and foremost explanation is connected to the country's isolation of several decades (self-imposed isolation until 1988 and the isolation that occurs following the demand made by the opposition). That isolation closed the doors of international exposure in every sense for the lives of the people of Myanmar, the ruling junta as well as the opposition, armed and un-armed.

2. The second explanation reflects the increased deterioration in the country, the economic and social crisis, the melting of middle classes which created a security-obsessed military regime uneasy toward their own position, and made the opposition lose the overview of its own political position in the chaos. Hence, the time for reconciliation is still far away.

3. The third explanation is linked to the abuse of the media, reflecting the imbalances between the national and exiled media that is misleading the people to a large extent.

4. The fourth type of explanation examines the role of the international community, which has two varieties: first, that which insists on some kind of 'political correctness' as a goal, and the second variety insists on helplessness of the in-

ternational community that has resulted from just focusing on a Western favoured political icon, Aung San Suu Kyi, but fails to look at human society in Myanmar as a whole.

The key element in the transition is the transfer of political legitimacy from one system of government to another. Failure to consolidate that popular loyalty in support of a democratic system of government can obstruct, divert or even reverse the democratisation process. There is no guarantee or inevitability about democratisation succeeding as if by some process of unstoppable evolution. The work here concludes that democratic civil peace is imperfect in several ethnically divided democracies and that it is not justified to expect that democratisation would lead to the disappearance of domestic ethnic violence in all countries. Even if one were to imagine a hypothetical scenario where the army leadership, possessed by a sudden change of paradigm, or forced by pressure from outside, stepped aside and let the Parliament elect an NLD executive, it would be naive to suppose that a change to a fully democratic society had thus been accomplished and other developments would naturally follow as a matter of course. Nelson Mandela closed his memoirs with the words,

> "I have walked that long road to freedom [....] but I have discovered the secret that after climbing a great hill, there are many more hills to climb [....] for with freedom comes responsibilities" (see Mandela 1996: 751).

This emphasises that the responsibilities before freedom consisted of finding rational ways and means to get to the top of the hill and putting them judiciously into effect. Applying this metaphor to the situation in Myanmar one can have the impression that some are in despair, some are hopeful but lack effective means and yet others are confident they will make it to the top, at a stride, after friends and sympathisers have cleared the way. Then there are those engaged spectators applauding and cheering the climbers. There is no lack of suggestions of assistance, of which not all are suitable for the purpose. At the same time, forces are busy trying to set up even stronger obstacles.

Bibliography

Books and Monographs

A Study by Burmese Economists (ed). *Economic Development of Burma: A Vision and Strategy.* Singapore: The Singapore National University Press, 2000.

A Study Commissioned by Bank Austria. *Prospects for Development in South-East Europe: Business Opportunities.* Vienna: WIIW, 2001.

Anand, V. K. *Insurgency and Counter-Insurgency: A Study of Modern Guerrilla Warfare.* New Delhi: Deep and Deep Publications, 1985.

Anderson, Benedict. *Imagined Communities: Reflections on the Origin and Spread of Nationalism.* London: Verso Editions, 1983.

______. *The Spectre of Comparisons: Nationalism, South-East Asia, and the World.* London and New York: Verso Books, 1998.

Aung Lwin. *Burma: The Struggle for a Common Future (Panglong Agreement and the Struggle of the Ethnic Nationalities of Burma).* Köln: Burma Büro e. V., 1997.

Aung San Suu Kyi. *Aung San of Burma: A Biographical Portrait by his Daughter.* 1991, 2nd ed., Edinburgh: Kiscadale Publications, 1995.

______. *Freedom from Fear and Others Writings.* intro. and ed., by Michael, Aris. 1990. London.: Viking, 1991.

______. *Voice of Hope: Conversations with Alan Clements.* New York: Seven Stories Press. 1997.

Aung San. *Burma's Challenge 1946.* Rangoon: U Aung Gyi, 1968.

Ba Maw. *Breakthrough in Burma: Memoirs of a Revolution, 1939-1946.* New Haven: Yale University Press, 1969.

Ball, Desmond. *Burma and Signet Intelligence.* White Lotus: Thailand, 1998.

Begović, Boris, and Mijatović, Boško (ed). *Four Years of Transition in Serbia.* Belgrade: Center for Liberal Democratic Studies, 2005.

Berman, Bruce, Eyoh, Disckson, and Kymlicka, Will (ed). *Ethnicity and Democracy in Africa.* Oxford, Athens: James Currey, Ohio University Press, 2004.

Bhutto, Zulfikar Ali. *The Third World: New Directions.* London: Quartet Books, 1977.

Bogdan, Denitch. *Ethnic Nationalism: The Tragic Death of Yugoslavia.* rev. ed., Minnesota: University of Minnesota Press, 1996.

Briggs, Asa, Isaacs, Alan, and Martin, Elizabeth. comp. and ed., *Who's Who in the Twentieth Century?* Market House Books. Oxford: Oxford University Press, 1999.

Burma Project, the (Open Society Institute). *Voice of '88: Burma Struggle for Democracy.* New York: Open Society Institute, 1998.

Butwell, Richard. *U Nu of Burma.* 1963. Stanford: Stanford University Press, 1969.

Callahan, Mary P. *Making Enemies: War and State Building in Burma.* Ithaca and London: Cornell University Press, 2004.

Chelabi, H. E. and Linz, Juan J. (ed). *Sultanistic Regimes.* Baltimore, the Johns Hopkins University Press, 1998.

Chomsky, Noam, and Edward S. Herman. *Manufacturing Consent: The Political Economy of the Mass Media.* New York: Pantheon Books, 1988.

Cohen, Leonard, and Warwick, Paul. *Political Cohesion in a Fragile Mosaic: The Yugoslav Experience.* Boulder: Westview Press, 1983.

Constitution of the Burma Socialist Programme Party. Rangoon: Burma Socialist Programme Party, 1973.

Cviic, Christopher. *Remaking the Balkans.* London: The Royal Institute of International Affairs, Pinter Publisher, 1991.

De Vos, George, and Romanucci-Ross, Lola (ed). *Ethnic Identity: Cultural Continuities and Change* California: Mayfield Publishing Company, 1975.

Dell, Elizabeth (ed). *Burma: Frontier Photographs, 1918–35.* London: Merrell Publishers, 2000.

Dun, Smith Gen *Memoir of the Four-Foot Colonel.* Ithaca: Cornell University Press, May 1980.

Duncan, Wilson. *Tito's Yugoslavia.* Cambridge: Cambridge University Press, 1979.

Durovi'c, Dragoljub. *Verfassung der Sozialistischen Föderativen Republik Jugoslawien.* Belgrad: Sekretariat für d. Informationsdienst d. Bundesversammlung, 1974.

Dusan I. Bjelic, and Obrad Savic (ed). *Balkan as a Metaphor. Between Globalisation and Fragmentation.* Cambridge: MIT Press, 2002.

Dutschke, Rudi. *Geschichte ist machbar.* Berlin: Verlag Klaus Wagenbach, 1980.

Earle, Valeria. *Federalism: Infinite Variety in Theory and Practice.* Itasca, IL: F.E. Peacock, 1968.

Elazar, Daniel J. *Exploring Federalism.* Tuscaloosa: University of Alabama Press, 1987.

Elazar, Daniel J., and Kincaid, John (ed). *The Covenant Connection: From Federal Theology to Modern Federalism.* Lanham: Lexington Books, 2000.

Elliott, Patricia. *The White Umbrella*. Bangkok: Post Books, 1999.

Fellowes-Gordon, Ian. *Amiable Assassins: The Story of the Kachin Guerrillas of North Burma*. London: Robert Hale, 1971.

Finer, S. E. *The Man on Horseback*. New York: Prager, 1962.

Freidrich, Carl J. *Trends of Federalism in Theory and Practice*. New York: Praeger, 1968.

Friedrich, Carl, J. (ed). *Totalitarianism*. Harvard University Press: Cambridge, 1954.

Gellner, Ernest. *Nations and Nationalism*. New York: Routledge, 1998.

Giddens, Anthony. *The Nation-State and Violence* Cambridge: Polity, 1985.

Gilhodes, C. *The Kachins: Religion and Customs*. Calcutta: Catholic Orphan Press, 1922.

Glenny, Misha. *The Balkans: Nationalism, War and the Great Powers, 1804-1999*. New York: Penguin, 2001.

______. *The Fall of Yugoslavia*. New York: Penguin, 1994.

Government of Burma, Economic and Social Board. *A Study of the Social and Economic History of Burma (The British Period). Part V: Burma under the Chief Commissioners 1886-7 to 1896-7*. Yangon: Office of the Prime Minister, 1957.

Gowing, Nik. *Real-Time Television Coverage of Armed Conflicts and Diplomatic Crises: Does it Pressure or Distort Foreign Policy Decisions?* Harvard: Shorenstein Center, 1994.

Gravers, Mikael. *Nationalism as Political Paranoia in Burma: An Essay on the Historical Practice of Power*. Richmond: Curzon Press, 1999.

Greenberg, Edward S. The Struggle for Democracy. University of Colorado, Boulder: Longman, 2003.

Grugel, Jean. *Democratisation: A Critical Introduction*. Basingstoke: Palgrave, 2002.

Gubrium, Jaber, F., and Holstein; James, A. (ed). *Handbook of Interview Research: Context and Method*. London, New Delhi: Sage Publication, 2002.

Gurr, Ted Robert, and Harff, Barbara. *Ethnic Conflict in World Politics*. Boulder, Colorado: Westview Press, 1994: 15.

Hamilton, Ian F. E. *Patterns of Economic Activity*. New York: Prager Publishers 1969.

Heinrich, H-G (ed). *Institution Building in the New Democracies: Studies in Post Communism*. Budapest: Collegiums Budapest, 1999.

Houtman, Gustaaf. *Mental Culture in Burmese Crisis Politics: Aung San Suu Kyi and National League for Democracy.* Tokyo: ILCAA, 1999.

Htilar Sitthu. *A Review of Myanmar History (1920-1962).* Yangon: University Press, 2004.

Htin Aung. *A History of Burma.* New York. Columbia University Press. 1967.

Huntington, Samuel. *The Clash of Civilisations and the Remaking of World Order.* New York: Simon and Schuster, 1998.

______. *Political Order in Changing Societies.* New Haven: Yale University Press, 1968.

______. *The Third Wave: Democratisation in the Late Twentieth Century.* Oklahoma: University of Oklahoma Press, 1991.

______. *The Soldier and the State: the Theory and Politics of Civil-Military Relations.* New York: Random House, 1975.

Ivanov, Andrey (ed). The Balkans Divided: Nationalism, Minorities, and Security. Euro-Atlantic Security Studies. Frankfurt am Main a. u.: Peter Lang, 1996.

Jacobson, Amanda. *Inherent Contradictions: The Failed Case of Socialist Federalism in Yugoslavia.* Chapel Hill: University of North Carolina, 2002.

Judah, Timothy. The Serbs, History, Myth and the Destruction of Yugoslavia. Yale: Yale University Press, 1998.

Jung, Kim Dae. *Building Peace and Democracy: Philosophy and Dialogues.* New York: Korean Independent Monitor, 1987.

Kaldor, Mary. *New and Old Wars: Organised Warfare in the Global Era.* Cambridge: Polity, 1999.

Kellas, James G. *The Politics of Nationalism and Ethnicity* (2nd ed., Revised and Updated). New York: St. Martin's Press INC., 1998.

Kennedy, Paul. *The Rise and Fall of the Great Powers: Economic Change and Military Conflict from 1500 to 2000.* New York: Vintage Books, 1989.

Keohane, Robert O., and Nye, Joseph S. *Power and Interdependence: World Politics in Transition.* Boston: Little Brown, 1977.

König, William J. *The Burmese Polity, 1752-1819: Politics, Administration, and Social Organisation in the Early Kon-baung Period.* Michigan: The University of Michigan, 1990.

Koyama, Yoji. *South Eastern Europe in Transition.* Niigata: Niigata University, 2003.

Kux, Stephan. *Soviet Federalism: A Comparative Perspective.* New York: Institute for East-West Security Studies, 1990: 7.

Laothamatas, Anek (ed). *Democratisation in South-East and East Asia.* Chaing Mai: Silkworm Books, 1997.

Leach, Edmund. *Political Systems of Highland Burma: A Study of Kachin Social Structures.* London: G. Bell and Son, 1954.

Lintner, Bertil. *Aung San Suu Kyi and Burma's Unfinished Renaissance.* Bangkok: White Lotus, 1991.

______. *Burma in Revolt: Opium and Insurgency since 1948,* 2nd ed., Chiang Mai: Silkworm Books, 1999.

______. *Land of Jade: A Journey through Insurgent Burma.* Edinburgh: Kiscadale, 1990.

______. *Outrage.* London, Bangkok: White House, 1990.

______. *The Kachin: Lords of Northern Burma.* Chiang Mai: Teak House, 1997.

Linz, Juan J. *Totalitarian and Authoritarian Regimes.* Boulder, Colo.: Lynne Rienner, 2000.

Linz, Juan J., and Stepan, Alfred. *Problems of Democratic Transition and Consolidation.* Baltimore and London: The John Hopkins University Press, 1996.

Lonsdale, Michael. *The Karen Revolution.* 2nd ed., Singapore: Sam Art, n. d.

Man, Che W. K. *Muslim Separatism: The Moros of Southern Philippines and the Malays of Southern Thailand.* Oxford: Oxford University Press, 1990.

Mandela, Nelson. *Long Walk to Freedom: The Autobiography of Nelson Mandela.* London: Little, Brown and Company (UK), 1996.

Maung Maung Gyi. *Burmese Political Values: The Socio-Political Roots of Authoritarianism.* New York: Prager Publishing, 1983.

Maung Maung. *Burma and General Ne Win.* London: Asia Publishing House, 1969.

______. *Burma's Constitution.* The Hague: Martinus Nijhoff, 1959.

______. *The 1988 Uprising in Burma.* New Haven: Yale University South-East Asian Studies Press, 1999.

Maung Yin Hmaing. *Daw Suu Kyi, NLD Party and Our Ray of Hope and Selected Articles.* Yangon: News and Periodicals Enterprise, September 2003.

Mayall, James (ed). *The New Interventionism: 1991-1994: United Nations Experience in Cambodia, Former Yugoslavia and Somalia.* Cambridge: Cambridge University Press, 1996.

Musgrave, Thomas D. *Self-Determination and National Minorities.* Oxford: Oxford University Press, 1997.

Muslim, Macapado Abaton. *The Moro Armed Struggle in the Philippines the Non-violent Autonomy Alternative.* Marawi: Mindanao State University Press, 2004.

National Coalition Government of the Union of Burma (NCGUB), the. in Weller, Marc (ed). *Democracy and Politic in Burma: A Collection of Documents.* Manerplaw: The National Coalition Government of the Union of Burma (NCGUB), 1993.

Ne Win. *A History of Anti-Fascist Revolution or a History, which was written by Aung San.* 1955. Yangon: Okkar Press, 1997.

New Light of Myanmar, the (ed). *The Collection of News and Statements, Years 1988-89 (Burmese Version).* 2nd ed., 1996. Yangon: The New Light of Myanmar Press, 1989.

O'Brien, Harriet. *Forgotten Land: A Rediscovery of Burma.* London: Michael Joseph Ltd., 1991.

Oberschall, Anthony. *Social Islam and World Revolution.* New Jersey: Prentice-Hall, 1973.

Olin Pye. *Panglong Paper.* Yangon: Sabai Oo Press, 1984.

Pickles, John, and Smith, Adrian (ed). *Theorising Transition: The Political Economy of Post-Communist Transformations.* London: Routledge, 1998.

Pridham G., Herring E., and G., Sanford (ed). *Building Democracy*, London: Leicester University Press, 1994.

Pye, Lucian W. *Asian Power and Politics.* Cambridge: Harvard University Press, 1985.

Press of the Head Office of the State Law and Order Restoration Council, the. The Union of Myanmar. *The Collection of Short Notices of the Speech and Statement of Sr. General Than Shwe, the Chairman of the State Law and Order Restoration Council: From Years 1992 to 1995 (Burmese Version).* Yangon: Photo Ltd. Press, 1996.

Riker, William. *Federalism: Origin, Operation, Significance.* Boston: Little, Brown and Company, 1964.

Roggemann, Herwig. *Die Verfassung der SFR Jugoslawien.* Berlin: Berlin Verlag, 1980.

Sadkovich, J. *The US Media and Yugoslavia, 1991–1995.* Westport: Preager Publishers, 1998.

Said, Edward W. *Orientalism: Western Conceptions of the Orient.* 1978. London: Penguin Books, 1995.

Saw Myat Sandy. *Burma: A Country in Meaningful Transition.* Muenster: n. p., 2003.

Schmitz, G., and Gillies, D. *The Challenge of Democratic Development: Sustaining Democratization in Developing Societies.* Ottawa: North-South Institute, 1992.

Seekins, Donald M. *The Disorder in Order: The Army-State in Burma since 1962.* Bangkok: White Lotus, 2002.

Sfikas, Thanasia D., and Williams, Christopher. *Ethnicity and Nationalism in East Central Europe and the Balkans.* Singapore: Ashgate, 1999.

Shwe Lu Maung. Preface. *Burma: Nationalism and Ideology – an analysis of society culture and politics.* Dhaka: The University Press Ltd. 1989.

Silber, Laura, and Little, Allen. *Yugoslavia: Death of a Nation.* rep. ed., New York: Penguin, 1997.

Silverstein, Josef. *Burma: Military Rule and the Politics of Stagnation.* Ithaca and London: Cornell University Press, 1977.

______. *Burmese Politics: The Dilemma of National Unity.* New Jersey: Rutgers University Press, 1980.

______. comp. and ed., *Independent Burma at Forty Years: Six Assessments.* Ithaca: Cornell University Press, 1989.

______. *The Struggle for National Unity in the Union of Burma.* Ithaca and Michigan: Cornell University, 1960.

Smith, Anthony D. *National Identity.* London: Penguin, 1991.

______. *Nations and Nationalism in a Global Era.* Cambridge: Polity Press, 1995.

______. *The Ethnic Origins of Nations.* New York: Basil Blackwell, 1987.

______. *Theories of Nationalism.* London: General Duckworth and Company Limited, 1971.

Smith, Anthony D., and Hutchinson, John (ed). *Ethnicity (Oxford Readers).* Oxford: Oxford University Press, 1996.

Smith, Martin. *Burma: Insurgency and the Politics of Ethnicity.* London and New Jersey: Zed Books Ltd. 1991.

South, Ashely. *Mon Nationalism and Civil War in Burma: The Golden Sheldrake.* London: RoutledgeCurzon, 2002.

Steinberg, David (ed). *In Search of South-East Asia: A Modern History.* New York: Prager Publisher, 1971. rev. and ed., Honolulu: University of Hawaii Press, 1985.

______. *Burma: The State of Myanmar.* Washington, DC: Georgetown University Press, 2001.

Taylor, Robert H. *The State in Burma.* Honolulu: University of Hawaii Press, 1987.

Tegenfeldt, Herman. *A Century of Growth: The Kachin Baptist Church of Burma.* South Pasadena: William Carey Library, 1974.

Thant Myint-U. *The Making of Modern Burma.* Cambridge: Cambridge University Press, 2001.

Tinker, Hugh. *The Union of Burma: A Study of the First Year of Independence,* 4th ed., London: Oxford University Press, 1967.

Tito, Broz Josip. *Tito Speaks in India and Burma.* New Delhi: Yugoslav Embassy, 1955.

Trager, Frank. N. *From Kingdom to Republic, a Historical and Political Analysis.* New York: Frederick A. Praeger,1966.

Trgo, F., Leković, M., Bojić, M., and Kljaković, V. (ed). *Tito's Historical Decisions 1941-1945.* Beograd: Narodna Armija, 1980.

Tutu, Bishop Desmond M. (Archbishop Emeritus of Cape Town, Nobel Peace Prize Laureate - 1984) and the Honorable Vacláv Havel (Former President of the Czech Republic). *Threat to the Peace: A Call for the UN Security Council to Act in Burma.* 20 September 2005.

Ullman, Richard H. *The World and Yugoslavia's Wars.* New York: Council on Foreign Relations Press, 1996.

Universities Historical Research Centre (ed). *The 1947 Constitution and the Nationalities.* Vol. I and II. Yangon: Pyi Zone Publishing House, 1999.

Vatikiotis, Michael R. J. *Political Changes in South-East Asia: Trimming the Banyan Tree.* 1996. London: Routledge, 1998.

Wachman, Alan M. *Taiwan: National Identity and Democratisation,* New York: M.E. Sharpe, 1994.

Weber, Max. *Economy and Society: An Outline of Interpretive Sociology.* Guenther Roth and Claus Wittich (ed). 2 Vols. Berkeley: University of California Press, 1968.

West, Richard. *Tito and the Rise and Fall of Yugoslavia.* New York: Carroll and Graf, 1994.

Wheeler, Mark. C. *Britain and the War for Yugoslavia, 1940-1943.* New York: Columbia University Press, 1980.

Woodward, Susan L. *Balkan Tragedy: Chaos and Dissolution after the Cold War.* Washington, DC: The Brookings Institution, 1995.

Yannis, Alexandros. *Kosovo Under International Administration: An Unfinished Conflict.* Greece: Hellenic Foundation for European and Foreign Policy (ELIAMEP), 2001.

Yawnghwe, Chao-Tzang. *The Shan of Burma: Memoirs of a Shan Exile.* Singapore: Institute of South-East Asian Studies, 1987.

Addresses, Articles, Essays, Papers, Reports, and Speeches

"City's Burma Policy an Endless, Bad Idea." Editorial. *Seattle Post-Intelligencer.* 18 August 1997.

"Going Slow on Embargoes." Editorial. *Rocky Mountain News.* 11 August 1997.

"Think before Sanctioning." Editorial. *Chicago Sun-Times.* 17 September 1997.

Ah, Oh Yoon. "State, Christian Church and Generation Gap in Ethnic Identity Formation: A Case Study of Insein Karen Community," unpublished paper presented at the Burma Study Conf. on "Burma-Myanmar Research and its Future: Implications for Scholars and Policy-makers." Gothenburg, Sweden. 21 - 25 September 2002.

Ahmed Buric. "The Media War and Peace in Bosnia" in Alan Davis (ed). *Regional Media in Conflict.* London: Institute for War and Peace Reporting, 2000.

ALTASEAN-Burma. *A Peace of Pie? Burma's Humanitarian Aid Debate (Special Report)* (ed). 13 October 2002.

Anderson, Stuart. "Self-inflicted Wounds." *Journal of Commerce.* 18 February 1997.

______. "Stop the Sanctions Game." *Journal of Commerce.* 23 July 1996.

Aung San. "Burma's Challenges in 1946," in Josef Silverstein (ed). *The Political Legacy of Aung San.* Ithaca: Cornell University South-East Asia Program Publications, 1993 [1972].

Aung Zaw. "The King Who Never Dies." *The Irrawaddy.* Vol. 9, No. 3, March-April 2001.

Baker, Peter. "US to Impose Sanctions on Burma for Repression." *Washington Post.* 22 April 1997.

Bakic-Hayden, Milica. "Nesting Orientalism: The Case of Former Yugoslavia." *Slavic Review 54.* 1995.

Bandow, Doug. "The Folly of Economic Warfare." *The Foundation for Economic Education, Inc.,* Vol. 48, No. 10, October 1998.

Barth, Fredrik. "Ethnic Groups and Boundaries (1969)" in Sollors, Werner (ed). *Theories of Ethnicity: A Classical Reader.* Houndmills, Basingstoke, Hampshire and London: Macmillan Press Ltd., 1996.

Beaudrillard, Jean. "La guerre de Golfe n'a pas eu lieu." *Libération.* 29 March 1991.

Bechert, Heinz. "To be a Burmese is to be a Buddhist," in Bechert, Heinz and Gombrich, Richerd (ed). *The World of Buddhism.* London: Thames and Hudson, 1984.

Blagojevic, Marina. "War in Kosovo: a victory for the media?" *Central European Review.* Vol. 1, No. 12, 13 September 1999.

_____. "War in Yugoslavia: Even Better than the Real Thing." *Belgrade Circle Journal.* 1-2, 1995.

Boutros Boutros-Ghali. "An Agenda for Peace Preventive Diplomacy, Peacemaking and Peace-keeping." *Report of the Secretary-General.* Pursuant to the statement adopted by the Summit Meeting of the Security Council on 31 January 1992.

Bozic, Agneza. "Democratisation and Ethno-political Conflict: The Yugoslav Case," in Cordell, Karl (ed). *Ethnicity and Democratisation in the New Europe.* London and New York: Routledge, 1999: 117-130.

Brooks, Stephen. "ASEAN Has No Choice but to Ignore US on Myanmar." *Asia Times.* 3 May 1997.

Burg, Steven L. (ed). "Negotiating a Settlement: Lessons of the Diplomatic Process," in Blank, Stephan J. *Yugoslavia's Wars: The Problems from Hell.* Carlisle Barrackes: US Army War College, 1995.

Burma Fund, The. "Breaking the Curse: The Rise and Fall of Military Strongmen and their Impact on Democracy in Burma." *Policy Brief.* No. 8, October 2004.

Callahan, Mary P. "State Formation in the Shadow of the Raj: Violence, Warfare and Politics in Colonial Burma." *South-East Asian Studies.* Vol. 39, No. 4, March 2002.

Carpenter, Ted Galen. "Foreign Policy Masochism: The Campaign For US Intervention In Yugoslavia." *The Cato Institute. Foreign Policy Briefing.* No. 19, 1 July 1992 .

Corzine, Robert, and Dunne, Nancy. "US Business Hits at Use of Unilateral Sanctions." *Financial Times.* 16 April 1997.

Daković, Nevena. "Cinematic Balkans: Balkan Genre." *NEXUS Research Projects.* Belgrad: n. p. 2002-2003.

David, Martin. "Croatia's Borders: Over the Edge."*New York Times.* 22 November 1991.

Dean, Karin. "Kachin Territorial Place vs. Social Space: Constructing, Contesting and Crossing Boundaries", unpublished paper presented at the Burma Study Conf. on "Burma-Myanmar Research and its Future: Implications for Scholars and Policy-makers." Gothenburg, Sweden. 21 -25 September 2002.

Dimitrova, Antoaneta. "The Role of the EU in the Process of Democratic Transition and Consolidation in Central and Eastern Europe" paper presented at the Third ECSA-World Conference "The European Union in a Changing World." Brussels, Belgium. 19 -20 September 1996.

Dvorakova, Vladimira. "Phases of Transitions to Democracy." *O prechodech k demokracii.* Prague: SLON, 1994.

Economides, Spyros, and Taylor, Paul. "Former Yugoslavia," in Mayall, James (ed). *The New Interventionism: 1991-1994: United Nations Experience in Cambodia, Former Yugoslavia and Somalia.* Cambridge: Cambridge University Press, 1996: 59-94.

Elazar, Daniel J. "Federal Democracy in a World Beyond Authoritarianism and Totalitarianism," in A. McAuley (ed). *Soviet Federalism, Nationalism and Economic Decentralisation.* Leicester: Leicester University Press, 1991.

______. "From Statism to Federalism: A Paradigm Shift." *Publius: The Journal of Federalism.* Vol. 25, No. 2, Winter 1995: 5-18.

______. "International and Comparative Federalism." *PS: Political Science and Politics.* Vol. XXVI. No. 2, June 1993.

Faulder, Dominic. "Any Hope for Myanmar?" *Asia INC.* March 2006.

______. "What are Burma's main problems today?" *Asia INC.* March 2006.

Finch, James. "Investors Can Help Break Myanmar's Political Gridlock." *Asiaweek.* 6 June 1997.

Forest, Jim. "The Serbian Orthodox Church: Not What We Have Been Led to Believe," in *Communion.* July 1999.

Friedrich, Carl J. "The Evolving Theory and Practice of Totalitarian Regimes," in C. Friedrich, M. Curtis, and Benjamin R. Barber (ed). *Totalitarianism in Perspective: Three Views.* New York: Praegar, 1969.

Fuentes, Carlos. "Federalism is the Great Healer." *Los Angeles Times.* 16 December 1990.

Gagnon, V. P. Jr. "Ethnic Conflict as Demobiliser: The Case of Serbia." *Institute for European Studies - Working Paper.* No. 96.1, 10 May 1996.

Gordy, Eric. "The Milošević Trial, Justice, and Reconciliation." *War Guilt and Responsibility: The Case of Serbia II.* Social Science Research Council, March 2003.

Greenberg, Robert D. (ed). "New Balkan Policy Needed" in Barry, Tom (IRC) and Honey, Martha (IPS). *Foreign Policy in Focus.* University of North Carolina-Chapel Hill. Vol. 6, No. 11, April 2001.

Gurr, Ted Robert. "Why Do Minorities Rebel?" in Günther Bächer (ed). *Federalism against Ethnicity? Institutional, Legal and Democratic Instruments to Prevent Violent Minority Conflicts.* Zürich: Verlag Rüegger, 1997.

Hadar, Leon T. "US Sanctions Against Burma: A Failure on All Fronts." *Executive Summary.* Cato Institute, March 1998.

______. "US Sanctions Backlash." *Business Times (Singapore).* 21 March 1997.

Hale, Henry E. "Divided We Stand: Ethno-federalism as Problem and Solution in Divided Societies" paper Competition of the Project to Combat Political Violence sponsored by Columbia University's Institute of War and Peace Studies, Columbia University, New York, USA. February 2003.

Halliday, Fred. "Nationalism" in Baylis, John, and Smith, Steve (ed). *The Globalisation of World Politics.* 2nd ed., Oxford: Oxford University Press, 2001.

Hauswedell, Christian, Ambassador, Dr, Director General (ret.), Asian and Pacific Affairs, Federal Foreign Office. Address. Speech at a Conference on "Round Table Discussion between Burma/Myanmar Experts: Constitution and Reconciliation" Friedrich Ebert Foundation (FES), Berlin, 14 December 2005.

Havel, Václav. "Five Years Later." *Written for World Media.* November 1994.

Hegre, H. "Toward a Democratic Civil Peace? Democracy, Political Change, and Civil War, 1816-1992." *American Political Science Review 95.* 2001.

Heintze, Hans-Joachim. "Autonomy and Protection of Minorities under International Law" in Günther Bächer (ed). *Federalism against Ethnicity? Institutional, Legal and Democratic Instruments to Prevent Violent Minority Conflicts.* Zürich: Verlag Rüegger, 1997.

Huntington, Samuel P. "Cart before the Horse." *Financial Mail.* Johannesburg, Vol. 129, No. 5, 30 July 1993.

Imle, John F. "A Case for Investment in Burma." *International Herald Tribune.* 6 February 1997.

Institute for European Studies. "Inter-Ethnic Conflict and War in Former Yugoslavia." *Research School of Pacific Studies: Working Paper.* No. 140, Canberra: The Australia National University Press, November 1993.

International Crisis Group (ICG). "Fehler! Hyperlink-Referenz ungültig.." *Europe Report N°170.* 17 February 2006.

Iyer, Venkat. "Federalism and Self-Determination: Some Reflections." *Legal Issue on Burma Journal.* No. 11, April 2002

Jagan, Larry. "Truce with Rebels would give Yangon Junta a Boost." *Asia Times.* 30 January 2004.

Jukic, Paul. "Russia and the South Slav Republics: The Contemporary Relationship." *Historical Roots of Contemporary International and Regional Issues.* International Security Studies at Yale University, Occasional Paper Series No. 5, June 1997.

Kaplan, Robert D. "History's Cauldron." *Atlantic.* June 1991: 93-104

Kecskemeti, Paul. "Totalitarianism and the Future." in Friedrich, Carl, J. (ed). *Totalitarianism.* Harvard University Press: Cambridge, 1954: 345-360.

Keyserling, Hermann. "Der Balkan." *Das Spektrum Europa.* Heidelberg, New York: Harcourt, Brace, 1928.

Khin Maung Win. "Federalism and Burma." *Legal Issue on Burma Journal.* No.11, December 2001.

Kirschten, David. "Chicken Soup Diplomacy." *National Journal.* 4 January 1997

______. "Economic Sanctions: Speaking Loudly . . . But Carrying Only a Small Stick." *National Journal.* 4 January 1997.

Kramer, Tom. "People's Power in Belgrade." *The Irrawaddy.* Vol. 8, No. 10, October 2000.

Kyaw Nyein. "He Made A Dream Come True." in Maung Maung, comp. and ed., *Aung San of Burma.* The Hague: Martinus Nijhoff; Yale University: South-East Asia Studies, 1962.

Kyaw Zwa Moe, and Seng Naw. "Pressing Forward: Media in Exile." *The Irrawaddy.* Vol. 10, No. 9, November 2002.

Lake, D. and D. Rothchild. "Containing Fear: the Origins and Management of Ethnic Conflict." *International Security.* 21-2, 1996.

Lavin, Frank L. "Asphyxiation or Oxygen? The Sanctions Dilemma." *Foreign Policy* Vol. 104 (Fall 1996): n. d., 146.

Layne, Christopher. "Blunder in the Balkans: The Clinton Administration's Bungled War against Serbia." *Policy Analysis.* No. 345, 20 May 1999.

Lintner, Bertil. "Paper Tiger." *Far Eastern Economic Review.* 7 August 1997.

______. "Transitions to Democracy." *The Washington Quarterly.* Vol. 13, 1990.

Linz, Juan, J. "An Authoritarian Regime: The Case of Spain" in Erik Allard, and Yrjo Littuen (ed). *Cleavages, Ideologies and Party Systems*: Helsinki, Finland: Transactions of the Westermarck Society, 1964.

Losman, Donald L. "Good Intentions Gone Bad." *Washington Post.* 6 October 1996.

Malik, Mohan J. "Sino-Indian Rivalry in Myanmar: Implications for Regional Security." *Contemporary South-East Asia.* Vol. 16, No. 2, September 1994.

Manning, Robert A. "U.S. Bullying Tactics Alienating Asian Allies." *Los Angeles Times.* 27 July 1997.

Min Zin. "Burma Changing Power Equation." *The Irrawaddy.* Vol. 10, No. 2, February 2002

Mirante, Edith T. (ed). "Burma's Environmental Devastation." *How You Can Help Burma's Struggle for Freedom.* The Free Burma Coalition. Washington DC: The NCGUB, 1997.

Mircev, Dimitar. "Balancing the Socio-Economic Discrepancies as Source of Security and Political Stability: Views and Experiences in the Republic of Macedonia," paper presented at Europe-Russia Conference Series – Conference on "South-Eastern Europe, Moving Forward." The Centre for European Studies (CES) and Canadian Forum on South-Eastern Europe (CFSEE), Ottawa, 23 -24 January 2003.

Moncreif, John S. "Shan Ceasefire Groups: Not Happy, But Not Ready to Fight Either." *The Irrawaddy.* Vol. 10, No. 2, February-March 2002.

Mozaffar, Shaheen, and James R. Scarritt. "Why Territorial Autonomy is Not a Viable Option for Managing Ethnic Conflict in African Plural Societies." *Nationalism and Ethnic Politics.* Vol. 5, No. 3 and 4.1999, 230-51.

Nagora, Bunn. "Home Issues Shape US, ASEAN Policies on Myanmar." *Asiaweek.* 4 July 1997.

National Bureau of Asian Research, The. "Reconciling Burma/ Myanmar: Essays on US Relations with Burma." *NBR Analysis.* Badgley, John H. (ed). Vol. 15, March 2004.

Neumann, Franz L. "Federalism and Freedom: A Critique," in Karmis, Dimitrios, and Norman, Wayne (ed). *Theories of Federalism: A Reader.* New York: Palgrave MacMillan Press Ltd., 2005.

O'Donnel, Guillermo. "Delegative Democracy." *Journal of Democracy.* Vol. 5, No.1, January 1994.

_____. "Delegative Democracy" in Larry Diamond, and Marc F. Plattner (ed). *The Global Resurgence of Democracy.* Baltimore: John Hopkins University Press, 1996.

Osamba, Joshia O. "Violence and the Dynamics of Transition State, Ethnicity and Governance in Kenya." *Africa Development.* Vol. XXVI. No. 1 and 2, 2001.

Oxford Analytica. "Serbia—Opposition Division," in *Perspective: The Weekly Column from Oxford Analytica.* 6 October 1999

Paddock, Richard C. "Tutu, Havel asks UN Intervention in Myanmar." *Los Angeles Times.* October 2005

Pantev, Plamen. "Multiethnic State, Ethnically Homogeneous State and the Future of the Nation-State in the Balkans." *Crisis Management in South-East Europe: Multi-ethnic State or Ethnic Homogeneity – the Case of South-East Europe.* 2nd Reichenau Workshop of the PfP Consortium Working Group, Chateau Rothschild, Reichenau, Austria. 18 -21 May 2001.

Pavlovic, Dusan. "Gold Bars Of Power." *Vreme.* August 1998: 32-33.

______. "Nine Theses on Milošević's Future." *Vreme.* February 1998: 8-9.

Phillips, Frank. "Massachusetts to be Warned on Burma Law." *Boston Globe.* 15 April 1997.

Pinheiro, Paulo Sérgio. "Interim report of the Special Rapporteur of the Commission on Human Rights on the situation of human rights in Myanmar." *Human Rights Questions: Human Rights Situations and Reports of Special Rapporteurs and Representatives.* 25 July 2005.

Plate, Tom. "Capitalism vs. Moralism in Burma." *Los Angeles Times.* 24 September 1996.

Pridham, Geoffrey. "On the Cusp between Democratic Transition and Consolidation in East-Central Europe? Regime Change Patterns and External Impacts Reassessed," paper for Conference on "Early Lessons from the Post-Cold War Era: Western Influences on Central and Eastern European Transitions" organised by the Centre for Applied Policy Research, Munich, and the Institute for Public Affairs, Bratislava, in Bratislava. 12-13 October 2000.

Raj, Shekhar. "Gandhi, Aung San Suu Kyi and Burma's Democratic Movement," unpublished paper presented at the Burma Study Conference on "Burma-Myanmar Research and its Future: Implications for Scholars and Policy-makers." Gothenburg, Sweden. 21-25 September 2002.

Robert J. Kerner (ed). "Constitution of the Federal People's Republic of Yugoslavia, 1946; Article 1," in *Yugoslavia* (Berkeley: University of California), Appendix, 487. n. p., n. d.

Roberts, Paul Craig. "A Growing Menace to Free Trade: US Sanctions." *Business Week.* 24 November 1997.

Rodden, Jonathan. "Comparative Federalism and Decentralisation: On Meaning and Measurement," in Journal of *Comparative Politics.* Cambridge: Cambridge University Presee, 2004.

Rodman, Peter. "The Burma Dilemma." *Washington Post.* 29 May 1997.

Ronen, Dov. "The Origins of Ethnic Conflict: Lessons from Yugoslavia." *Research School of Pacific Studies: Working Paper.* No. 155, Canberra: The Australia National University Press, November 1994.

Sambanis, Nicolas. "Do Ethnic and Nonethnic Civil Wars Have the Same Causes?" *Journal of Conflict Resolution.* 45(4), 2001: 259-82.

Scarritt, James R., and Shaheen Mozaffar. "The Specification of Ethnic Cleavages and Ethno-political Groups for the Analysis of Democratic Competition in Contemporary Africa." *Nationalism and Ethnic Politics.* Vol. 5, No. 1, 1999: 82-117.

Schiff, Rebecca. "Civil-Military Relations Reconsidered: A Theory of Concordance." *Armed Forces and Society.* Vol. 22 (1), 1995.

Schmahmann, David, and Finch, James. "The Unconstitutionality of State and Local Enactments in the United States Restricting Business Ties with Burma (Myanmar)." *Vanderbilt Journal of Transnational Law 30.* No. 2, March 1997: 184-202.

Sen. V. K. "Secession and Self-Determination in the Context of Burma's Transition." *Legal Issue on Burma Journal.* No. 11, December 2001.

Seth, Andrew. "Burma's Intelligence Apparatus." *Working Paper.* No. 308, Strategic and Defence Studies Centre, Australian National University, Canberra, 1997.

Sheridan, Michael. "The general who would be king menaces Burma." *The Sunday Times.* 7 May 2006

Silverstein, Josef. "Federalism as a Solution to the Ethnic Problem in Burma," in Günther Bächer (ed). *Federalism against Ethnicity? Institutional, Legal and Democratic Instruments to Prevent Violent Minority Conflicts.* Zürich: Verlag Rüegger, 1997.

_____. "Politics in the Shan State: The Question of Secession from the Union of Burma." *Journal of Asian Studies,* XVIII. November 1958: 43-57.

_____. "The Idea of Freedom in Burma," in Kelly, David, and Reid, Anthony (ed). *Asian Freedoms: The Idea of Freedom in East and South-East Asia.* Cambridge: Cambridge University Press, 1998.

Smith, Alan. "Burma/Myanmar: The Struggle for Democracy and Ethnic Rights," in Will Kymlicka, and Gaogang H. (ed). *Multiculturalism in Asia.* Oxford: Oxford University Press, 2005.

_____. "Ethnic Conflict and Federalism," in Günther Bächer (ed). *Federalism against Ethnicity? Institutional, Legal and Democratic Instruments to Prevent Violent Minority Conflicts.* Zürich: Verlag Rüegger, 1997.

_____. "Ethnic Problems and Constitutional Solution," Legal Issues on Burma Journal. No. 15, August 2003.

Smith, Martin. "Burma (Myanmar): The Time for Change." *Minority Rights Group International (MRG).* May 2002.

Son, Vum. "Drafting the Constitution of the Union of Burma." n. p. 3 June 2003.

Steinberg, David. "The Burmese Political Economy: Opportunities and Tension," paper presented at a conference on "Myanmar towards the Twenty-first Century". Chaing Rai, Thailand. 1-3 June 1995.

Taylor, Robert, and Pederson, Morten. "Supporting Burma/Myanmar's National Reconciliation Process: Challenges and Opportunities." *An Independent Report for the European Commission.* January 2005.

Tutu, Desmond M. "Burma as South Africa." *Far Eastern Economic Review.* 16 September 1993.

Vanhanen, Tatu. "Democratic Peace and Ethnic Violence," prepared for delivery at the 4th Pan-European International Relations Conference, ECPR Standing Group on International Relations, Section 5: Analytical Politics and Public Choice in International Relations, at the University of Kent at Canterbury, 8-10 September 2001.

Vankovska, Biljana. "Civil-Military Relations in the Third Yugoslavia." *Copenhagen Peace Research Institute.* August 2000.

______. "NATO War over Yugoslavia: Civilian Control in Focus." *Copenhagen Peace Research Institute.* July 2000.

Veljo, Vujacic. "Serbian nationalism, Slobodan Milošević and the origins of the Yugoslav War." *The Harriman Review.* Vol. 8, No. 4, December 1995.

Wamala, Augustine. "Federalism for Africa." *De Villiers.* 1994: 251-67.

Wendt, Allan. "Futility of Sanctions against Burma." *Washington Times.* 29 June 1997.

Will, Gerhard. "Wege aus der Isolation." *SWP-Studies.* Berlin, August 2003.

Yawnghwe, Chao-Tzang. "Burma and National Reconciliation: Ethnic Conflict and State-Society Dysfunction." *Legal Issues on Burma Journal.* No. 10, December 2001.

______. "Burma: State Constitutions and the Challenges Facing the Ethnic Nationalities." *Role of State: Report of the Institute for Democracy and Electoral Assistance (IDEA).* 3 March 2003.

______. "Political and National Reconciliation: A Peace of Pie?" in ALTSEAN-Burma. *Burma's Humanitarian Aid Debate: Special Report.* 13 October 2002.

______. "Politics in Burma: Activism and Scholarship," lecture given at the Burma Study Conf. on "Burma-Myanmar Research and its Future: Implications for Scholars and Policy-makers." Gothenburg, Sweden. 21-25 September 2002.

Yawnghwe, Harn, "Burma: Ways into Democracy." Address. at a Conf. Friedrich-Ebert-Foundation, Bonn. 4 September 2002.

Young, Christopher. "The Role of Media in International Conflict." *Canadian Institute for Peace and Security, Working Paper.* No. 38, 1991.

Zarni, and Oo, Naw May. "Common Problems, Shared Responsibilities: Citizens' Quest for National Reconciliation in Burma/ Myanmar." *Free Burma Coalition.* October 2004.

Zizek, Slavoj. "The Spectre of Balkan." *The Journal of the International Institute.* 1998.

On-Line Articles and Broadcast Media[150]

"Aleksandar Rankovic, Yugoslavian History, Biographies." The Columbia Electronic Encyclopaedia: Columbia University Press, 2003
http://reference.allrefer.com/encyclopedia/R/Rankovic.html

"Alija Izetbegović." *Wikipedia: The Free Encyclopedia.* 11 October 2006
http://en.wikipedia.org/wiki/Alija_Izetbegovic

"Background Biographies." Research Pages of *the Irrawaddy.* October 14, 2006
http://www.irrawaddy.org/res/bio.html

"Balkan since 1815" *The New York Times.*
http://www.nytimes.com/specials/bosnia/context/yugo1815.GIF.html

"Balkanization." *Wikipedia: The Free Encyclopedia.* 11 October 2006
http://en.wikipedia.org/wiki/Balkanization

"Brief Biographies of Exiled Members of Parliament of Burma." Web Page of the *Democratic Voice of Burma Radio.* 27 July 2004
http://english.dvb.no/e_docs/217bio_mp.htm

"Brief Biography of Aung San Suu Kyi." *US Campaign for Burma.* n. d.
http://www.uscampaignforburma.org/assk/biography.html

"British Empire: British acquisitions in Burma." Encyclopedia Britannica.
http://www.britannica.com/eb/art-3397

"Burma: Country in Crisis." *The Burma Project.* Open Society Institute.
http://www.burmaproject.org

"Burma's Hard-line Generals." *BBC News.* 26 May 2006
http://news.bbc.co.uk/2/hi/asia-pacific/3755684.stm

"Count Hermann Alexander Keyserling: The Founder of the School of Wisdom." *School of Wisdom.* n. d. http://www.schoolofwisdom.com/count.html

---

[150] Last access to the most of the Web-Pages here: 13 October 2006.

"Croatian Spring." *Wikipedia: The Free Encyclopedia.* 11 October 2006
http://en.wikipedia.org/wiki/Croatian_Spring

"Daw Aung San Suu Kyi." *Heroes of the 20th Century.* 17 June 2006
http://www.moreorless.au.com/heroes/suukyi.html

"Dayton Agreement." *Wikipedia: The Free Encyclopedia.* 12 October 2006
http://en.wikipedia.org/wiki/Dayton_Agreement

"Democratic Opposition of Serbia." *Brainy Encyclopaedia.* n. d.
http://www.brainyencyclopedia.com/encyclopedia/d/de/democratic_opposi
tion_of_serbia.html

"Demokratska stranka Srbije." http://www.dss.org.yu

"Đinđic Proposes Kosovo Federation." *Orthodox News.* 27 February 2003
http://www.orthodoxnews.netfirms.com

"Đjilas, Milonvan." *Political Science Biographies: The Columbia Encyclopaedia.*
6th ed., Columbia University Press, 2006
http://www.encyclopedia.com/html/D/Djilas-M1.asp

"Dr Zoran Đinđic 1952-2003." *Personal Biography Page of Dr. Zoran Đinđic.* n. d.
http://www.zorandjindjic.org

"Former Burma Dictator Ne Win dies." *BBC News.* 5 December 2002
http://news.bbc.co.uk/2/low/asia-pacific/2544975.stm

"Franjo Tuđman." *Wikipedia: The Free Encyclopedia.* 11 October 2006
http://en.wikipedia.org/wiki/Franjo_Tudjman

"Josip Broz Tito." *Wikipedia: The Free Encyclopedia.* 13 October 2006
http://en.wikipedia.org/wiki/Josip_Broz_Tito;

"Ljubljana." Institut "Jožef Stefan". n. d. http://www.ijs.si/slo/ljuljana

"List of Cease-fire Agreements with the Junta." The Irrawaddy
http://www.irrawaddy.org/research_show.php?art_id=444

"Map 1. Burma: States and Divisions." *People's Tribunal on Food Scarcity and
Militarization in Burma.* n. d. http://www.foodjustice.net/burma/1996-
2000tribunal/report/map1.htm

"Map Serbia and Montenegro." *War in Europe.*
http://www.pbs.org/wgbh//pages/frontline/shows/kosovo/etc/map.html

"Marina Blagojević." Enwise valorisation Conference: "Enlarging Europe with/for
Women Scientists,"Sihtasutus Archimedes. 9 - 10 September 2004,
Tallinn, Estonia
http://www.archimedes.ee/enwise/speakers/blagojevic.html

"Myanmar (Burma) Map." *AsiaTour.Net*
http://asiatours.net/burma/info/burma_map.html

"Myanmar (Burma) Map." http://asiatours.net/burma/info/burma_map.html

"Obituary: Zoran Đinđic." *BBC News.* 13 March 2003 www.bbc.co.uk

"Perry-Castañeda Library Map Collection." *The University of Texas at Austin.*
http://www.lib.utexas.edu/maps

"Republic of Macedonia." *Balkan Info Home: Places We Hold Dear.*
n. d. http://www.b-
nfo.com/places/Macedonia/republic/images/citiesSkopje.shtml

"Research Page." *The Irrawaddy.* http://www.irrawaddy.org/res

"Rice Names 'Outposts of Tyranny'." *BBC News.* 19 January 2005
http://news.bbc.co.uk/2/hi/americas/4186241.stm

"Sarajevo." *Wikipedia: The Free Encyclopedia.* 13 October 2006
http://en.wikipedia.org/wiki/Sarajevo

"Serbia and Montenegro." *The World Factbook.* March 2006
http://www.cia.gov/cia/publications/factbook/geos/yi.html

"Serbia Opposition Division." *Oxford Analytica.* 6 October 1999
http://www.ciaonet.org/pbei/oxan/oxa991006.html

"Slobodan Milošević." *Wikipedia: The Free Encyclopedia.* 13 October 2006
http://en.wikipedia.org/wiki/Slobodan_Milosevic

"SSE Security Monitor: The Serbia and Montenegro Political Environment." Centre of South-East European Studies, 2004-2005. http://www.csees.net

"The Burma Project." *Open Society Institute.* http://www.burmaproject.org

"The Former Yugoslavia: Chronology." The European Graduate Organisation
(EGO), University of Pennsylvania, 11 September 2006
http://www.sas.upenn.edu/~mercerb/chyugo.html

"Time for Soul Searching." Editorial. *The Irrawaddy.* August 2000: Vol. 8, No. 8,
www.irrawaddy.org

"Timeline Myanmar [formerly Burma]." *Timelines of History.* 30 July 2006
http://timelines.ws/countries/BURMA.HTML

"Timeline Serbia 1998-1999." http://timelines.ws/countries/SERBIA_B.HTML

"Titoism." *Wikipedia: The Free Encyclopedia.* 13 October 2006
http://en.wikipedia.org/wiki/Titoism

"Vojislav Koštunica." *Wikipedia: The Free Encyclopedia.* 13 October 2006
http://en.wikipedia.org/wiki/Vojislav_Kostunica

"Yugoslavia." *Wikipedia: The Free Encyclopedia.* 13 October 2006
http://en.wikipedia.org/wiki/Yugoslavia

Ash, Timothy Garton, "Beauty and the Beast in Burma." *The New York Review of Books.* 25 May 2000 http://www.nybooks.com

_____, "Eastern Europe: The Year of Truth." *The New York Review of Books.* February 15 1990: Vol. 37, No. 2, http://www.nybooks.com

Associated Press, The. "Myanmar names new prime minister: Meaning of shift remains unclear." *International Herald Tribune.* 27 August 2003 http://www.iht.com/articles/107896.html

Aung Naing Oo. "The Road Home to Pang Long." *Himal South Asian.* October 2002 http://www.himalmag.com/2002/october/burma_perspective_3.html

Balalovska, Kristina. "Between 'the Balkans' and 'Europe': A study of the contemporary transformation of Macedonian identity, 1991-2002." *The New Balkan Politics: Journal of Politics, Issue.6.* 2000 http://www.newbalkanpolitics.org.mk/OldSite/Issue6.asp

Bechev, Dimitar. "Building South-Eastern Europe: the Politics of International Co-operation in the Region." The Kokkalis Programme on South-eastern and East Central Europe, JFK School of Government, Harvard University. 13 February 2002 www.ksg.harvard.edu/kokkalis/GSW4/BechevPAPER.PDF

Brunner, Borgna, and Johnson, David. "Timeline: Yugoslavia." *From World War I to the new State of Serbia and Montenegro.* 19 December 2004 http://www.infoplease.com/spot/yugotimeline1.html

Đinđić, Zoran. "Platform for Kosovo." Democracy Party. Belgrade: 29 January 1998 http://www.balkan-archive.org.yu/politics/kosovo/html/platf_ds_e.html

Elazar, Daniel J. "Will Federalism Preserve Yugoslavia." *Federalism.* Jerusalem Centre for Public Affairs. n. d. http://www.jcpa.org/dje/articles2/yugoslavia.htm

German Embassy, London. "Notion and Historical Background of Federalism in Germany" http://www.german-embassy.org.uk[151]

Golubovi, Zagorka. University of Belgrade. "What sociological analyses of nationalism reveal in ex-Yugoslavia. Why Nationalism is Contreproductive vs. a Democratic Transition?" *Pages Balkans du GSsA.* Groupe Pour Une Suisse Sans Armée. 25 October 2000 http://www.gssa.ch/balkans/forbalk/golubovi.htm

Gross, Jane. "On This Day." *The New York Times.* 29 September 1989 http://www.nytimes.com

Kazmin, Amy. "UN Envoy Urges More Aid to Spur Burma Reform." *Financial Times.* 31 October 2002 at *BurmaNet News.* http://www.burmanet.org/bnn_archives/2002/20021031.txt; http://six.pairlist.net/pipermail/burmanet/20021031/000011.html

---

[151] Last access to this Web-Page was in December 2002.

Lučić, Ivo. "Security and Intelligence Services in Bosnia and Herzegovina." *National Security and the Future.* Vol. 1, No. 2, Zagreb, Summer 2000
http://www.nsf-journal.hr/issues/v1_n2/NSF-2-pdf/05Lucic.pdf

Matic, Veran. "How Milošević was Finally Defeated." *Global Beat Syndicate.* 10 October 2000 http://www.nyu.edu/globalbeat/syndicate/Matic101000.html

McMahon, Robert. "Bosnia: U.S. Secretary Of State Hails Bosnian Pledge On Reforms." *Radio Free Europe: Radio Liberty.* 22 November 2005 http://www.rferl.org/featuresarticle/2005/11/07ca1344-dc7b-4365-becc-87ce91f281ff.html

Pavlovic, Dusan. "Can Real Democracy Exist After A Sultanate?" *Cyber Izdanje "reči".* No. 001, June 1999 http://www.b92.net/casopis_rec/arhiva/pavloviceng.html[152]

Peranic, Barbara. "Croatia: The 'Greatest Croat'." *Columbia International Affair Online: Policy Briefs.* 6 -12 January 2004 http://www.ciaonet.org

Popovic, Dragan M. "Political System of Yugoslavia under Tito: 1945-1974." n. d. http://www.grupa.org.yu/political_system.html

Pryce-Jones, David. "Remembering Milovan Djilas." *The New Criterion.* Vol. 18, No. 2, October 1999 http://www.newcriterion.com/archive/18/oct99/djilas.htm

Rich, Roland. "Recognition of States: The Collapse of Yugoslavia and the Soviet Union." *European Journal of International Law.* 14 October 2003 http://www.ejil.org/journal/Vol4/No1/art4.html

Robertson, Philip S. "In Focus: US Policy Regarding Burma" in Barry, Tom (IRC), and Honey, Martha Honey (IPS) (ed). *Foreign Policy In Focus.* Vol. 5, No. 31, September 2000. http://www.ciaonet.org

Rusinow, Dennison. "Yugoslavia." Microsoft® Encarta® Online Encyclopedia 2006 http://encarta.msn.com/text_761567145___7/Yugoslavia.html

Schwarz, Benjmin, and Layne, Christopher. "The Case Against Intervention in Kosovo" *The Nation.* 19 April 1999 http://www.thenation.com/doc/19990419/schwarz

Senigalliesi, Livio. "The Yugoslavian Issue." n. d. http://www.liviosenigalliesi.com/oltre_immagini_en/testo_foto_02.html

Special Report. "The Milošević Indictment." *The Guardian.* 29 June 2001 http://www.guardian.co.uk/yugo/article/0,2763,514466,00.html

Stepan, Afred. "Federalism and Democracy." *Democratic Invention Lecture Series.* 2 November 1998 http://www.ned.org/events/deminvention/stephan.html

---

[152] From the Page of the B92 Youth Radio Broadcasting, Belgrade.

Tesoro, Jose Manuel, and Faulder, Dominic. "Changing of the Guard." *ASIAWEEK*. 28 November 1997 http://www.asiaweek.com

Tharckabaw, Saw David. "Choosing to engage: strategic considerations for the Karen National Union," in Ricigliano, Robert (ed). *Conciliation Resources' Accord: An International Review of Peace Initiative*. London: 2005 http://www.c-r.org/our-work/accord/engaging-groups/karen-national-union.php

Van Bik, Rollin. "Chin National Front and Chin Nationhood." *Online Burma/Myanmar Library*. February 1997 http://www.burmalibrary.org/reg.burma/archives/199702/msg00067.html

Wilson, Michael. "Burma Opium Lord." *IWAR - Information Warfare*. 26 November 1997 http://lists.jammed.com/IWAR/1997/11/0003.html

Win, Kanbawza. "Will the Junta live up to its Rhetoric?" *Rebound 88*. 9 March 2002 http://rebound88.tripod.com/sp/junta/srhetoric.html

Zaw, Aung "The Talk of the Town." *The Irrawaddy*. 9 November 2004 www.irrawaddy.org

Web Sources:

- "Country Information." *US Department of State*. http://www.state.gov/p/eur/ci

- *Burma On-Line Library, the* http://www.burmalibrary.org

- *Columbia International Affair Online*. http://www.ciaonet.org/

- *Wikipedia: The Free Encyclopedia*. http://en.wikipedia.org

- *World Fact Book, the*. http://www.cia.gov/cia/publications/factbook

Dictionaries:

- *Myanmar-English Dictionary*. Yangon: Yangon University Pressed, 2001

- *Oxford Advanced Learner's Dictionary*. Oxford: Oxford University Press, 2003

Interviews:

- Professor Paulo Sérgio Pinheiro, UN Special Rapporteur of the Commission on Human Rights, on BBC "Hardtalk." 1 September 2005 http://news.bbc.co.uk/1/hi/programmes/hardtalk/4216736.stm

- Interviewed with U Lwin (NLD). by Min Zin, Radio Free Asia. 2 June 2006 www.rfa.org

Appendix I

The Constitution of The Socialist Republic of Yugoslavia (1974)

The Constitution of The Socialist Republic of SFR Yugoslavia, which was promulgated in 1974, can be structured as follows:

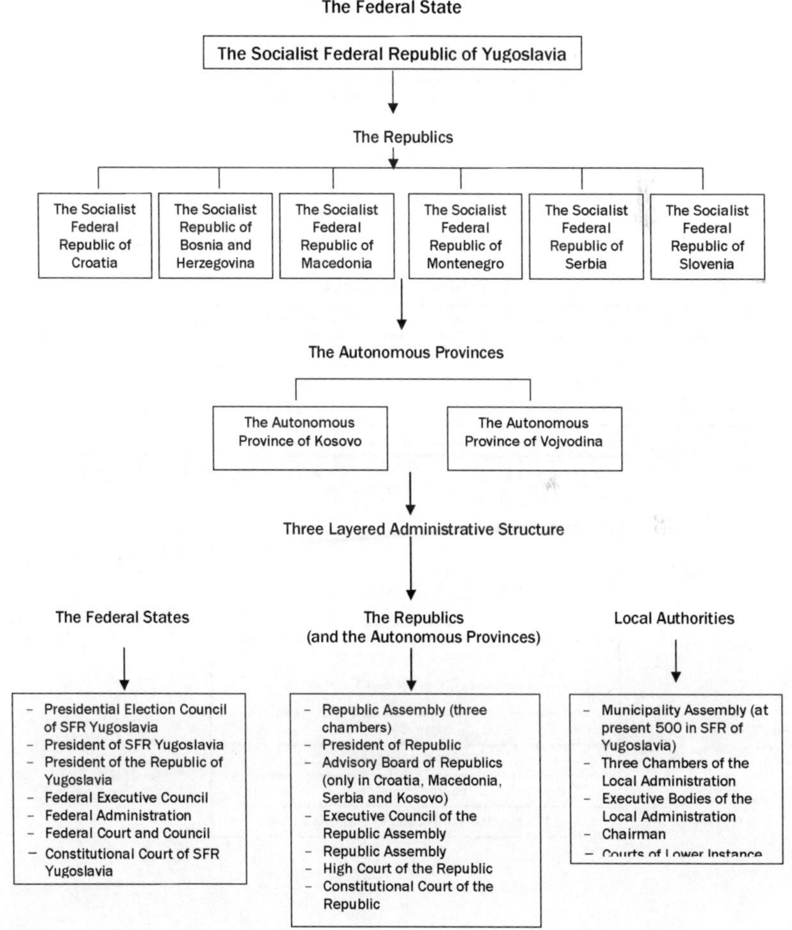

Federal Organisations

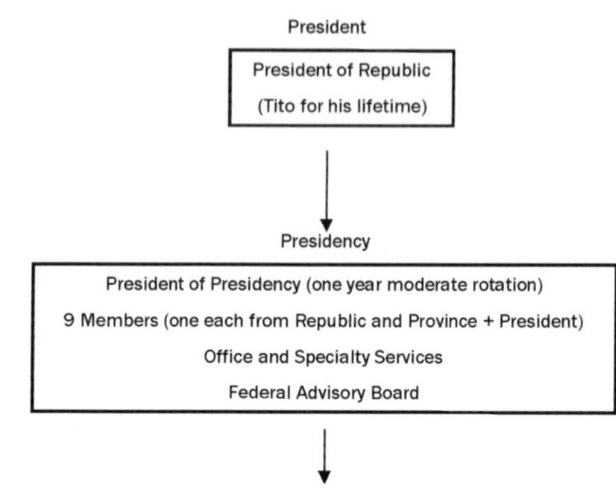

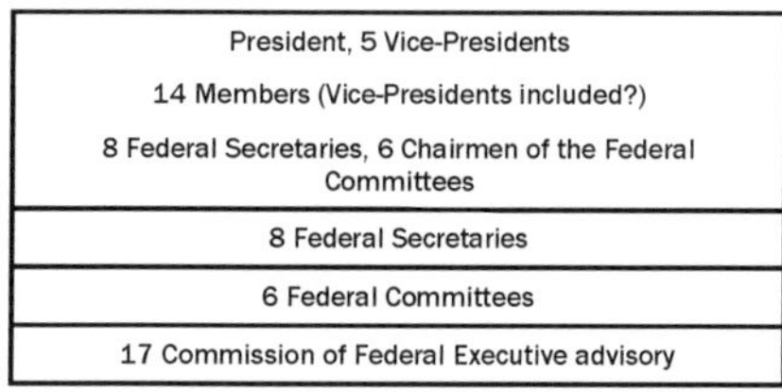

The Panglong Agreement

Panglong, 12th February 1947

A conference having been held at Panglong, attended by certain Members of the Executive Council of the Governor of Burma, all Saohpas (*Saw Bwas*) and representative of the Shan States, the Kachin Hills and the Chin Hills. The Members of the conference, believing that freedom will be more speedily achieved by the Shans, the Kachins and the Chins by their immediate co-operation with the Interim Burmese Government:

(1) A Representative of the Hill Peoples, selected by the Governor on the recommendation of representatives of the Supreme Council of the United Hill Peoples (SCOUHP), shall be appointed as Counsellor for Frontier Areas and shall be given executive authority by similar means.

(2) The said Counsellor shall also be appointed a Member of the Governor's Executive Council, without portfolio, and the subject of Frontier Areas brought within the purview of the Executive Council by Constitutional Convention as in the case of Defence and External Affairs. The Counsellor for Frontier Areas shall be given executive authority by similar means.

(3) The said Counsellor shall be assisted by two Deputy Counsellor's representing races of which he is not a member. While the two Deputy Counsellors should deal in the first instance with the affairs of their respective areas and the Counsellor with all the remaining parts of the Frontier Areas, they should by Constitutional Convention act on the principle of joint responsibility.

(4) While the Counsellor, in his capacity as Member of the Executive Council, will be the only representative of the Frontier Areas on the Council, the Deputy Counsellors shall be entitled to attend meetings of the Council when subjects pertaining to the Frontier Areas are discussed.

(5) Though the Governor's Executive Council will be augmented as agreed above, it will not operate in respect of the Frontier Areas in any manner which would deprive any portion of those Areas of the autonomy which it now enjoys in internal administration. Full autonomy in internal administration for the Frontier Areas is accepted in principle.

(6) Though the question of demarcating and establishing a separate Kachin State within a Unified Burma is one which must be relegated for decision by the Constituent Assembly, it is agreed that such a State is desirable. As a first step towards this end, the Counsellor for Frontier Areas and the Deputy Counsellors shall be consulted in the administration of such areas in the Myitkyina and the Bhamo Districts as are Part II Scheduled Areas under the Government of Burma Act of 1935.

(7) Citizens of the Frontier Areas shall enjoy rights and privileges which are regarded as fundamental in democratic countries.

(8) The arrangements accepted in this Agreement are without prejudice to the financial autonomy now vested in the Federated Shan States.

(9) The arrangements accepted in this Agreement are without prejudice to the financial assistance which the Kachin Hills and the Union Hills are entitled to receive from the revenues of Burma, and the Executive Council will examine with the Frontier Areas Counsellor and Deputy Counsellors the feasibility of adopting for the Kachin Hills and the Chin Hills financial arrangement similar to those between Burma and the Federated Shan States.

Shan Committee.	Kachin Committee.	Burmese Government.
(Signed) Saohpalong of Tawngpeng State.	(Signed) (Sinwa Naw, Myitkyina)	(Signed) (Aung San)
(Signed) Saohpalong of Yawnghwe State.	(Signed) (Zau Rip, Myitkyina)	
(Signed) Saohpalong of North Hsenwi State.	(Signed) (Dinra Tang, Myitkyina)	
(Signed) Saohpalong of Laihka State.	(Signed) (Zau La, Bhamo)	
(Signed) Saohpalong of Mong Pawn State.	(Signed) (Zau Lawn, Bhamo)	
(Signed) Saohpalong of Hsamonghkam State.	(Signed) (Labang Grong, Bhamo)	

(Signed)
Representative of Hsahtung Saohpalong (Hkun Pung)

(Signed) (U Tin E)	(Signed) (U Htun Myint)	Chin Committee
(Signed) (U Kya Bu)	(Signed) (Hkun Saw)	(Signed) (U Hlur Hmung, Falam)
(Signed) (Sao Yape Hpa)	(Signed) (Hkun Htee)	(Signed) (U Thawng Za Khup, Tiddim)
		(Signed) (U Kio Mang, Haka)

The Constitution of the Union of Burma (1948)

Constituent Assembly of Burma
Rangoon, Supdt, Govt. Printing and Stationery, Burma (1948)

PREAMBLE

WE, THE PEOPLE OF BURMA including the Frontier Areas and the Karenni States, Determined to establish in strength and unity a SOVEREIGN INDEPENDENT STATE, to maintain social order on the basis of the eternal principles of JUSTICE, LIBERTY AND EQUALITY and to guarantee and secure to all citizens JUSTICE social, economic and political; LIBERTY of thought, expression, belief, faith, worship, vocation, association and action; EQUALITY of status, of opportunity and before the law, IN OUR CONSTITUENT ASSEMBLY this Tenth day of Thadingyut waxing, 1309 B.E. (Twenty-fourth day of September, 1947 A.D.), DO HEREBY ADOPT, ENACT AND GIVE TO OURSELVES THIS CONSTITUTION.

The 1947 Constitution and the Nationalities
Framework of Indirect Rule
Immediate and Near Future

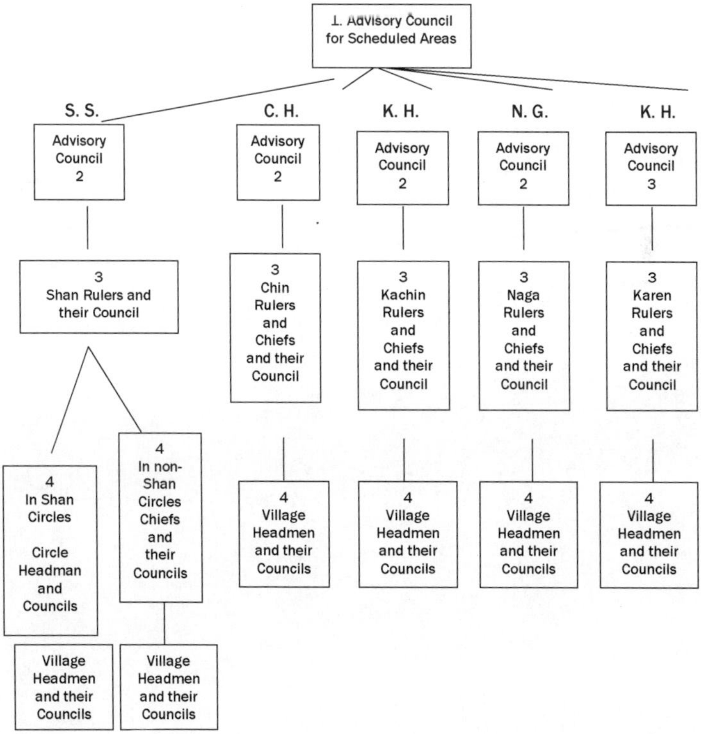

In the first stages of re-organisation after re-occupation, to facilitate efficient action, stage 1 and 2 will remain purely advisory to the directorate of Scheduled Areas Administration, the President and the assistant Presidents respectively. But for the future, say 5 years, stages 1 and 2 will be given carefully graded executive powers and responsibility, officers under the Directorate of Scheduled Areas Administration assuming a more advisory and less participant role.

FUTURE

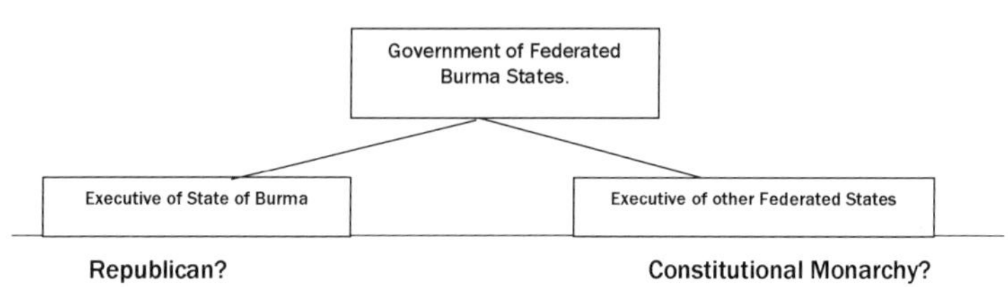

Republican?   Constitutional Monarchy?

Appendix II

List of Cease-fire Agreements with the Junta
Main Cease-fire Organisations (in order of agreement)

No	Name of organisation	Abb:	Leader	Date	Region
1	Myanmar National Democracy Alliance Army (Kokang)	MNDAA	Phone Kyar Shin	21 Mar 1989	Special Region-1, Northern Shan State
2	United Wa State Army (Myanmar National Solidarity Party)	UWSA	Pao Yuchang & Kyauk Nyi Lai	9 May 1989	Special Region-2, Shan State
3	National Democratic Alliance Army (Shan/Akha Armed National Groups)	NDAA	Sai Lin & Lin Ming Xian	30 June 1989	Special Region-4, Eastern Shan State
4	Shan State Army (Shan State Progress Party)	SSA	Col. Loi Mao	2 Sept 1989	Special Region-3, Shan State
5	New Democratic Army (Kachin)	NDA-K	Sakhone Ting Ying	15 Dec 1989	Special Region-1, North-East Kachin State
6	Kachin Defence Army (KIO 4th Brigade)	KDA	Mahtu Naw	13 Jan 1991	Special Region-5, Northern Shan State
7	Pa-O National Organisation	PNO	Aung Kham Hti	11 April 1991	Special Region-6, Southern Shan State
8	Palaung State Liberation Army	PSLA	Aik Mone	21 April 1991	Special Region-7, Northern Shan State
9	Kayan National Guard (breakaway group from KNLP)	KNG	Gabriel Byan & Htay Ko	27 Feb 1992	Special Region-1, Kayah(Karenni) State
10	Kachin Independence Organization	KIO	Lamung Tu Jai	1 Oct 1993	Special Region-2, Kachin State
11	Karenni State Nationalities Peoples' Liberation Front	KNPLF	Sandar & Htun Kyaw	9 May 1994	Special Region-2, Kayah(Karenni) State
12	Kayan New Land Party	KNLP	Shwe Aye	26 July 1994	Special Region-3, Kayah(Karenni) State
13	Shan State Nationalities Peoples' Liberation Organization	SSNPLO	Ta Kalei	9 Oct 1994	Southern Shan State
14	New Mon State Party	NMSP	Nai Shwe Kyin	29 June 1995	Mon State

(source: see "List of Cease-fire Agreements with the Junta.")

ibidem-Verlag

Melchiorstr. 15

D-70439 Stuttgart

info@ibidem-verlag.de

www.ibidem-verlag.de
www.ibidem.eu
www.edition-noema.de
www.autorenbetreuung.de